THIS BOOK WILL DRAW YOU
CLOSER

Patty LeMoine

Dotty McNairn

Having Coffee With Jesus

By Patty LeMoine

Longstockings
PUBLICATIONS
ANDERSON, CA

ISBN-10: 1499663633
ISBN-13: 978-1499663631

Longstockings
PUBLICATIONS

ANDERSON, CA

Acknowledgements

I must first give thanks to my Lord and Savior Jesus Christ, and the Holy Spirit who now lives in me, for inspiring this devotional/testimony. What, to me, seemed like an impossible task has become a reality, all because of You! **I give You all the glory!**

My husband, Dave, has been the one prodding and pushing me along to final completion with his encouraging words and praise. His carefully chosen criticisms have been such a help in the final editing process as well. **Thank you, Dave!**

My dear friend, Lindy Checchi, who the Lord gave me right after my salvation experience, has been such a trusted sister, confidant, and coconspirator as we have worked on our books and studies together over the years. Without her encouragement, this would still be sitting in my computer somewhere. **Thank you, Buddy!**

Alice Ballou took the drawing I had sketched roughly as a non-artist, and managed to convey my thoughts so beautifully in her first-ever book cover. Her artistry put "legs" on the Scripture, Colossians 3:1,2 *"Since, then, you have been raised with Christ, set your hearts on things above, where Christ is seated at the right hand of God. Set your minds on things above, not on earthly things."* **Thank you, Alice!**

Rob Henslin took Alice's artwork to new heights, as he designed the cover, making it a professional presentation I am extremely pleased with. **Thank you, Rob!**

Introduction

As with any book, you will find words dancing across the pages, carefully placed with the intent of the author to express his or her personal views as seen through the lens of their own life experiences. You may not always agree with those statements or the way they present themselves, but that is the beauty of it. May I encourage you to step out and place your own expressions on paper, strung together with your particular slant on things, for others to ponder. You and I may be surprised at the reactions we get from various readers.

My close friends and family members have been hearing about this proposed book for at least half a decade; it is a bit like being pregnant for five, long years. As I have been dabbling in writing, this baby has grown larger and larger, until it feels like giving birth to an elephant. And, worse, I suffer like Miss Prissy in Gone With The Wind. "But I don't know nothin' 'bout birthin' babies!" she cried in hysteria.

I now find myself at the inevitable end of the journey, and do not know what to do with the finished product. I use the term "finished" loosely because I could go on forever writing, writing, endlessly writing. Will it ever be completed, with a book like this one? After all, life is not over yet. There is always *something* around the next bend, whether it is a joyful, exciting, or traumatic event. But, there comes a time when you need to cut it off, wrap it up, and present it to the world, not knowing what the reaction might be, if any. Will it even cause a ripple in the life of the reader?

Only God knows, literally. And, since He put this idea on my heart, encouraging me to get my thoughts on paper, even waking me up in the middle of the night with creative inspirations, I must comply. Isn't that what this project is all about? Letting God be God of all, including the results of our obedience to Him?

The Lord gave me the desire to write even before I knew Him, when I was in high school, while creating a new ending to an old, classic novel. My teacher challenged me to do my best and was surprised at the outcome, as was I. That spark of creativity, over the years, became a burning ember while raising my two children. Finally, the fire engulfed my life as I began writing about my relationship with my Lord.

These writings are intended to be read in bite-sized chunks of time to be savored a little each day. The journal entries were written over the last ten or eleven years. While my stand-alone stories often are not in any particular time frame, the topical entries flow together that pertain to the scriptural life lessons. The beginning entries, in particular, pertain to my coming to the Lord and, hopefully, will explain the salvation experience to those who are unfamiliar with spiritual things.

Having Coffee With Jesus

After reading my devotional for the morning, I felt compelled to do what it said, "Ask, and keep on asking." I began talking to the Lord about the great desire I had in my heart to share all that He taught me over the years as we spent time together. I know there are many women out there just like me. These women have been hurt in the past, feeling the pain of rejection, confusion, and facing the uncertainty of the future. *Lord, maybe You could help them through my experiences. Maybe they could come to know and trust You the same way I do. Isn't there some way we could get the word out?*

This dream had been put on a shelf but, every once in awhile, I would take it down, pull out my cloth, dust it off, look longingly at it, and then give it back to the Lord. And wait... Today was one of those days.

Then, as I listened, I heard a nudging in my spirit, *"Come away, down to the river."* Quickly gathering my Bible, glasses, journal, and a pen, I started out the door. Oh! My coffee! I always need to have my coffee with Jesus. Walking across the lawn down to the river was an enjoyable experience, the cool, damp grass on my feet, the sun rising above the trees along the bank, and wildlife scampering in surprise to see me at daybreak.

Carefully wiping off the morning dew from a chair, positioning myself facing the rushing river, I said, "Lord, I am ready. Please let me hear from You today."

Isaiah 53 immediately came to mind.

Yes, Lord, I am very familiar with this prophecy about your death. As I began to read it, I let the words graphically, painfully, penetrate my soul. Wiping away the tears, I expressed the gratitude that filled my heart for what Jesus did for you and me. He gave His <u>all</u> for us, everything He had to give. *Thank You, Jesus, thank You.*

I heard a quiet, gentle response, *"Wasn't that enough?"* A pause followed and then, again, *"Wasn't that enough?"* I could almost feel His eyes searching my soul.

Yes, I realized, You are enough; Your healing, salvation, and eternal home prepared for me, Your love poured out for us. *Oh, Lord, I am overwhelmed with gratitude. I simply cannot put it into words.* Realizing that He is answering my prayer by giving me this book to share with other people who have gone through similar circumstances, I am so grateful.

Thank You, Lord, for touching my heart and changing my path as I had coffee with You throughout the years. I am content to sit at Your feet, knowing that You are God, and I am not.

The Roman Road To Salvation

Romans 3:10 *As it is written: "There is no one righteous, not even one."*

We were all born with the sinful nature.

We came into this fallen world as infants screaming for our own way. "It's cold and too bright out here! Put me back

2

into that warm, dark cocoon---now! I can't hear my mother's heart beating anymore!"

And that was just the beginning. As a parent, I learned about the demands of my children all the way into adulthood. My job was to temper my sons and to help them see that they could not have everything they desired, because so much of what they wanted was not good for them.

Like our Heavenly Father... He wants to hold us so close we can hear His heart. He wants to mold us and shape us into what He created us to be, no matter how painful it is at times. He wants to have His way in our lives. Will we let Him?

Lord, reveal Your love through these pages. Please encourage and enlighten those that need You. Fill that God-shaped vacuum in a way that only You can.

The Roman Road To Salvation (Cont.)

Romans 3:23,24 *...for all have sinned and fall short of the glory of God, and are justified freely by his grace through the redemption that came by Christ Jesus.*

We were all born with that sinful nature, but there is an answer.

We all sin. Nobody is perfect this side of heaven. The only thing that allows us to be seen as perfect is the blood covering of the Son of God, Jesus Christ. Covered by the blood of Jesus, our sin is no longer visible to God. My life was in a shambles, and I could never seem to find God.

That is precisely why He came to me, to provide the way. Notice I said *the* way, not *a* way. There is only *one* way to the Father, in spite of what some people may say. Personally, I believe that the Word of God (the Bible) is true. It holds the key for us to live righteously here on earth, as well as the key to eternal life with God.

Lord, I'm so far from perfect; You are the glorious and sinless One. My life is hidden in You. Please put my hand into Your glove of perfection.

Death Entered Through Sin

Romans 5:12,8 *Therefore, just as sin entered the world through one man, and death through sin, and in this way death came to all men, because all sinned... But God demonstrates his own love for us in this: While we were still sinners, Christ died for us.*

Death entered the world through Adam.

These were two of the first Scriptures that the Lord showed me as His plan of salvation. It is not too hard to grasp, yet difficult to personalize. Adam was the first man and, when he sinned, death entered the earth. His sin opened the floodgate for sin to enter all men throughout history. So, God sent His Son, Jesus, to repair the damage. He actually died for all the sin and death which was prevalent throughout the earth. He made a way for men to die to sin and have eternal life, by personally believing in what Jesus did for them.

Father, thank You for sending Jesus to cover our sin, to die and rise again, that we may have an abundant life in You now and forever. I turn away from my selfish lifestyle, to see what You have for me in place of the ugliness I have created. I give myself wholly to You and ask You to forgive every sinful thing in my past. Open my eyes and my heart to Your life-giving love.

Letting Christ In

The concept of allowing God to indwell us can be explained in this way: Suppose you are a golfer and desperately want to improve your game. You can watch golf on television, and it may or may not give you some tips. Or, as in the days when I first thought about this, you could meet Arnold Palmer out on the golf course, and he could tell you how to improve your swing. Better yet, he could wrap his arms around you and help you to hit that ball. But, if you want to be like Arnold Palmer in golf, the best way would be for him to step inside your body and live in you on the golf course to give you the near-perfection you desire. Unfortunately, that is not possible.

But, in Christianity, it is possible. We can go to church and read Bible stories about Jesus to get an idea of who He is. But, the best thing we can ever do is ask the Author of the book to completely and fully live in us. God wraps His loving arms around us, explains the intent of the Scriptures, helps us to live, and convicts us of sin. He speaks to us about the issues of life. He helps us grow and teaches us how to show more love. He helps us accomplish every task. As we surrender to Him, He gives us an entirely new life.

A New Song To Sing

Psalm 40:1–3 *I waited patiently for the Lord; he turned to me and heard my cry. He lifted me out of the slimy pit, out of the mud and mire; he set my feet on a rock and gave me a firm place to stand. He put a new song in my mouth, a hymn of praise to our God. Many will see and fear and put their trust in the Lord.*

This is my story! This is my song!

God heard my cry for help and gently, slowly lifted me out of the pit in which I found myself. If He had yanked me, the change would have been too much. If He had let me remain, I would have been discouraged. He knew precisely what I needed and how much time it should take. Though it seemed like an eternity, His schedule was exactly right. His plan is always perfect. He placed my feet upon a rock, The Rock, Jesus Christ. He is my firm foundation. He has given me a new song to sing---not a song of lament, but a song of unceasing praise to my God and Savior. Many will see and hear as I write my story, and we will all sing a glorious hymn throughout eternity!

Oh, my Lord, I am so thankful for You, and for Your steady hand upon the rudder of my life. We're on this journey together, though I know not our earthly destination. As we round the bends in the stream, I look with anticipation to see the surprises You hold for me. What's behind this rock that I keep bumping up against as I eddy in the quiet stillness? Will there be turbulence or a swift, unobstructed current? Only You know, Lord. The ferns and flowers that grow along the shore give me such joy as You carry me along. Suddenly, I rush headlong over the rocks, dropping into a waterfall that seems it will take my very life. You are there to catch me, tenderly guiding me into a safe place, a place of rest and quiet where I can commune with You and grow through that unexpected experience. The exhilaration that I feel comes from You, the Giver of Life. I don't want to waste a moment that You have given me; my time spent with You is so precious. Those quiet moments drifting down the lazy stream fill me with the energy I need to meet the tasks at hand. If You hadn't filled me, I would have nothing to give others. Thank You, Lord, for this beautiful picture of a life lived in You.

I Was Once Dead But Now I Am Alive

Ephesians 2:1,2 *As for you, you were dead in your transgressions and sins, in which you used to live when you followed the ways of this world and of the ruler of the kingdom of the air, the spirit who is now at work in those who are disobedient.*

How many ways can it be said, "You must be born again"?

One cannot overemphasize this truth, and, in fact, the Word is full of Scriptures on this subject, in one form or another. Therefore, it must be very close to God's heart. He wants all of us who are dead in our trespasses and sins to come alive, like in Ezekiel 37, the dry bones coming to life. Our dry bones need to come to life. He wants to breathe His existence into us, not just for the here and now, but for

7

eternity. We only have a set number of days on this earth, in these frail bodies. The ones who accepted Christ's death and resurrection for themselves in their formative years have a much longer time to serve God and to bring others to Him. For those like myself, who didn't really begin to know Him until middle adult years, we need to grow on a much faster level. We have no time to throw away. After all, we already wasted half our lives serving the devil, even though we refused to recognize it at the time. All we knew was that our lives were not fulfilling. The days, even the good ones, were empty; we had habits that controlled us, and there were many times we were ashamed of things we did.

Now, for those who may be reading this out of curiosity, you do not know how much time you have. You could die tonight. All those people on 9/11/01 never dreamed their time was up. Only God knew. He is calling you, right here, right now. He loves you and has special gifts, just for you. The first is a life that is satisfying, and will last forever, with Him. He is giving you the gift of Himself. How can you not accept Him?

Father, I pray that You will draw people to Yourself. Show them Your love for each and every one of them. Let them see Your goodness, Your mercy, Your heart for them. Give them a spirit of repentance so that they will turn and run into Your arms of love. I know that You removed that empty, hollow feeling in my life as soon as I finally gave in to Your beckoning call.

God Begins To Get My Attention

We owned a very small duplex, and the tenant in the back unit, Kevin, was involved in real estate. He came over on a Sunday evening, excitedly telling us about this great house he had looked at in Menlo Park. He had put his name in the hat, so to speak, to see if he could possibly acquire it.

Kevin explained, "Housing and Urban Development (H.U.D.) comes in and fixes up older homes that are in complete disrepair. Then, instead of selling them, H.U.D. draws lots to see who will be the new owners. The price is always well below market value but, for the most part, the homes are in less than attractive neighborhoods." He added, "I've done this many times before, but my name was never drawn. This particular house is the best one I've ever seen with H.U.D. It's in a pretty good neighborhood, and I think it would be fun to take you by to see it."

Off we went to look at the property by flashlight. He was right. The inside was clean and neat with gold carpeting and attractive gold, orange and brown vinyl in the kitchen (remember... it was the 70's). Everything inside had been completely redone to look like brand new. We fell in love with this place. The backyard was large, fenced in, and mature walnut trees provided shade from the hot summer sun. I could easily visualize the bamboo garden without the weeds. It would be a wonderful place for our children to play and be creative.

After we got back home to the front unit of our duplex, I began looking around at our dismal 700 square feet of living space and realized how cramped we were. I was pregnant with Erik, and we had plans to turn our son, Chris', closet into a nursery. I had previously been excited about this transformation, but now the prospect did not seem nearly as appealing. I kept thinking about that roomy, three-bedroom, two-bath house that actually had a garage.

Later Kevin came over to ask us, "Well, what do you think? Do you want to put your name in for the drawing tomorrow?"

Declining at first, "We probably can't even afford the down payment." Then we pondered the possibilities, "Well, maybe it's worth a shot," and finally, "Let's do it! We can get the money somehow." We anxiously awaited the outcome. What chance could we possibly have, anyway, that our name might be drawn, out of all the people who would be interested in such a great place?

I could hardly sleep that night but, just before dozing off, I remember talking about the house to God. *Lord*, I prayed, *if it's possible for me to have a healthy baby and that house too, I'll give my life totally to you someday.*

The following morning, Kevin called. I will never forget his words:

"Patty, I don't believe it, but they drew your name for the house. I have tried over and over again, and you got the best one the very first time." His voice was positively quivering with excitement.

I went berserk, running outside, screaming and jumping up and down in the middle of the street like a mad woman. I cannot even imagine *any* six months pregnant woman behaving in such a fashion, much less *me*! Of course, my neighbors all came running to find out what had happened. I was very thankful for our beautiful house, but went on my way, doing my own thing for several more years. I really had no concept of what "serving the Lord" meant at the time. I look back at my utter selfishness with great embarrassment and dismay.

That house in Menlo Park certainly was a blessing to us. As it turned out, we only had to come up with $1200 to move in, and then the monthly payments were well within our budget. In addition, we were able to keep the duplex and rented the front unit to a very nice family. To his chagrin, Kevin remained our tenant in the back unit for at least a year until he acquired an H.U.D. property of his own. I thoroughly loved that house, but we only stayed there for a short time because the location, as it turned out, was so undesirable. Things are not always as they seem at first glance. There were stabbings, drugs, and alcohol related attacks just a few blocks from us, and they overflowed into our quiet little neighborhood. I loved to work in the front yard, but had to especially watch Chris, who was three at the time. Some of the passersby would throw rocks or broken bottles at him if I wasn't on guard.

The joy of giving birth to my second healthy son was quickly dampened. We brought Erik home from the hospital to find that someone had broken into our house.

We put more security on our windows and doors, but that did not lessen the fears I felt when my husband traveled with his job, which was often. We had other incidents that left us angry with the community, which pushed us into putting our lovely little home on the market. In the nine months we were there, the property values had increased tremendously, and of course, we had paid much less than the market value in the first place. We were able to purchase an even nicer home in a better neighborhood a few miles away in Redwood City. It was in this home that I ultimately gave my heart to the Lord, six years later.

Oh, Lord, six wasted years. I would not have waited so long if I knew then what I know now. I am so sorry I delayed in giving my heart to the One who created it.

The Gift Of Faith

Ephesians 2:8,9 *For it is by grace you have been saved, through faith---and this not from yourselves, it is the gift of God---not by works, so that no one can boast.*

Even faith to believe is a gift.

Isn't it amazing? We cannot claim any of this as our own doing. First God gave us His means of rescue, then He gave us the faith to accept that rescue. We can't brag about how we came to know Jesus; it had nothing to do with us. It is as if you were on a cliff and fell off, to land on a small ledge 20 feet below. You laid there facing certain death because it was impossible to save yourself. Along came a Man with a rope who threw it down for you to grasp. All you had to do was reach up and grab onto His rope to attain life. <u>All</u> have fallen but only those who grab the rope will be saved.

Jesus, thank You for rescuing us! Now help us to be a rope in Your hands.

God Speaks To Us So We Can Get It

Genesis 40:9 *So the chief cupbearer told Joseph his dream. He said to him, "In my dream I saw a vine in front of me..."*

Genesis 40:16 *When the chief baker saw that Joseph had given a favorable interpretation, he said to Joseph, "I too had a dream: On my head were three baskets of bread."*

The Lord speaks to us in ways that mean something to us. The wine bearer saw a grapevine and the baker saw a loaf of bread.

He knows how to get our attention, by using illustrations (or dreams, in this case) that make sense to each of us. He speaks to us individually in our own language of understanding. He used these dreams to point them to the future and to shine His light on Joseph, who had success in whatever he did (Genesis 39:23). This opened the door, albeit two years later, for Joseph to interpret Pharaoh's dreams. This put Joseph in the number two position over all of Egypt, even over Potiphar who threw him into prison in the first place!

As I remember, when I was about 30 years of age, I had a deep yearning in my soul that I could not explain. A Peggy Lee song* on the radio that was popular during my early twenties prompted it. This tune exposed the vacuum in my spirit, turning my blood cold. "Is that all there is?" she lamented in verse after verse. I recognized that *that* was what I was feeling! Life seemed empty, my experiences so insubstantial. I had a yearning for a more fulfilling life, but I did not know what to do.

I was very afraid of death from the moment I learned about it as a little girl. I remember having the realization that I would die one day, and my mother, a nonbeliever, could not give me the comforting words I needed to hear. As an adult at this pivotal point in my life, I had a vivid dream where God spoke to me in a way that meant something to me. This dream was so lifelike and frightening, I knew it would never be forgotten. I had died and my body was laying in a casket. Somehow, I was also hovering overhead watching people filing by, hearing them saying all the appropriate things, "She was so young; how sad; her poor children..."

I began shrieking, "I'm alive! I'm up here. Please, won't somebody hear me? Listen!"

But my screaming fell on deaf ears. I woke up in a cold sweat, wondering what the nightmare was all about. Gradually I became aware of what some have called a "God-shaped vacuum," slowly realizing that it could not be filled with fun, relationships, or money. God successfully used this event, in addition to many others, to get my attention about my need for Him in my life.

Thank You, Lord, for Your persistence in reaching me for the Kingdom of God. You know just how to pursue each of us in a way that we will understand Your calling. We can then trust that You are doing the same for our loved ones.

*"Is That All There Is" was written by Jerry Leiber and Mike Stoller, and composed by Randy Newman. It was released in 1969.

Clothe Yourself In Jesus

Romans 13:12-14 *The night is nearly over; the day is almost here. So let us put aside the deeds of darkness and put on the armor of light. Let us behave decently, as in the daytime, not in orgies and drunkenness, not in sexual immorality and debauchery, not in dissension and jealousy. Rather, clothe yourselves with the Lord Jesus Christ, and do not think about how to gratify the desires of the sinful nature.*

We have spent plenty of time doing those negative things if we were saved later in life.

The past is just that… it is over. We have gone through it and have come out the other side. If we have come under the Lordship of Jesus, it is all covered with His blood. He has forgiven us and we need to forgive ourselves. This is sometimes the hardest part. Stop and think about that [Selah]. Forgive yourself; God already has. Do not allow guilt to rob you of your joy. We are now clothed in His righteousness and are new creatures in Christ Jesus.

Thank You, Lord Jesus. Your blood continually cleanses us from all unrighteousness, past, present, and future, as we ask for Your forgiveness.

15

⌁ Can You Hear Him?

Revelation 3:20 *Here I am! I stand at the door and knock. If anyone hears my voice and opens the door, I will come in and eat with him, and he with me.*

Can you hear Him? He is knocking!

You know when He is drawing you. Life is not that great anymore. You begin questioning those things you lived for ---that shiny new car, your next vacation, the promotion, and recognition at work. Somehow, they now seem empty. You are aware of things you had not seen before. When Jesus is mentioned, your heart is drawn to that name. If you have been reading things like Christian materials or the Bible, they are beginning to make more sense than ever before. Open the door to Him; let Him come in! Let Him feed you and give your spirit new life.

Father, I lift those who are reading this up to You. Touch their hearts, draw their spirits to Yourself. Please give them new life.

⌁ The Suffering Of Jesus

Psalm 22:14 *I am poured out like water, and all my bones are out of joint. My heart has turned to wax; it has melted away within me.*

This prophetic word was written hundreds of years before Christ's birth. It foretold His death on the cross.

Psalm 22 is such a clear picture of what Jesus endured for us. The suffering He went through is unimaginable. How can we deny Him? How can we say, "Thanks, but I am not

16

interested"? Jesus suffered and died for all humanity, that they might live forever. Mankind has only to accept His gift personally, and yet, their hearts are hardened in unbelief.

Oh, my Lord and my God! I am sorry that I wasted so much time before coming to You. You don't deserve what I've done in the past, but You opened Your arms of love to me, forgiving my filthy life and letting me in. Thank You, Lord. Help me to show others the way. May my life be a testimony of Your constant goodness and faithfulness. Lead the way and I will follow.

✈ The Early Church

Matthew 9:35 *Jesus went through all the towns and villages, teaching in their synagogues, preaching the good news of the kingdom and healing every disease and sickness.*

Jesus is a Jew, which should not be a big surprise. He went to the synagogues.

Today's church fails to recognize that the early church was comprised of Jews. At Pentecost, the first 3,120 were all Jewish believers. He was not recognized by the leadership in many places, but the common people loved and pursued Him. The crowds followed Him into the countryside and clung to His words.

Do we follow You so closely, Lord? Do we cling to Your Word for our very lives? We want to be like that; we long to rest at Your feet, but our lives are so busy, too busy in fact. You are all we really need, Jesus. Your blood covers us and we yearn for You. Help us to find those quiet places of rest in You. Thank You for this morning.

✝ The Apple Of His Eye

Romans 2:9-11 *There will be trouble and distress for every human being who does evil: first for the Jew, then for the Gentile; but glory, honor, and peace for everyone who does good: first for the Jew, then for the Gentile. For God does not show favoritism.*

God places the Jewish people first, but He does not show favoritism. He wants _all_ men to come to know Him.

Men get their just reward---trouble and distress for the evil doer; glory, honor, and peace for the ones who do good. He treats Gentiles and Jews the same, though the Jews are the "apple of His eye." We may have a favored child, but we know it is unfair to treat them so. However, by their behaviors, both good and bad, they are rewarded. It is just natural to want to bless those that bless, honor, and respect us.

Lord, I want to bless You; I want to draw near to You and never step back again. My pattern has been to press in only so far and then draw away. I know now that it does not have to be that way. I can remain close always. It is up to me. Draw me close to You; never let me go.

✝ Will You Take Care Of My Dog?

Who would have ever thought that Je'**tam**, one obnoxious poodle, could open the gateway to heaven? But she is only the first piece of a giant jigsaw puzzle the Lord used to

18

draw me to Himself. Let me begin in 1979, which was not an easy year for me. My husband had quit his well-paying job to go into partnership with a friend building spec houses in the Oakland hills. What appeared at first to be a great idea, began many years of financial trials. The more positive side of these trials was that they produced spiritual growth in my life.

At the time, I really wanted to put my younger son, Erik, into preschool, but that was a luxury I could no longer afford. My neighbor, a devoted Christian, told me about putting her son into a free preschool that was starting in September. He and Erik were best buddies, so I told Pam I would like to look into the school also. There was a hitch. As it turned out, the mothers would spend one morning a week working on projects for the children's classes and finish up with a Bible study. My hard-drinking friends howled when I told them I was going to be attending a Bible study---me! But, for a free preschool, I would give it a try.

I cringe when I think about who I was at that point in my life. Alcohol had become a real crutch, and I found myself drinking two or three glasses of wine in the evenings when the kids went to bed. My language was peppered with profanity; I used the Lord's name in vain throughout my conversation, never even realizing how coarse I sounded to others. The adorable ladies in my Bible study just loved me through it, and it was not long before I was ashamed about my speech, at least around them. They questioned me about whether I had ever asked Jesus into my life. My immediate response was, "Yes! When I was in fifth grade, I asked

Him into my heart and was given a King James Bible to prove it." I am afraid that was about as far as my walk went; I had never allowed Jesus to make any life-changing transformations, even though He had given me plenty of opportunities to call on Him during a life-threatening illness, and now these financial crises. I started reading the Good News Bible with the ladies and, for the first time in my life, it began to make sense. I really did look forward to those weekly Bible studies, but being "born again" seemed like a silly, unnecessary formality that I was not ready to commit to.

The year went by and, the following September, Erik started kindergarten. Pam again approached me about helping with the preschool and attending the Bible study. By this time, despair over our finances had so swallowed me, that I could not even reach for the help God would have provided. I chose to sink deeper into depression. A couple of months later, Pam showed up on my doorstep and, during the course of our conversation, proceeded to tell me about the Rapture of the church. "One day Jesus is going to come back in the clouds and take those that belong to Him out of this world," she said. Then she turned to me and, in all seriousness, asked, "When the Lord takes me to heaven, will you take care of my dog?"

Now *that* got my attention. Pam had the previously mentioned yappy, annoying poodle that I simply could not tolerate. In utter amazement, I asked myself, *what makes her think she's going to heaven and I'm not. After all, when I was in fifth grade....*

At the same time, God placed another Christian woman in my life. Patty had invited me to a Christmas program that her Bible study group was putting on the following day. I had already agreed to attend and, in my own abrupt way, challenged God to prove that the Rapture was really in the Bible. There were probably 350 women in attendance that frigid, damp, winter's morning. The Lord first began penetrating the hardness of my heart as we sang many of the favorite Christmas carols I had loved as a child; tears were softening my soul by the time the leader seated us and began to teach. She had only made a few comments when she had us turn to 1 Thessalonians 4. She began reading in verse 1 and read through to verses 16 and 17,

"For the Lord himself will come down from heaven, with a loud command, with the voice of the archangel and with the trumpet call of God, and the dead in Christ will rise first. After that, we who are still alive and are left will be caught up together with them in the clouds to meet the Lord in the air"...

Looking up, she finished with, "Some people call this the Rapture."

I almost could not breathe and was awestruck that God would answer my prayer so quickly and completely. I did *not* want to be left behind to take care of Pam's pesky poodle. I began studying the Bible in earnest again and enjoyed the new friends I was making. Several weeks later, alone at home, I recommitted my life to Jesus, asking Him to become Lord of my life, to make me clean and forgive my sins. I knew I had really made a mess of things and finally saw the necessity of being "born again." At that moment, the Holy Spirit was so present in my room; I felt, if I turned around quickly enough, I could actually see Him. His presence has never left me since that January of 1981, and my life has never been the same, thankfully!

Contrary to what I first believed, things did not immediately become rosy when I accepted Christ. Our finances did not dramatically change, but *I* changed. I learned that money could not make or destroy my happiness. After Jesus became a part of my life, my mind was refocused and I became engrossed in learning all about Him. The emptiness disappeared and the fear of death left, just like it says in 1 Corinthians 15:55, *"Where, O death, is your victory? Where, O death, is your sting?"* I found what had eluded me for my entire life. Satisfaction did not rest on what was happening in the circumstances going on around me anymore. The truths in the Bible were finally becoming absorbed because the Author of the Book, who now lived in me, gave comprehension that wasn't formerly available. Our spiritual life is what goes on forever. I chose to live in the Holy Spirit, where heaven awaits me after this life is over.

Jesus, The King

Matthew 2:2 *At Jesus' birth the Magi asked, "Where is the one who has been born king of the Jews?"*

Luke 23:38 *There was a written notice above him, which read: "THIS IS THE KING OF THE JEWS."*

Jesus – The King of the Jews.

From His birth to His death, and now after His resurrection and throughout eternity, Jesus is the King of the Jews, but also the King of all mankind, the King of the universe!

Thank You, Father, for sending Your Son to die and be raised again to bring eternal life for all mankind. That was His whole purpose of coming to earth, so that we could know Him, accepting Him as Lord. He brought with Him the gift of salvation for all who believe. Thank You for this wondrous reward! Thank You for completing the gift with the outpouring of the Holy Spirit.

God Does Not Show Favoritism

Acts 10:34 *Then Peter began to speak: "I now realize how true it is that God does not show favoritism but accepts men from every nation who fear him and do what is right."*

God is not prejudiced.

Since He created the world and everything in it, He wants all to know Him as He is. It is incredible to realize that He is reaching out to all humanity, every race, tribe, color, and tongue. He is drawing us all to Himself. He loves those who have accepted other faiths, and is working to get their attention, though He has also given everyone free will. He loves the Muslim people who are bound up in their fanaticism, laws, coverings and man-made religion; He loved me though I was trapped in unbelief and a selfish lifestyle. He wants to set us all free from the chains that hold us in self-imposed prisons.

Lord, You so love Your creation, all of mankind. It must grieve You to see humanity's loss, their hatred of You, and hatred of those who follow You. Please save them!

✝ ## God's Plan Of Salvation

Galatians 1:11,12 *I want you to know, brothers, that the gospel I preached is not something that man made up. I did not receive it from any man, nor was I taught it; rather I received it by revelation from Jesus Christ.*

Man did not make up a new religion one day. God laid down the plan, first for the Jews. Then He sent His Son, Jesus, to complete the picture.

The Holy Spirit presented the gospel message to men over many hundreds of years. He gave His words to those He handpicked, to write down, and pass on to future generations. Our Bible is God-breathed, written by man, first to the Jews and then to the Gentiles. The Bible tells how the world came about, how sin entered God's creation, and how good and evil have been battling ever since. It is God's plan, not man's plan. It is a plan for salvation through His Son. Nothing can change that. The first blood covering for sin came in the third chapter of the Bible when God killed an animal to provide clothing for the very first sin, called the fall of man.

Thank You, Lord, for Your plan of salvation. Thank You that it's still being carried out thousands of years after You created the universe. Thank You that it will be carried out until the end of time.

You Must Say "Yes, Lord!"

Luke 14:24 *I tell you, not one of those men who were invited will get a taste of my banquet.*

We *must* accept the invitation!

The Holy Spirit is constantly searching for people to invite into the kingdom of God. There are those we continually pray for, our friends and loved ones. He places people in their paths, to speak into their lives, to get their attention. He orchestrates events to soften their hearts, to cause them to cry out to Jesus. I look back at my life and realize that He was there all along, way before I began to be truly interested in Him. Eventually I started going to a Bible study and then to church. It was not until I totally gave my heart to Him and became born again that I finally said "yes" to His invitation.

After asking Jesus into my heart, I returned to my Bible study class the following week. I first told the ladies how Jesus had become my Lord, and bubbled on animatedly about how present He now was in my life. Of course they were thrilled that God had answered their prayers. (And I had no idea they were even praying for me.) While doing our study, I had learned about my personal sin, and my heart and mind were quickly changed in one moment as repentance flooded over my life. Then I finished telling them about the many other blessings the Lord had poured out upon my family and me that infamous day. What was funny about all this was that, what I read was not what the rest of the class had read at all! Somehow, though I was concentrating on doing the assigned work, I had gotten into a different book of the Bible. It may have been wrong according to our lesson plan, but it was what the Holy Spirit designated for that particular moment. Upon learning of my "mistake," I realized how much the Lord loves us. He can orchestrate our lives in a way we never expect. It took my finally saying "Yes, Lord!" to His invitation to make that permanent, eternal change in my life.

Lord, many who sit in churches aren't going to be at the Marriage Supper of the Lamb. They think they've been serving You all this time, but they've never been totally sold out for You. Please, help them to seal the deal. Give them understanding.

 ## Sin Starts At Birth

Genesis 8:21 *"Never again will I curse the ground because of man, even though every inclination of his heart is evil from childhood..."*

People are born with the sin nature.

Proud parents cater to the whims of their newborn infant. Then, as the child grows, they need to tame that temper, quiet the screaming, refocus the child's desires. Children do not need to be taught how to be self-centered, egotistical, and selfish. It comes naturally through the sin nature. They must be taught not to touch, not to use bad language, not to misbehave. If the child is fortunate enough to be born to Christian parents, he will, perhaps, come to know the Lord. Without the Holy Spirit, sin runs rampant through all of our lives on into adulthood.

Father, thank You for sending the Holy Spirit, the Helper, into the world to convict us of sin and to make us suitable for Your kingdom.

✝ ## The Promised Gospel

Romans 1:1-6 *Paul, a servant of Christ Jesus, called to be an apostle and set apart for the gospel of God---the gospel he promised beforehand through his prophets in the Holy Scriptures regarding his Son, who as to his human nature was a descendant of David, and who through the Spirit of holiness was declared with power to be the Son of God by his resurrection from the dead: Jesus Christ our Lord. Through him and for his name's sake, we received grace and apostleship to call people from among all the Gentiles to the obedience that comes from faith. And you also are among those who are called to belong to Jesus Christ.*

This entire chapter speaks to me!

Verses 1-6 give the gospel clearly about Who God is and why He sent His Son, and then the Holy Spirit, to indwell us. I, like Paul, am not ashamed of the gospel because it is the power of God for salvation of everyone who believes: first for the Jew, then for the Gentile (vs. 16). I continued to read verse 18 to the end and saw today's humanity portrayed clearly: darkened hearts, foolish thinking, depravity of all kinds, idolaters of themselves. God gave them over to their shameful lusts for homosexuality, greed, murder, and all kinds of shameful behavior. The last verse ties it up, *"Although they know God's righteous decree that those who do such things deserve death, they not only continue to*

27

do these very things but also approve of those who practice them." God help us!

Lord, we see that only the gospel of Christ can save us from the sin that surrounds us. Please give us the words to speak and the boldness to follow through; then open the ears of our listeners.

Jesus, I think about how you left the safety and glory of heaven to come down here to live life as a human, knowing that You would be hunted down, spat upon, treated as a common criminal, and die a horrible, painful death. Thank You, Jesus. What can I say, but thank You? We await our eternal home, even as You ascended back to the glory and safety of Your Father as a demonstration to us.

God Answers A Parent's Prayer

One thing that I could not seem to get a handle on in the spiritual realm was my anger and temper with my boys. They knew how to push my buttons, usually by fighting with one another, which always brought the desired result. I would scream and cry and use foul language; there was no control at all when this anger came over me. Afterward, alone in my room, I would cry out to the Lord for His forgiveness. The guilt was overwhelming and my heart would be so repentant.... until the next time. Then the cycle would start all over again. But on December 1, 1983, the Lord reached down and touched me to begin a healing that would take place over the next several months.

I had been invited to a one-day mini-retreat at a friend's home where I began to hear distinctly from the Lord. After breakfast we were to pick a favorite Christmas story and find a quiet corner to meditate for the balance of the morning. I picked The Littlest Angel by Charles Tazewell, and began thinking about what the birth of Christ must have truthfully been like compared to the picture-perfect cards we send one another. They usually depict a sweet smelling barn with darling farm animals gathered around a tiny baby with a halo. *Can you imagine what Mary must have had to go through convincing Joseph and her parents that she was carrying God's Son? Initially, they were most likely convinced she was insane. Then, riding on the back of a donkey all those miles while nine months pregnant; I cannot grasp what that must have been like. Poor Joseph probably felt like a total failure when he could not find a nice, clean place for them to stay. Then, later, what about the wise men, filthy after traveling all those miles trying to find the Christ child?* Other puzzling questions arose, *I wonder what it was like for Mary raising Jesus? Did He go through the terrible two's? Were the other children jealous of Him? Did they argue? Did she have a hard time not showing favoritism?*

Suddenly it was time for lunch. My racing mind could hardly break away, but I joined the other ladies and shared a little bit about what I had been pondering. They thought it was very interesting, and I enjoyed hearing what they were learning as well. Little did I know that this day would have a profound impact on my life. As we went back to our private corners, I began writing about the difficulties of what I desire for the Christmas season versus what actually transpires, leading to varying disappointments in my life. I remember writing about wanting to take the children in the car to see the lights all over town, only to have them become cranky and cry to go home. Then there was the desire to spend time reading the Christmas story around the fireplace and singing carols (Isn't that a lovely picture, sort of warm and glowing?), merely to have spilled hot chocolate on the carpet and the kids fighting over which cookies they wanted. It just was not what I anticipated, sorry to say.

Unexpectedly, I was writing as fast as my fingers would go in a way that I can only explain as "taking dictation from God." The words flowed as God moved my pen:

> *See the light of Jesus in your children. Know that I am in them; when you hurt them, you are hurting Me. When you are able to see and love them the way I do, they will receive you the same way. Give them warmth and understanding, enfold your arms around them, embracing them with My love. Realize that they are children, My children as well as yours. Just as you are My child and are far from perfection in My eyes, yet I do love you. Do not berate and belittle them, for they are very tender. You can damage them with your harsh voice and harmful ways. Just as I am gentle with you, you shall be gentle with them. I will give you the strength to deal with them; just seek Me in times of need.*

Wow! I had never experienced anything like this. I could not bear to share my treasure with the other ladies. This beautiful gift could not have possibly been more cherished and, for the time being, I did not want to step out of the sweetness of the Lord's presence by talking about it.

That evening, when getting ready for bed, I timidly asked my husband if I could share what the Lord had given me that day. When I read it to him, he just sat there dumbfounded. His first response was, "I know you, and I know you did not write that."

Even though most people would find these words a little less than flattering, his response was exactly what I needed to hear. The Lord gave me the desire to live out His revelation, but it was not until the following spring that He actually enabled me to be successful by a supernatural touch at yet another women's retreat.

Several months after receiving this writing, I went to bed early one night because my husband was out of town. Feeling somewhat guilty about my lack of accomplishment that evening, I laid there wondering, *what should I do instead of going to bed?*

At that exact moment, Erik got out of bed and came to my side with one comment, "Mom, you should write a story about how God answered your prayer with us kids."

I believe he heard from the Lord right then. I did write a short story before going to bed, sent it to a national writing contest, and was turned down flat. That was the last time I submitted any of my writing for many years. But I have found that it is very important to put the Lord's blessings down on paper for future reference, especially in times of discouragement. Then we can look back and remember all the things He's done in the past, which helps us to have faith for our uncertain futures. He's there through it all, no matter what.

 Share With Your Instructor

Galatians 6:6 *Anyone who receives instruction in the Word must share all good things with his instructor.*

When you are taught something in the Word, be sure to share with your instructor how it has blessed you. It is good to let our teacher know the impact it had on our lives so that they can be blessed as well.

I remember attending Bible study when Erik was in preschool. That is how I got interested in reading God's Word and that is where it really began making sense to me. It was after I left that study that I finally gave my heart to the Lord. Later, I felt like I needed to go to the first teacher to let her know the impact she had on my life, but I did not realize it was scriptural. She, of course, was thrilled to hear that her efforts were not in vain.

Lord, thank You for moving me to share what a blessing she had been in my life. I am sure that it encouraged her and helped her to continue in faithfulness to Your Word.

God's BIBLE: Basic
Instructions
Before
Leaving
Earth

 In The Stillness You Are There

Luke 5:16 *But Jesus often withdrew to lonely places and prayed.*

Jesus longed to be with His Father.

Why must I always be on the go; running here, doing there, never content to sit at the feet of my Heavenly Father? I must force myself to be still and have quiet times. My heart wants it, but I am always busy. I long to hear the Lord speak to me, but I do not stay quiet long enough to hear His voice. This morning, though, in my devotional, I distinctly heard Him say, "No, read here!" As I did, He answered my written prayer of salvation for my family with a word of encouragement.

Going through the hard times of financial stress for seven years and then divorce, I learned to sit at the feet of Jesus. I could not have survived if I hadn't. I would get up early, watch the sunrise, and have a cup of coffee with my Lord. Sometimes I would put on quiet, beautiful music that would assist me in entering into worship. There were many times that He would speak to me through His Word or through a song. At other times I could hear Him in my spirit. He gave me hope and direction, leading me through His Word to a place of quietness and rest. I look back at those times, marveling at the growth I experienced during the most difficult days of my life. He does allow us to go through these things so that we can get to know Him on a deeper level. We learn to trust Him and to believe that He means what He says. How else can He build our faith unless we really need Him to provide for us?

Lord, I know I need to withdraw to a quiet place to pray now more often than I do. My life would be so much more satisfying, as it was back then when it was just You and me.

 ## Give And It Will Be Given

Luke 6:38 *Give, and it will be given to you. A good measure, pressed down, shaken together and running over, will be poured into your lap. For with the measure you use, it will be measured to you.*

Give good, valuable things.

We do not give to get, but the principle still holds true according to Jesus: You reap what you sow. As we give, it will be given back to us. This applies not only to good things, but to everything we give. If we give criticism, anger, lies, or gossip, these things will be given back to us. If we give prayer, love, kindness, goodness, finances, and time, these things will also be given back to us. Give God the time that He asks for and it will be given back in one form or another. He will even help you not to waste hours in frustration during the day, while looking for lost car keys or a cell phone, for example.

In the case of finances, though God has blessed me abundantly more in later years than I could have ever hoped or dreamed, we had a lot of stress due to lack of money during the early 1980's. At one point, we unexpectedly received a windfall of $200, which we really needed. I felt impressed to give half of that money to our friends who also needed to make ends meet. So, out of obedience and with real excitement to bless someone else, we put an unmarked envelope in their mailbox with a crisp $100 bill in it. My friend called and was so thrilled. She wondered who could have possibly done this good deed. Part of her comments contained a sentence that really tickled me. "I'm sure it was not you because you are as broke as we are!"

But, unknowingly, something wonderful was right around the corner for us. In the mail that week came a registered envelope with a $12,000 check. We had carried a Second Trust Deed on the house we sold in Redwood City that was due and payable in March of 1986. The borrowers had paid off the note three full years early! The saying, "You cannot out-give God" seems so trite, unless you are on the receiving end of God's generosity. I will never forget it, and our friends that received the $100 still have no idea to this day who helped them.

Lord, encourage us to be mindful of what we are giving throughout our lives. We only want to give good things away. Teach us to be generous sowers.

Give To The Lord

At the end of 1986, a Christian radio program offered a beautiful leather-bound Bible if listeners sent in a year-end gift of $50. As my Good News version was becoming increasingly tattered, I sent in a gift of $50. My boys also decided to order a sports magazine subscription to get the magazine's offer of a free pair of binoculars.

Both of our gratis gifts arrived around the same time. I received the most beautiful NIV, gold-edged, full concordance, mapped, illustrated, leather-covered Bible, and was absolutely delighted. The boys, on the other hand, received a petite, plastic pair of binoculars that almost enabled them to see across the living room! I remember laughing with a comment about the fruit of giving to the world versus giving to the Lord. They didn't appreciate that very much, but I can only hope they learned a lesson there. By the way, it is that same Bible, which is all marked up and highlighted today, that I used to write this book.

Who Do You Say That I Am?

Luke 9:18 *Jesus asks, "Who do the crowds say I am?"*

Luke 9:20 *"But what about you?" he asked. "Who do you say I am?"*

There is scarcely anyone in our country who has not at least heard of Jesus Christ.

People have an opinion about Him, be it good or evil. So many think He was a good teacher and had great things to

36

say, but that is as far as it goes. Others say He was a prophet with much wisdom, and that is as far as it goes. Both are right but they do not go far enough. When I say Jesus is the Son of God, that He died and rose again, and is still alive today, I may get looks of disdain or questioning unbelief. But, that is who He is. I am willing to stand on that, with the help of the Holy Spirit who resides within me.

In 1981, while preparing for our move from Redwood City to Walnut Creek, one of my friends handed me a little green card saying, "When you are ready to meet ladies and are all settled over there, just send this card in and someone will call you for a Bible study." When she handed me the card, I heard in my spirit, "*special gift.*"

We moved to a rental home in Walnut Creek on Father's Day. I spent the summer with the boys getting acquainted with our new community. In September, when they went back to school, I spotted that little card in my Bible. I immediately filled it in and mailed it the next day with anticipation to see what the Lord was going to do. Lindy, who called me about the new Bible study that was starting, continues to be a dear friend to this day. She was a more mature Christian, and I grew tremendously through our close relationship. She helped me to have a greater depth of understanding about Jesus and what His purpose is for my life. She encouraged me to get to know Him on a deeper level and also taught me about the Holy Spirit. In other words, I not only gained a wonderful friend, but I gained a closer relationship with my Lord, getting to know Him better as well.

Oh, God, how can it be that You, Creator of the universe, could dwell in one such as I? It is amazing to think about. But ... that is who You are!

The Fickleness Of Man

Luke 4:22 *All spoke well of Him [Jesus] and were amazed at the gracious words that came from his lips ...*

Luke 4:28 *All the people in the synagogue were furious when they heard this.*

People are so fickle! In one moment they love Jesus and are totally enamored with Him. Then, only a few verses later when He speaks a hard truth, they turn on Him and try to kill Him!

It is not easy being a follower of Christ. As people first turned to Him and then turned on Him, we can expect the same treatment. Christ stands for truth, then and now. Apparently, He did not care how the truth was received by His hearers. Can I be so bold? Or am I afraid of man's rejection? Will fear cause me to keep my mouth closed when I should be speaking with certainty?

I had known the Lord for almost a year before I finally broke it to my husband. Realizing that he was so against the term "born again," I chose my words carefully. I asked if he had not noticed a change in me over the last several months, and he did respond that I did not seem to be so fearful over our finances any longer. I tried to live my life before my husband without saying too much about Jesus' influence for two more years after that. At one point he claimed that he also had accepted Christ into his life.

Wrongly seeing that as an open door, I began to share freely about my faith and what the Lord was teaching me through life experiences. He seemed interested, but I cannot say that I saw much fruit in his personal life through his own spiritual transformation.

Several years later, as he walked out the door for the last time, he told me, "You have been the perfect wife, but I just don't love you anymore."

As it turned out, he blamed my relationship with Jesus for ending his love for me. It was Christ that gave me love for my husband through thick and thin and, believe me, it had been very thin for the last seven years of financial ruin. It was Jesus that helped me to be the wife I needed to be. It was Jesus he was rejecting and, in the process, he also rejected me.

Lord, give me boldness to stand for You, even when it is hard. How can I run away if You are bidding me to speak? Give me Your strength and words.

Religion vs. Relationship

Acts 17:22 *Paul then stood up in the meeting of the Areopagus and said, "Men of Athens! I see that in every way you are very religious!"*

People who are religious stand out in a crowd.

Religious people sometimes do stand out, but not in a good way. By their legalism and puffed up head knowledge, they place themselves on a pedestal to prove that they are the most serious about their faith. Religion is not what God

39

wants from us. Jesus came to set us free from all the backbreaking laws. He wants to spend time with us, to talk to us through the Holy Spirit that we now have living in us. He wants a personal relationship with each of us as we read His Word. A simple, quiet relationship with Him gives us what we need to help others know Him as well.

Lord, I do not want to be considered legalistic or religious. Please temper that. Religion repulses the observer while relationship warms them to You.

Jesus, The Healer

Luke 13:12,13 *When Jesus saw her, he called her forward and said to her, "Woman, you are set free from your infirmity." Then he put his hands on her, and immediately she straightened up and praised God.*

Obedience brings blessing.

Jesus saw the woman's infirmity and decided to bless her by calling her forward. What would have happened had she been too embarrassed to be obedient to His instruction? How many times have I missed out when I did not obey that small, still voice? Maybe I was tired, lazy, or intimidated. If we see these challenges as opportunity for blessing, for us or for others, we will jump at His voice and do what He says!

Thank You, Lord, for Your touch upon my life and for reminding me of the following story. How awesome You are!

Jesus Heals Today

In 1985, we had a family reunion at my sister's house in Santa Barbara County, and were all gathered on their ranch enjoying a wonderful meal in the bright days of summer. They had horses and a fuzzy, floppy-eared burro named Bucky, who was very adorable. The kids took turns riding him, and I thought it might be fun to ride him also. After all, I had ridden horses a few times in the past. As soon as I climbed on the saddle, my brother-in-law slapped Bucky on the fanny and he took off running like a racehorse (That is what it felt like to me anyway!), heading directly for the side of the barn. In addition to the imminent danger of hitting the wall, the saddle began slipping to the side with me clinging and screaming for dear life. Everyone was laughing hysterically, except me. When that burro dumped this passenger, I was one fuming woman! Not only was I furious, there was excruciating pain in my lower back. Take a lesson from me; never ride <u>any</u> animal with the name of Bucky.

In addition to the utter humiliation of it all, I ended up going to a Chiropractor for almost a year after that. I never even knew what a number 4 lumbar vertebrae was prior to this time, but quickly became very familiar with the medical jargon. In the beginning, I was being seen three times a week; after several weeks, I was down to twice a week; after many more months, I saw him just once a week. This experience caused me a lot of discomfort and trouble, not to mention the additional expense which, of course, we did not need.

In May of 1986, I was also meeting once a week with a group of about five ladies from Zion Fellowship, Jim Hayford's church. They were a bunch of great women and we would have Bible studies, watch teaching videos, or pray when we got together on Fridays in one of our homes. One morning we began watching a video with a wonderful teacher in a large auditorium. The principles were fantastic and pertained to Luke 13:10-13, *"On a Sabbath Jesus was teaching in one of the synagogues, and a woman was there who had been crippled by a spirit for eighteen years. She was bent over and could not straighten up at all. When Jesus saw her, he called her forward and said to her, 'Woman, you are set free from your infirmity.' Then he put his hands on her, and immediately she straightened up and praised God."*

We really got a lot out of his excellent teaching, and afterward the speaker asked everyone in the large amphitheater to stand and sing a familiar song. Being obedient, we five ladies stood up too, and began singing along to "Jesus Loves Me." Within a few moments after we started singing, my back straightened up, as my shoulders simultaneously squared off. I realized that the Lord had healed me! A second later, our video teacher spoke these words: "The Lord is here to heal tonight, and especially to heal backs."

As I cried softly, my friends continued singing the little song, never even realizing that Jesus had touched me in such a beautiful way. When they finished worshiping the Lord, they noticed that God had moved in our own small group and we all were jubilant as I shared what He had done. Notice that He had already healed me <u>before</u> the teacher made the declaration, so I knew it was not a "mind over matter" event. It truly was an awesome experience.

On my way home that afternoon, I drove right by the Chiropractor's office and was tempted to stop to see him to confirm what God had done in my body. However, my regular appointment was on Monday, so I decided to put it off until then. That weekend I slaved away in the yard for hours pulling weeds, bending, stooping, and stretching my back in a way that I had been unable to do for almost a year. It was wonderful!

Monday morning, I drove to my appointment and determined not to tell my doctor what had happened, to see if he could observe the difference. Laying on the table in my usual fashion, he began pressing on my lower back in the same familiar spot he had worked on in the past. He pressed once, then pressed in a slightly different way; pressing a third time, he finally uttering a puzzled, "Hmmmm?"

At last I told him, "The Lord healed me on Friday!"

His response was, "He sure did."

Afterward he suggested that I return in a couple of weeks to see how I was doing. I did go back even though I felt absolutely fantastic. When the doctor determined that my back was still in great shape, I informed him that I would not need any more appointments. In fact, I did not have back problems again for over 20 years.

There is a side note that pertained to the Scriptures we studied the day I was healed; Jesus simply talked to the woman and then laid hands on her. Do not put Him in a box. Listen and do what He tells you. In my case, no words were even spoken, except for triumphant praise from five little ladies who love Jesus!

Lord, You are so awesome! I am blessed that You healed me. You are the Healer, the Savior, the Creator, You are a Shield about me and the Lifter of my head. Your grace is sufficient.

✝

God's GRACE: God's
Riches
At
Christ's
Expense

The Kingdom Of God Is Here

Luke 17:20,21 *Jesus replied, "The kingdom of God does not come with your careful observation, nor will people say, 'Here it is,' or 'There it is,' because the kingdom of God is within you."*

These days people are running to and fro searching for manifestations of the Holy Spirit.

They are in error. The kingdom of God is within those of us who have the Holy Spirit indwelling them. As we read the Word, or as we listen to His voice, the presence of God is available. We do not need to go here or there to find Him. If we sit quietly, meditating on the Scriptures that He highlights to our minds, we have found Him. We need to trust Him with a childlike faith and follow what He shows us. It is so easy, yet people make it difficult.

One day, quite unexpectedly, the Lord showed me His presence. I was leaving for a women's retreat at my friend's church and simply prayed for the safety of my family while I was away. At that moment, as I was driving my car, I was instantly transported to a cloud with Jesus at my right arm. We were looking down on the earth and I could see hundreds of angels all around.

I asked, *"Lord! What is this?"*

He replied, *"Even though you were afraid of circumstances in your life, those angels have been there all along to protect you; you just couldn't see them."*

Although this vision probably took only a second or two, it transformed my life. Now don't get me wrong; visions are not a part of my normal lifestyle, in fact the Lord has only given me a few in my entire Christian walk to this point. That is why it had such a profound effect on my relationship with Him. What a beautiful, graphic picture that I will always remember. Elisha had a similar experience as God opened his eyes in 2 Kings 6:16, 17:

"Don't be afraid," the prophet answered, *"Those who are with us are more than those who are with them."* And Elisha prayed, *"O Lord, open his eyes so he may see."*

Then the Lord opened the servant's eyes, and he looked and saw the hills full of horses and chariots of fire all around Elisha.

Lord, even as I'm cleaning or cooking, I anticipate Your speaking to me. You have stunned me with Your presence at the most unexpected moments. The words may be quite simple, but they are always impactful to my life.

God Rescues Us

Titus 3:5,6 *He saved us, not because of righteous things we had done, but because of his mercy. He saved us through the washing of rebirth and renewal by the Holy Spirit, whom He poured out on us generously through Jesus Christ our Savior.*

God saved us because He first loved us. He rescued us from our path of unrighteousness and destruction.

The Holy Spirit was poured out on us to bring us into this new life of forgiveness and fullness in the Lord. Am I wasting the life that God has provided for me, or am I walking in that fullness? I want to operate in the gifts of the Holy Spirit.

Thank You, Lord, for the Holy Spirit's life in us. Fill us up, draw us close, and use us as You give us Your abundance. The overflow will touch others, drawing them to Yourself, giving them new life and hope in You.

Splinter Ministry

Again in 1985, I experienced another healing that led to what I laughingly called my "splinter ministry." In re-staining our front door, I managed to get a large sliver jammed into my right thumb near the fingernail. After careful examination, I was able to pull it out with some tweezers; however, after about a week of more pain and apparent infection, it was determined that there was still a piece of wood in my thumb well below the surface. Not wanting to go to the doctor, I asked my husband if he could please dig it out for me. The pain was excruciating and, keeping my eyes tightly shut so as not to see what was going on, I began pressing on the underneath side of my thumb while he dug around next to the nail trying to find the blamed sliver. I was silently praying and asked the Lord to bring that sliver out just like a submarine comes out of the ocean. In wanting to keep my mind off of what was happening, I simply concentrated on a submarine resurfacing. After a few minutes, my husband decided it was way too deep and could not get it out; he told me to make a doctor's appointment because it was impossible for him.

Determined that I would <u>not</u> go see a doctor (guys aren't the only stubborn ones), I continued praying, asking once more to surface that splinter just like a submarine, as I pressed on the underneath side. The Lord, again, had given me faith to believe that He was going to remove it in my behalf. Even so, after pressing and praying a few more moments, I looked down in utter amazement. That sliver was emerging right out of my skin. I took a pair of tweezers and pulled the piece of wood out with absolutely no effort. *Thank you, Lord*!

When my husband came back home, I showed him the 1/3 inch sliver laying on a magnifying glass and he, too, was amazed. I kept it for several weeks until one of the boys needed the magnifier to look at something and lost it. I guess it is a good thing because I might have built a shrine for that little piece of wood.

A few days later, I stopped at a friend, Pat's, home to pick up Erik. She was gardening and complained that a pyracantha thorn had gotten embedded in her hand. She was a nurse, so tried her remedies for removal with no results. Well I, of course, had to tell her about my sliver experience and, consequently, had no qualms about praying for her also to see what might be done in this situation. We did not observe any immediate results, and I have to admit I was more than a little disappointed.

Within that week, I went to kiss Chris goodnight and noticed that he had a terrible, prickly rash all over his back and sides. When asked what on earth had caused it, he responded that, while playing ball with the boys, he threw his shirt off onto a cactus. Not thinking about it, he put the shirt back on after the game was over, and now it was very uncomfortable for him. Upon close scrutiny, I could see probably hundreds of fine little cactus spines all over his skin. There was simply no way to pull every one of them out. I told him I would pray for him but that was about all we could do that night, and he should probably sleep on his stomach. He, of course, knew about my sliver story so was willing to pray to see what might happen during his sleep.

The following morning, Chris woke up and the rash was completely gone; there were no more spines in his skin at all. We were very grateful for that experience.

After about a week, I happened to talk to Pat again and asked her about her pyracantha thorn.

Her response was simply, "Oh, yes; I meant to call you. The following morning after I saw you, I was taking a shower and the tape fell off. The thorn was gone."

These three incidents took place during one week, and increased, not only my faith, but also the faith of my family and my friend. The Lord does care about even the smallest details in our lives, and proved it by giving a "splinter ministry" to a lady with childlike faith. This, then, brought glory to Himself as well as relief to the benefactors of His goodness.

Be An Exhorter

Titus 2:15 *These, then, are the things you should teach. Encourage and rebuke with all authority. Do not let anyone despise you.*

God's Word tells us to live godly lives, to say no to ungodly passions, to be self-controlled.

As we encourage others in this way, helping them to be the Spirit-filled people God created them to be, we lift them up and give them hope. God gave us the authority, by His Spirit, to speak into others' lives those loving words of rebuke and/or encouragement. We need to take that authority and use it for His kingdom, not remaining silent on issues He is showing us to address.

Lord, would people despise me for speaking up or <u>not</u> speaking up? Help me to be bold in You and not to worry about others' reactions when You are leading. Help me to grow in grace in Your Spirit. Give me the love I need to represent You.

⅄ **Patty, The Presbyterian**

Even after receiving that previous beautiful vision of angels (on page 45), I was a little nervous about attending this retreat because it was "full gospel" and, after all, I was still a Presbyterian! Just to be sure that everyone else realized that I, too, knew I wasn't one of them, I introduced myself the entire weekend: "Hi, I'm Patty; I'm a Presbyterian."

The singing was heavenly and the teaching was something extraordinary at that gathering of women. It was the beginning of learning about the Holy Spirit and the great impact He wants to have on our lives and the lives of those around us. The Holy Spirit wants to work in and through us; the gifts did not die out with the first saints of the church as I had been taught. Leaving Him out of your life is like leaving your Bible up on a shelf covered with dust.

The teacher that had been brought in for this year's retreat taught about forgiveness toward people who had hurt us in the past, about cleansing those dark areas of our lives, and being filled with the Holy Spirit. All I knew was that I wanted more of the Lord and I wanted to be a good mother to my children. I needed Him to give me more love for them; it just did not exist on my own.

After the teaching, we broke off into two's to pray for each other's needs. As Lindy prayed for me, that I would be cleansed of all the unforgiveness in my life and be filled with the Holy Spirit, the Lord gave me my second vision. With my eyes closed, a very crudely made brown pottery bowl, with a gaping hole in the side, came to mind. Out of the hole poured a black, oily, lumpy substance. A lovely clear, crystal vase with a fluted edge at the top and delicate etchings in the fine glass stood next to the bowl. The vase began filling up from the bottom with beautiful clear, sparkling water. When the prayer ended, so did the vision. I knew Jesus had done something supernatural relating to making me a new person at that moment, but did not realize how much He did until later.

After the retreat, I went home to find my once clean house in a state of disarray. The boys, now 10 and 13, were running through the family room wrestling all over the house, and their dad was not even around. Apparently he had an offer to go out onto the Bay in a sailboat, leaving them alone all day. I simply told Chris and Erik, with a new, quiet authority, that they needed to clean up their mess. Normally, after being nurtured in a retreat setting, the real world would seem a little overwhelming, especially when it was so chaotic just walking through the door. I did not cry, or yell; I responded in a way totally foreign to those hooligans.

When we were eating dinner that evening, I explained that God had made me a whole new mom; I was going to be able to treat them the way I should have all along, and they had better be prepared to do some changing also because they were not going to push my buttons anymore. But, believe me, they tried. They tried that night, they tried that week, they tried for the next three weeks to make me explode, and it just did not happen. Finally, Chris had to admit that I had been changed.

To this day, they know God did something wonderful for their mom that weekend. I cannot explain it, but He gave me a loving way that I had never known before by filling me with His love. It was true, as His letter to me stated, that when I treated my boys with more respect and love, they responded to me in kind.

Thank You, Lord, for the gift of Your Holy Spirit. I am a new woman! Words cannot express my gratitude for this life-changing transformation.

<u>Childlike Faith</u>

<u>Luke 18:16,17</u> *But Jesus called the children to him and said, "Let the little children come to me, and do not hinder them, for the kingdom of God belongs to such as these. I tell you the truth, anyone who will not receive the kingdom of God like a little child will never enter it."*

We must have simple faith, similar to that of a child.

This is what makes it so difficult for the much-educated ones. They think they have the answers already. Therefore, why would they need Jesus? They say He's only a crutch for those who believe. "After all, I am a self-made person; I do not need Him," they say. Little do they know, but, not only are they <u>not</u> self-made, they are actually God-made, along with everything else in the universe. Pray for the gift of childlike faith for your family. It helps to have that to become true believers.

Lord, thank You for showing me this simple truth as I pray for our loved ones this morning.

Be A Light Where God Places You

Leviticus 20:23,26 *You must not live according to the customs of the nations I am going to drive out before you. Because they did all these things, I abhorred them... You are to be holy to me because I, the Lord, am holy and I have set you apart from the nations to be my own.*

We must be different as we move into the places God gives us. He removes people who are not His followers and fills those places with people who love and serve Him.

God removed the people from our home, people who had hard hearts toward Him, and moved us in. He wants us to occupy the land and use it for His glory, and He wants us to be a light in our neighborhood.

Thank You, Lord, for this great opportunity. Help us to live here in a way that is pleasing to You.

Gluttons In The Spiritual Realm

Hebrews 5:12 *In fact, though by this time you ought to be teachers, you need someone to teach you the elementary truths of God's word all over again. You need milk, not solid food.*

So many people just want to be fed and fed and fed... yet they need to be sharing what God has already taught them.

God's Word is so important to all of us. We need to get the elementary truths down first, and then go deeper into the Word to get the more complicated concepts. But what is the purpose of learning, except to share with others and to help them grow as well? We must not be spiritual gluttons.

Father, the most important thing I have to give people is the concept of dying to self. When we are successful in that area, we give You complete control over our lives. There may be times when You will call upon us to do the impossible. But, at those times, You will supernaturally equip us to do the job. You bring the life we need. I find that I will die to self for a season, only to be bumping my head on the top of the casket when I want to take control again. Ouch! What a gruesome picture! Help me to be pliable and at rest in Your Spirit.

Our Unbelievable God

Psalm 8:3,4 *When I consider the heavens, the work of your fingers, the moon and the stars, which you have set in*

54

place, what is man that you are mindful of him, the son of man that you care for him?

God, the Creator of the heavens, lives in us and cares for us!

Can you imagine? He is so big, awesome, powerful, and yet He lives in us and cares about all the details of our lives. It is inconceivable to me, but it is true. He loves us with an everlasting, compassionate love, even when we are unlovable. He has a plan and purpose for each one of us; He arranges "coincidences" to fulfill those plans and, when we give Him control, He carries them out with the help of the Holy Spirit He has provided to do the task. Again, it is all about Him.

Lord, I can't grasp Your goodness; You know that about me. It's more than I can comprehend but, because You said You care, I believe it!

✝ Hawaii, Here We Come

A radio station popular in the Bay Area began a contest called "The World Game," in which 50 people would win trips for two, all expenses paid, to Hawaii. I was such a new believer that I did not know a thing about the "name-it-and-claim-it" teachings. Asking God if He would give us one of those trips, He in turn gave me a simple, childlike faith to believe that He wanted to answer my prayer. My more mature Christian friends and our family members, however, were not quite so positive about the prospects of my winning a trip.

Not to be deterred, I decided to send in 12 cards. The radio station would give out new clues to the mystery sound every time the disk jockeys changed shifts. I began carrying a boom box everywhere I went, no matter how much my family protested. Every hour, KNBR would call a new contestant's name and the entrant then had a half hour to call back to the station with what they thought the mystery sound could be. I always taped the new clues just in case my name was called, so that I could listen to the sound and have all the clues together to make my guess. From the beginning my constant prayer was,

Lord, you know how hard we have been working, that our finances still aren't that great, and we haven't gotten to take a vacation in quite awhile. Please, would you give us one of those trips? Lord, could you make it late in the game so that I can learn patience and perseverance through this experience? I want it to be a testimony, that You do care about us. I promise to give You all the glory.

After about six weeks of this fanaticism, everyone was completely fed up with me. KNBR had managed to give away 48 of the 50 trips, and I was starting to get slightly nervous. One evening, as they were about to call the final contestant for that day, I pretended I was going in to check on the boys who were getting into bed. First I sneaked into the living room and quietly turned on the radio. Within moments, I heard, "Patty Wilson of Walnut Creek, you are our next contestant. You have 30 minutes to call back with the description of this mystery sound." With that, they played the sound and gave the latest clue. I became nearly hysterical. Playing my recorded clues and listening to the sound in frantic turmoil, I just could not figure out what it was. In desperation, I cried out, "Lord if you want me to win this game, you will have to give me the answer!" Within two minutes the phone rang. I quickly responded to hear an unfamiliar young man's voice asking, "Are you Patty Wilson of Walnut Creek? They are calling your name on KNBR!" Practically crying by this time, I told him I had heard, but did not have the answer to the puzzle. He eagerly responded, "I do! It's a pull chain on a lamp!" That was it! Of course!

The young man's name was Guy Shalin, a name I will never forget even though memory for such details has not been my forte'. I took his phone number and promised to call him back right after I had talked to the radio station. That was the correct answer! I was so grateful to Guy for helping me that I immediately called him. He was as excited as I was, and said that he had looked me up in his phone book, which just came out the week before. We were so new to the area that we were not in the previous edition. In answer to my prayer, they did not call my name earlier in the game so Guy was able to easily contact me. I really wanted to do something nice in return for him, so called his mother the following day to find out what I could bring him back from Hawaii. We had an enjoyable visit in which she told me that it was so unlike Guy to call a total stranger. When he knew I was also from Walnut Creek, he felt compelled to do it. In addition to a better gift we would bring from Hawaii, just as a joke, I decided to bring him 20 pounds of fresh pineapple, the standard KNBR prize to unsuccessful contestants. She laughed and said, "You will really like Guy. He is a nice, *Christian* boy."

I have had many opportunities to share this story, including the following year, while standing in my neighbor's tire shop waiting for my car to be finished. KNBR happened to be on the radio and, over the airwaves, came the familiar, "A-LO-HA! Get ready for this year's World Game!" Another customer in the crowded store remarked, "Well, you can bet none of *us* has ever won one of those games." What a perfect opportunity to speak, and the owner of the shop verified my saga. As an additional interesting detail, most of the winners we traveled with had sent in hundreds of cards, and were playing in teams to help each other win. The Lord was my only team member, and we won!

Oh, God, I am so grateful for how You've blessed me throughout my life! And, thank You for the opportunity of sharing my story once again. I never get tired of giving You the glory for Your blessings.

The Godly Belong To Him

Psalm 4:3 *Know that the Lord has set apart the godly for himself; the Lord will hear when I call to him.*

Those He loves, He hears.

The Lord has given all of us His Word. And He knows who will say yes to Him. It was He who gave us a searching heart, and it was He who gave us His Holy Spirit to make us godly once we accepted Him. Again, it is all about Him; it is not about us.

Lord, why was I so highly favored? You have poured out such a blessed life on me. You have given me so much, and I am thankful. As I keep serving You, and listening for Your voice, You show me the path of Your righteousness for I have no righteousness of my own. I know who I was before You came into my life, and so do You. Thankfully, that life is under Your blood covering, which You continue to pour out, day after day, minute by minute. My heart is full of gratitude.

 ## Obedience!

Acts 16:7 *When they came to the border of Mysia, they tried to enter Bithnia, but the Spirit of Jesus would not allow them to.*

But, Lord, my plans seem so good!

Sometimes, when we want something so badly, we turn a deaf ear to the Lord. He may be saying, "Not now," or "wait," or "never." That is not what we want to hear so we keep pushing at the door in front of us until we make it happen. We create our own Ishmaels in life by disobedience and obstinate hardness of heart. Then we suffer the consequences and ask God, *"Why did You allow this to happen?"* If we would be like sheep that obey their shepherd, life would go much more smoothly for us; we would not get stuck in the muck and mire of life, and we would be led to the streams of still water that He provides.

Lord, we want to be obedient not obstinate. Help us to be clear on hearing Your direction.

Make Jesus The Center

Psalm 16:8 *I have set the Lord always before me. Because He is at my right hand, I will not be shaken.*

We must make Jesus the center of our lives.

The Lord guides us as we trust in Him. When we put Him as our first priority, He blesses us and leads us where we should go. He gives us wisdom when we need it. When we encounter difficulties, we know He is there in the midst of our trials. The Lord uses those difficulties to strengthen our faith in Him. We will not be shaken for He is with us.

Jesus, I thank You that Your Holy Spirit is by my side and, at the same time, You are at the right hand of the Father. When things go wrong, I know You are there to rescue me. Lead me, Lord, to Your place of rest and refreshing.

The Stick That Produced Fruit

Numbers 17:8 *The next day Moses entered the Tent of Testimony and saw that Aaron's staff, which represented the House of Levi, had not only sprouted but had budded, blossomed and produced almonds.*

God often goes above and beyond our hopes and dreams.

God had told Moses that the staff of the man He chose would sprout. But, as stated, He did much more than promised. A stick that budded, blossomed, and actually produced fruit overnight is another one of God's miracles to prove that He means what He says, and often will exceed our expectations. This stick was placed in the Ark of the Covenant for safe keeping, and for all to remember what God did for them during their time in the desert. Do I have memories from the past that show God's faithfulness? You bet I do!

Lord, I remember how You brought me through many things; I also trust You to bring me through the current troubles. You are my strength and my song. I look for You throughout the day in so many ways. Remove the blinders that I may see You!

✝ Abundance!

Matthew 15:34–37 *"How many loaves do you have?" Jesus asked. "Seven," they replied, "and a few small fish." He told the crowd to sit down on the ground. Then he took the seven loaves and the fish, and when he had given thanks, he broke them and gave them to the disciples, and they in turn to the people. They all ate and were satisfied. Afterward the disciples picked up seven basketfuls of broken pieces that were left over.*

They only had seven <u>loaves</u> to begin with, but there were seven <u>basketfuls</u> left over.

Our Lord provides for our needs as we keep our eyes on Him. These 4,000 followers stayed with Him, listening intently for three entire days out in the wilderness. Food and provision were not their primary focus – Jesus was. He had compassion because of their faithfulness and provided, not only for their need, but in abundance – more than they could use.

Oh, Father, as we observe all the myriad of circumstances around the world pointing to the soon return of Jesus, we can become fearful. What about my finances? What about my healthcare? What about my home, my debt? What about our country crumbling down around us? What about the Middle East and Israel? Who is going to protect them? Lord, I am keeping my eyes on You, and not just for the answers. We need to be about Your business and You will take care of the rest. We ask You for provision, for wisdom, for direction. Your Word is very clear about the last days so we are aware of what is happening... if we are in Your Word. Lord, guide me to the right Scriptures to prepare for the future. Give me the wisdom and relationship to hear and follow You.

Sifting Happens

Luke 22:31,32 *"Simon, Simon, Satan has asked to sift you as wheat. But I have prayed for you, Simon, that your faith may not fail. And when you have turned back, strengthen your brothers."*

We will be sifted, but God will use our sifting to help others.

Those that think the road to glory will be paved in gold are sadly mistaken. Because of original sin, it is a very rough path down here. We will have sickness, financial woes, and relational problems, all in spite of what we had hoped for when we first became Christians. That golden road is up in heaven, <u>after</u> we are done growing and stretching through the trials of life. Our faith may fail at times and we will ask

God, "Why?" But, if we are truly rooted and grounded in Him, we will get back on track and hang on.

Lord, we pray that our faith will not fail in the difficulties. Please hang onto us, even if we let go for a moment.

✝ He Is The Lifter Of My Head

Psalm 3:3 *But you are a shield around me, O Lord; you bestow glory on me and lift up my head.*

Persecutions and trials come, but keep looking to God for guidance and direction.

Our Heavenly Father has plans for our lives and sometimes He takes us through deep valleys for our spiritual growth. These troubles are things that we usually do not ever want to go through again, but we eventually realize their vital importance in the spiritual realm.

Lord, those were some of the hardest years in my life and I felt like you slayed me. What you really did was kill my stubborn will and give me a desire to know You deeply and fully in the midst of the trials. I had no idea how much I wanted my own way and tried to manipulate a fantasy life into reality. Thank you for bringing me through, in spite of myself. Your gentle hand was firmly guiding.

Financial Distress And Spiritual Growth

No matter what comes your way, keep trusting the Lord through it all. Things often do not turn out as planned. I found that I would unknowingly write a script in my head and then was devastated when family members, or the Lord did not follow that story line the way I authored it. Such was the case with all the losses that occurred during a low point in my life in the early 1980's.

We did not pick the best of times to go into a construction business, but how do you know without asking God? It seemed so grand when we decided to give up a successful engineering career to build houses in the Oakland Hills. We had always wanted to build our own home and this would be a great way to have our dream come true at a fraction of the cost. Little did we know that it would cost us our investments, our marriage, and almost my sanity before it was finished. Years later, I realized that the Lord was involved in all these things, and that I grew stronger through them.

I think it was Charles Stanley who remarked at the time, "Just when you think you see the light at the end of the tunnel, it turns out to be an oncoming freight train." That was about the way I felt and learned to trust God no matter what life brought our way. Though I was still asking the question, *"What good can come out of this?"*

Part of our great financial stress was due to the fact that there was an economic recession taking place and the latest property we built was just not selling, along with most houses on the market at that time. Because we had a construction loan on the house, which was costing us the prime rate plus three points, we could not afford to pay our crew and all the expenses of construction. Let me translate prime plus three points for you: At one stage, our $300,000 construction loan was costing us 25 percent interest! As you can imagine, it did not take long to put a small business under. We had needed to come up with some cash earlier. Our business partner had talked us into putting a $50,000 short-term, second mortgage on our own new home, "just to get us over the crunch," because he was already mortgaged to the limit. (This should have given us our first clue.)

While reading my Bible one morning, the words jumped off the page, and I knew that God was giving an advance warning of things to come. Psalm 55:12, 13, 20, and 21 stated,

"If it were an enemy making fun of me, I could endure it; if it were an opponent boasting over me, I could hide myself from him. But it is you, my companion, my colleague and close friend... My former companion attacked his friends; he broke his promises. His words were smoother than cream, but there was hatred in his heart; his words were as soothing as oil, but they cut like sharp swords."

Before leaving for a meeting with our business associate, my husband was advised about what I felt would be a very bad experience. I showed him the Scripture that the Lord had impressed upon my heart that day. A few hours later, his face was ashen as he told me how our partner turned on him, and said that the $50,000 loan on our home was our personal responsibility, not the company's. Since that loan was now due and payable, it became our obligation to pay it back. He basically walked away from all liability, leaving us with every bit of the debt. Psalm 55 was completely accurate, and I was so glad the Lord prepared us in advance. We managed to borrow the $50,000 from relatives so that we did not lose the roof over our heads.

But things got progressively worse when my husband was removed from the engineering division, the only part of the company that was making money. The other partners in engineering were told that my husband would continue to take a salary from the construction segment. Unaware that there was no income in that side of the group, they allowed our partner to cut my husband out of any payroll whatsoever, leaving us with a mountain of construction debt on top of it. Pride kept him from telling our other partners that he was now on the brink of financial ruin. He was completely devastated and, for the first time in our marriage, leaned on my faith to believe that God was even bigger than this.

"Coincidentally," we had been gifted with tickets to an outdoor Christian concert that Friday evening. We grasped with all our might onto the peace that became available to us. The rest of the weekend was very heavy with tears, "what if's" and questions about our future, but we got through it with grace. Monday morning, as I recall, my husband phoned his former employer. As it turned out, they had planned on calling him to see if he had time to do some engineering consulting work at an exceptionally good rate of pay. He started that very day and never went without a day of work! I praise the Lord for his mercy and goodness to us during that overwhelmingly heavy time.

Because the latest house that we had on the market still was not selling, there was no income and a lot of debt yet to be paid off. The final blow to our company was when the bank called our construction note and put the $550,000 house and 12 remaining view lots on the auction block. I had a lot of faith that the Lord would not allow us to lose those properties, and that we would be pulled through just as before. I fully believed there would be a buyer in the eleventh hour to bail us out.

I remember being at work the day I got the devastating news that our property had been auctioned off. Everything we had put our funds into was gone and there was no money that would come to us. I simply refused to believe it. The Lord would make a way; He <u>had</u> to! But it was true. All of our investment went back to the bank.

In tears, I called my friend, Lindy, and she came right over. My employer was out for the afternoon, fortunately, so she prayed with me and helped me to grow up with this one brutal lesson.

She told me, "The Lord is sovereign; He is not going to do something that is against His will. Thank God you have Him right now to hang onto; He is not controlled by your whims and desires. Keep looking to Him because Romans 8:28 says, '*We know that in <u>all</u> things God works for the good of those who love him, who have been called according to his purpose.*'"

What good could possibly come out of this? How could there be any good at all? As weeks grew into months, I realized that I had faith in my own faith, not necessarily faith in what God wanted to accomplish. Spoiled by the Lord's previous graciousness, I now needed to mature in my relationship with Him. In Job 13:15, Job said, *"Though He slay me, yet will I hope in him…"* Eventually I realized that the Lord had separated us from our unethical partner in one quick moment of time, and that things would have gotten much worse if we continued on that same path.

Father, even though these trials were so painful, I realize that You were sparing us from still greater sufferings by severing our relationship with that man. It took me years to forgive him, and then it was only by Your Spirit's nudging.

Ignorance, Not So Sweet

Proverbs 9:17,18 *"Stolen water is sweet; food eaten in secret is delicious."* But little do they know that the dead are there, that her guests are in the depths of the grave.

People are partying on their way to the grave.

I am looking at society all over the world. Life is tough, gas prices are going through the roof, people's jobs are in jeopardy, and houses are not selling. In some cases it is just easier to walk away. People muffle their pain with drugs and alcohol. They are dead on the inside and do not even know it. They gather in groups to party their lives away, pretending they have it all together. It is only because of Jesus living in me that I am any different. He is the hope of my life. He gives me peace in the turmoil.

Thank You, Lord, for putting my feet upon Your rock and giving me new life. My existence is in You, and that life will last throughout eternity. For those who call you a crutch, I must say that I would rather have You than anything this world has to offer. You hold me up when I should be falling down.

 Jesus Fulfills Everything

Luke 24:44 *He said to them, "This is what I told you while I was still with you. Everything must be fulfilled that is written about me in the Law of Moses, the Prophets and the Psalms."*

He fulfilled all the prophecies pertaining to His first coming. He will fulfill all the prophecies pertaining to His second coming.

Much has been written about the return of Jesus in the Word. You can be sure He will fulfill those, too. There have been many teachings about the odds of one man being the answer to so many prophecies. It is astounding, totally unbelievable (without the gift of faith), that He could have completed so much in the short season He walked on this earth. But, because He is God, He did it!

Lord, You have given me a clear picture that it is all about You, Your Word, Your prophecies which were written by Your prophets, and all on Your timetable!

69

✝ <u>A Hearing Ear</u>

I was Chris' team mother for his soccer team one year and it was quickly approaching the end of the season. Being the team mom, it fell on my shoulders to get a gift for each of the two soccer coaches. I ran an errand for my boss one afternoon, picking up his new stationery downtown. I had a distinct impression that I should go to the "Shirtique," just around the corner, to get two shirts for the coaches. At first I tried to ignore it. However, the impression just would not leave me, and I kept pushing it to the back of my mind while I waited for the print job to be finished. I thought, *When I have the time tomorrow, I plan on going to the bank and can run across the street to get those soccer shirts.* <u>Still</u> the idea would not leave me. *Oh, alright, if there is a parking space right in front...*

I looked at my watch to realize that the printing had taken longer than I expected; it was now 4:45, and I did not have time to get back to work anyway. With the thought in my mind about those shirts, I entered my car. Driving around the corner, I looked to see a vacant space in front of "Shirtique." *O.K, I give up. I'll go.* I went into the store and asked for two iron-on emblems of soccer balls to put on two shirts. The girl helping me said they had been out of those particular emblems for a month and that there did not seem to be any more left in the entire county.

Another employee looked over her shoulder and told her, "Yes, there are two left, in that bag under the counter."

The first girl was embarrassed when she found them right at her fingertips, whispering to me that she had sent people away empty-handed because she did not know they were available. I picked two shirts and had the emblems transferred. Feeling grateful for this obvious blessing, I told my family all about it at dinner.

The following morning our clock radio woke me up, as usual, to the news of the Bay Area. The first words I heard were, "'Shirtique' in Walnut Creek burned to the ground during the night; cause of the fire is unknown at this time." I was one of the store's last customers. The Holy Spirit really does have our best interests at heart, trivial as they may seem at the time.

Please, Lord, make me more aware of Your presence, and help me to know when it is You, not my own thinking. I actually thought I was arguing with myself but it was You guiding my life all along. You are awesome! Thank You.

Growth Through Trials

Psalm 40:1,2 *I waited patiently for the Lord; he turned to me and heard my cry. He lifted me out of the slimy pit, out of the mud and mire; he set my feet on a rock and gave me a firm place to stand.*

Waiting is one of the very hardest things we do as Christians.

I remember first reading this and wondering, *"How long, Lord, do I need to wait?"* It had been a great trial over many years and I was still waiting. Yet He did come to my rescue; he heard my cry. He lifted me out of that slimy pit of financial devastation after seven, long years. Divorce

71

followed immediately upon the heels of the first devastation, another three years of great pain. He set my feet upon a rock and gave me a firm place to stand. God's Word is true. If we wait patiently for Him, He changes our lives. Much as I hated these two experiences, I grew through them more than at any other time in my life. I learned to trust the Lord, no matter what.

Thank You, Lord, for giving me the Solid Rock to stand upon, You and Your Word! Thank You for opening my eyes to recognize Your presence, Your peace in the circumstances, and Your love for me and my family.

 ## Holy Spirit, Fall On Me

Deuteronomy 32:1,2 *Listen O heavens, and I will speak; hear, O earth, the words of my mouth. Let my teaching fall like rain and my words descend like dew, like showers on new grass, like abundant rain on tender plants.*

When the dew from heaven falls on me, am I like new grass that drinks it in, or am I like a rock along the path that sheds the water? I want to be a tender plant that soaks up God's Word and really hears His voice. Like a sunflower whose bloom follows the warmth of the sun, I want to turn toward the Light of the Son.

Lord, let Your warmth and light fall on me. Soften my heart and spirit to soak up the dew of the morning that falls like light rain. When You speak, I will incline my ear to Your voice. Help me to be obedient to Your call. I want to rest in

Your arms of love, worrying not about the frustrations of life.

✝ The Deposit Of The Holy Spirit

2 Corinthians 1:22 *He anointed us, set his seal of ownership on us, and put his Spirit in our hearts as a deposit, guaranteeing what is to come.*

He has done it and we will never be the same again!

Regardless of what people think, regardless of their reaction to me, I cannot, I will not, go back to what I was. The Spirit of the living God has come to reside in me and has changed me forever. If what I have experienced so far is only a deposit on what is to come, heaven is going to be more glorious than any of us could ever imagine.

Lord, thank You for placing Your Spirit in me. That is something I could never have received on my own. Even though people told me it was going to be wonderful, I couldn't envision what it would be like. Much like having children or grandchildren, one has no idea until they experience You for themselves. Your gifts are so precious, and we can't begin to have a grasp on spiritual matters without Your Holy Spirit.

✈ The Helper

In May of 1984, we had an opportunity to take a much needed vacation. My sister was a flight attendant, working for Western Airlines. She got us some round-trip passes to fly anywhere Western Airlines flew for a mere $60 per person! We were so excited and began planning a tour of Washington, D.C. We would need to take the boys out of school in order to use the passes by the deadline date, May 31, so thought an educational excursion would be just the right thing. Because our finances were still very tight, I did a lot of researching to find an inexpensive (probably seedy) hotel right downtown where we could catch the public transportation and not have to rent a car. I learned of an economical cafeteria there on the same block and prepared in every way to do this visit as cheaply, but safely, as possible.

The week before leaving on vacation was very hectic with my husband out of town on business; he was scheduled to arrive home late the night before we were to leave for Washington. I had begun reading a wonderful little book by Catherine Marshall entitled The Helper,* which opened my eyes tremendously to the role God wants to play in our lives, if we would get out of His way and ask Him for assistance. Through her writing, I began expecting that the Lord, in the person of the Holy Spirit, would help me with everyday details.

I felt rushed the day before our departure and had not yet started getting ready. I prayed for guidance and began packing everything a family of four would need for a vacation to the East Coast. We had lived in Maryland earlier in our married life so I knew the weather should not be too hot or humid this early in the season; however, in my spirit, I began hearing words like, *"sun block...shorts... sun visors...swimming suits* (even though there was no swimming pool at our hotel)...*sandals."* I was sure that it was God directing my hand as I began selecting all those items that I personally never would have even considered. *Going to be unseasonably warm I guess,* was my thought as I found the items after a long, dreary winter. Then I heard the word, *calculator.* Calculator? *Nope! Couldn't be; that just does not make sense...* So, in my own human wisdom, I left the pocket calculator on the desk. It was amazing how quickly I finished the task at hand. In addition to the afore-mentioned items, I brought jeans, sweatshirts, maps, small umbrella, tennis shoes, and socks for all the walking we would be doing around Washington.

My husband did not arrive home until 1:00 a.m., quite tired from his trip, but looking forward to our vacation with the family. We were to fly out of Oakland at 6:00 a.m. In addition, we realized that the excursion we had planned would put us on a dead run most of the week, which would not allow for rest in this very hectic, troubling time of our lives. We rationalized that it would be a wonderful experience for the kids. Traveling on passes can be tricky, but the first leg turned out well for us. We arrived in Salt Lake City, right on time to catch the next flight to Washington. But, when we walked into the terminal, we were met with literally a hundred people traveling on the same passes, all wanting to board a plane to Washington, D.C. This was simply unbelievable!

We settled in for a long wait with our hopes growing dimmer by the hour. Sitting in the crowded terminal, I pulled out The Helper once again to while away the time. After I began reading, the Lord increased my faith as I remembered to ask for help and direction in this mess. It appeared that all these people wanting to go to our destination would also be traveling back the same way we were, and just at the time that the passes would expire. If we did not get on a flight, we would have to pay full price to come home. This definitely was not a good situation. I prayed that the Lord would help us out.

In a few hours, a Western Airlines employee came up to us, out of all the passengers waiting at the terminal. Quite unexpectedly, he said, "You are never going to get to Washington at this rate. You know, Western flies to a lot of other places besides Washington, D.C. Why don't you come with me and we will look on the computer to see what else is available."

Oh, Lord, show us where you want us to go!

"What about Calgary? What about Seattle? What about..."

We shook our heads until, finally, he asked, "What about Ixtapa, Mexico?"

"Yeah!" We all responded in unison.

"Great! So let's see what's available for you."

There was a flight leaving first thing in the morning. Our mystery Western employee proceeded to tell us, "Since you're waiting for a flight that doesn't leave until tomorrow, we'll put you up in a hotel for the night. Here are dinner coupons for discount meals at their restaurant."

With that, he put us on a shuttle to a brand new Marriott Hotel that had a lovely pond with swans and paddle boats; the restaurant was poolside. It was absolutely fabulous and so much better than the old flea-bitten accommodations we would have been staying at in Washington. *Thank You, Lord, thank You! And thank You for telling me to pack those swimsuits!* While the boys swam, we ate a quiet, romantic dinner for two by the pool.

The following morning, we arrived in time to catch our flight to Ixtapa. A Western Airlines employee was amazed that we were being allowed to travel south again on our passes, flying over our original departure point. Someone the day before had been prohibited from doing that exact thing. Also, we did not have any passports or birth certificates for the boys, but they took our word for their having U.S. citizenship and let us on the flight (obviously pre-9/11).

Upon arrival in sunny, hot Mexico, we had no idea what to do next or where to stay. Every bit of my research pertained to the Washington, D.C. area. One of the airline workers suggested we catch a cab for Hotel El Presidente, right on the beach, and even made arrangements in advance for us there. When we arrived at this open, breezy, absolutely heavenly resort, we found that, since we were loosely affiliated with Western Airlines, they gave us a wonderful room overlooking the pools and ocean for only $18 per night. (The hotel in Washington would have been $52 per night.)

I saw this as another divinely inspired gift and remarked at the time, "I don't know if this is the beginning of the 'good life' or if we are being given a rest before more grueling things to come." (As you continue to read, you will find that it was the latter.)

We had the most glorious time relaxing, snorkeling, eating, and one hotel employee took the boys under his wing doing a lot of fun activities which left us time to relax and regroup after the business trials we had been experiencing. Fortunately, the Lord knew in advance where we were headed, and He had me put in all the items we needed for our trip....except the calculator, which would have been so handy to figure the exchange rate from pesos to dollars!

Father, I'll never forget how miraculous this vacation was. Thank You for the break and for the breath of fresh air You provided!

*The Helper by Catherine Marshall, published by Chosen Books, 1978

Keep On Track With The Lord

Jude 20,21 *But you, dear friends, build yourselves up in your most holy faith and pray in the Holy Spirit. Keep yourselves in God's love as you wait for the mercy of the Lord Jesus Christ to bring you to eternal life.*

No matter what anyone else says or does, no matter how they treat you, keep on track with the Lord.

Focus on Jesus as you walk through this life, and the cares of this world will fade in comparison. Have God's love for those that hurt you. You will not have enough love in your flesh to carry it off. Be filled with the Spirit so that you can pray for them and His love can be poured out.

Oh, God, we love You and desire to spend time with You. Give us those moments alone with You when we can't have the relationship with some loved ones that we so long for.

Prophetic Words

While laying on the beach in 1984, I simply could not tear my nose out of The Helper. It was so informative and I was certainly learning firsthand how the Holy Spirit wants to assist us in this life. Reading it in conjunction with my Bible, I was getting more acquainted with the Word as well. As I was reading a chapter on how He wants to teach us to pray, one of the references was Psalm 37. That Scripture really spoke to me about the personal situation we were in with our business partner, and a particular portion stuck in my mind. I could not let it go. Verses 35-36 read: *"I once knew a wicked man who was a tyrant; he towered over everyone like a cedar of Lebanon; but later I passed by, and he wasn't there; I looked for him, but couldn't find him."* (GNB) I read it to my husband and silently wondered if our partner was moving. He was definitely not trustworthy at this point, and lived in one of the houses that the company built before we became partners. This house was high on a hill with a beautiful view, and I felt that I was again getting advance news regarding our future.

We were on shaky ground in our relationship with our associate, Bob [fictitious name], and the business debts were now escalating faster than we could even begin to think of paying them. Psalm 37 became my life Psalm and, even though the Lord has spoken to me in various ways, this is almost like his personal love letter to me; He has used it to build up and encourage in more ways than I can count over the years.

Our vacation was the most wonderful, relaxing experience, giving us lots of time to clear our heads and plan for our return to the "real world." When we arrived back home, my husband was very depressed about our business, and knew he needed to talk to Bob about the way things were being run. Before he left for Bob's, I asked if we could pray about it. He really did not see how God would help him but agreed to pray. I decided to tell him about my feelings, that Bob would be moving and leaving the area because of what I read in Psalm 37.

He was angry in his response. He snarled, "He'll never leave. Why would he leave? Where would he go?"

After a couple of hours, my husband sheepishly returned from his meeting. "I can't believe it! There's a For Sale sign in front of his house. Nothing is selling in this recession right now. That doesn't mean he'll be going anywhere."

I knew his days were numbered on that hill, regardless of the economic situation.

These were only some of the events that took place before we were permanently separated from this unethical man, as I related in a previous story. We did see him be removed from his home, and he left the company with us holding the bag of monumental debts to be paid off.

Lord, again You prepared us in advance. Thank you for giving me Psalm 37, which is my life song even to this day. You strengthened me during the bill collectors' calls and helped us to pay all the debts instead of filing for bankruptcy, as most people would have done. Your prophetic word gave me the strength I needed to withstand the trials.

 ## Lord, Don't Waste My Sorrows

1 Peter 1:6,7 *In this you greatly rejoice, though now for a little while you may have had to suffer grief in all kinds of trials. These have come so that your faith---of greater worth than gold, which perishes even though refined by fire---may be proved genuine and may result in praise, glory and honor when Jesus Christ is revealed.*

We will suffer on this side of heaven.

God uses our sufferings to refine and purify our faith, if we let Him. I have often said, "Lord, don't waste my sorrows." What a shame it would be if we did not grow through our grief, if we let the circumstances weigh us down and distract us from our walk with Him. God helps us to draw near to Him during these times.

Lord, I'm asking that You hold us so tightly to Your bosom that the cares of this world won't matter anymore. Help us hear the beating of Your heart. We trust You, Your faithfulness, and goodness.

Go In Obedience

Joshua 8:1 *Then the Lord said to Joshua, "Do not be afraid; do not be discouraged. Take the whole army with you and go up and attack Ai. For I have delivered into your hands the king of Ai, his people, his city, and his land."*

Go with the Lord's direction and go in obedience to Him. He will give victory where you have failed in your own strength.

This same group of men had been soundly defeated at Ai on a previous occasion. It was because they had been disobedient to the Lord, by stealing and going in without checking with Him. They had it all together, thank you very much! Now, however, there was a spirit of repentance, and they had removed the evil from among them. Thus God gave them direction and favor, and they will now win the battle. I must not think that I can do things on my own. Even in the simplest of circumstances, the Lord wants to help me be successful.

Lord, thank You for direction, guidance, and victory in these difficult days. We can trust You to accomplish those tasks You've put before us.

82

God Keeps His Promises

1 Kings 4:20 *The people of Judah and Israel were as numerous as the sand on the seashore; they ate, they drank, and they were happy.*

God promised Abraham that he would be the father of such a people.

When God gives a promise, He keeps it. Usually, the promise has a condition: If you will, then I will. Of course the opposite is true as well: If you don't, then I won't. God has many plans for His people who love and serve Him. He wants to use us and draws us close to Himself in the process. As I think back to the time when the Lord gave me more love for my children, I know that He gave me the gift of a Spirit-filled life.

However, about three months later, my sister called to tell me that the Lord had told her I needed my prayer language. *Who does she think she is, anyway?* (She had just come to the Lord in a charismatic church, while I, after all, came to Him in a Presbyterian Church where we were not taught such things.) I got annoyed, telling her that I could hear from the Lord myself. He had not told me anything of the sort. After we hung up, I called my trusted friend, Lindy. "Can you imagine the gall? What nerve!"

Her response was not what I had anticipated. "I believe the Lord wants to give you this gift, too."

Oh no!

"Well, don't you desire everything God wants you to have?"

How can I say no to that? I admitted that I did want everything, but was not sure about this particular gift. She reassured me that it is scriptural and that I could trust God's promises to His believers.

"Do you want me to pray for you?" In response to my positive, though hesitant reply, she stated, "Hmmm, I'm seeing you kneeling next to your bed. Can you go do that?"

My answer sent chills up her spine: "That's exactly what I'm doing."

The Holy Spirit visited us during that telephone prayer in a way that I have never experienced again. I distinctly remember what happened as a sensation of warm honey being poured over my head and down my body. When I revealed what had happened during our prayer time, she confidently told me that I had received this Spiritual gift. I just needed to trust the Lord and go into further prayer after we hung up. She said she would continue to pray for me as well. I did receive my prayer language that day, and then searched the Scriptures so that I could know more about it. What a blessing to learn that God can pray His will through His Spirit when I do not even know how to pray. I am thankful for my birth sister's faithfulness to call me and for my spiritual sister's desire to pray for the Lord's blessing on my life. Thank You, Lord, for this "special gift!"

We Are Willing Slaves

Galatians 4:7 *So you are no longer a slave, but a son; and since you are a son, God has made you also an heir.*

We are children of the most high God. Therefore, we are His heirs.

Before we belonged to Christ, we belonged to this world. We were enslaved to the things that it had to offer, which often were not good and pleasing to God. Our lives were empty and unfulfilled. We kept running from one thing to the next to try and get lasting satisfaction. It never came. However, when we gave those empty lives to Christ, all that changed. The Lord gave us purpose and real direction. He gave us joy just by knowing Him. Not only that, we can look forward to seeing Him face to face. Our inheritance is that we get to spend more time with Him, forever in a beautiful place He's created for us. Oh, to be a slave for Jesus!

Thank You, Lord, that You are our inheritance, to worship, to adore, to give this life to, forever.

God Protects Those He Loves

Deuteronomy 20:1 *When you go to war against your enemies and see horses and chariots and an army greater than yours, do not be afraid of them, because the Lord your God, who brought you out of Egypt, will be with you.*

As I study the battles of Israel, both ancient and modern day, I see how God has been faithful to His Word.

They experienced many miracles of protection. In their modern wars, for instance, He had a powerful wind storm blow the sand to reveal land mines placed there by Israel's enemies. These enemies had much more artillery, but Israel won the battle because their God was with them.

As God protects and gives favor to Israel in their battles, he also protects believers all over the world. He exposes darkness when needed; He shows favor to us; He vindicates us. We do not need to be afraid because He is our Abba Father, our loving Daddy.

About a year after receiving Jesus into my life, I got very busy building our dream home. My job was to run errands, procuring floor samples, tile samples, stain colors, etc. It was just such a busy day in January of 1982. I had let life get in the way of my relationship with Jesus and had begun wondering if that "born again" experience was for real. I actually thought that I was swept up into an emotional phase for a season and now was getting more "normal" again.

Hurrying to pick the boys up at school after doing the home building chores, I was struck by a large truck as it attempted to change lanes while I was in the driver's blind spot to his right. Because the big rig was behind my shoulder as it moved over, I did not even see it until the truck was hitting the window behind my seat. I spun around in front of it, crossing three lanes of busy traffic, and bounced off the center divider of our bustling freeway system. As I was spinning, I remember hearing someone screaming, "Jeee-sus!" and later realized that it must have been me. I was unhurt, miraculously, though the car was totaled. Either I believed or I didn't. At that moment, I knew I <u>did</u> believe, even though the enemy of my soul had tried to convince me otherwise.

Thank You, Father, that Your Word not only applies to Israel, but to all those who love and follow You. Thank You for exposing the deception in my own thinking, and for saving my life.

 ## Do Not Be Deceived

1 Corinthians 10:12 *So, if you think you are standing firm, be careful that you don't fall.*

We can stumble in those areas in which we thought we were firm. G o o D

Our enemy looks for those places in our flesh that are weak. We may have been strong at one time but, being unaware of the weakness settling in, we are not prepared for the attack upon our soul. He is out to destroy us any way he can. First there is a little test in that area, to be followed by a larger test. If there is a definite vulnerability, he sets up something that will actually make us stumble. In our blindness, we push it out of our minds, not wanting to recognize the corruption that has taken place. Next comes the major attack that topples us like a tree in the forest. At that point, Satan has won the battle, but God has won the war for our souls if we truly are born again and repent, asking Him to forgive us.

Lord, You will always receive us back into Your loving arms if we purposely ask to be restored. Your mercy endures forever. I am so grateful for your loving kindness.

✝ Sing Unto The Lord

Psalm 13:6 *I will sing to the Lord, for he has been good to me.*

The Lord has been so good to me in my walk with Him.

He was even blessing me before I began my journey with Him. Yet, unaware of His presence, I made some bad choices. Some of those choices resulted in reaping the consequences while, in others, He protected me from the consequences. I know that He will do the same for our loved ones as we pray for them and the choices they make.

Oh, Lord, I do praise Your name. You have been so faithful all through the years. You have met my every need, even those needs that I was unaware of. You have been my Protection, my Covering, my Provider, my Husband, and my Father. You have wrapped Your arms around me when I was lonely and given me wisdom when I needed it. You gave me guidance when I was making wrong choices. I am so grateful for your continuing love and presence in my life. Without You, things would be so different, so pointless. Thank You, Lord.

<u>Live By The Spirit</u>

<u>Galatians 5:25, 26</u> *Since we live by the Spirit, let us keep in step with the Spirit. Let us not become conceited, provoking and envying each other.*

Live by the Spirit, not by the flesh.

Let the Spirit of God direct your path, actions, motives of the heart, and tongue. If all of us who belong to Jesus would act that way, there would not be so much agitation and irritation in our church families. We would love and care for one another as brothers and sisters in the Lord. We would go out of our way to be kind. Even with those difficult personalities, we would give grace and mercy. The talk among us would reflect the Spirit of God.

Lord, we thank You for Your mercy and grace that You've given to us. Help us to give that same grace to others.

<u>Family Disputes</u>

<u>Micah 7:6,7</u> *For a son dishonors his father, a daughter rises up against her mother, a daughter-in-law against her mother-in-law... A man's enemies are the members of his own household. But as for me, I watch in hope for the Lord, I wait for God my Savior; my God will hear me.*

When family members are not walking with the Lord, there is an invisible barrier seen only in the spiritual realm that causes the family to polarize.

Instead of drawing to one another, there is revulsion from the nonbeliever toward the Christian. The believer with discernment can sense it and, even though they long for a deeper relationship with the family member, they are rejected along with Christ in them. With the rejection of family, the believer will be drawn to another Blood relative... within the Bloodline of Christ. He is our source of comfort and He will place us in families of His choosing.

Along that line, I remember talking to a neighbor who had come to the Lord later in life, experiencing some hard times at Folsom Prison and San Quentin in his younger years. He expressed it in a way that has stuck with me all these decades later.

He said, "You know how you feel when you walk into a bar where there is a lot of drunkenness going on, or you're suddenly confronted with a sex scene in a movie? You are very uncomfortable, right?"

I nodded.

"Well, that's the way your loved one feels when they walk into your home. You don't need to mention Jesus at all, but they sense His presence there. It repulses your relative because the Holy Spirit confronts the spirit that rules their life. They'd rather not deal with it, so they avoid you altogether."

I continue to pray for family members, hoping that one day they will let down their barriers so that old wounds can be healed.

Lord, thank you for our church family and the ones that live the way we do; I want a relationship with my blood family members but, instead, You have given me family members that are connected because of the Blood of Your Son.

✝

Disagreements Within The Church

<u>**Acts 15:39**</u> *Paul and Barnabas had such a sharp disagreement that they parted company. Barnabas took Mark and sailed for Cyprus, but Paul chose Silas and left, commended by the brothers to the grace of the Lord.*

There were, and continue to be, disagreements in the church. Later these two patched it up but, for the moment, they went their separate ways.

There are people I am not always in agreement with, but I must not slander them or seek to undermine them. God is not pleased with that behavior, and He is the one I am setting out to gain approval from. I must try to keep my attitudes and heart pure before Him, regardless of what others might do.

Lord, these words are easy to write but much harder to live. Convict us when we are becoming bitter toward someone. We want to live a life pleasing to You, free from anger, strife, and hard feelings.

Struggles Between Believers

Galatians 2:11,12 *When Peter came to Antioch, I opposed him to his face, because he was clearly in the wrong. Before certain men came from James, he used to eat with the Gentiles. But when they arrived, he began to draw back and separate himself from the Gentiles because he was afraid of those who belonged to the circumcision group.*

The struggle between followers of Christ is not a new thing; we read about personality conflicts even in biblical times.

These two mighty men of God clashed over issues; they had their frailties, just as we do. Peter was a people pleaser at this time and did not stand up for his convictions. We all get intimidated occasionally, but I never think about our biblical heroes being flesh and bone like we are.

Lord, it's hard to get along with everyone all the time, but help us to stand up for what we believe in. Let Your Spirit rule over our lives and our actions. Help us to stand our ground in gentleness and love.

Bonzai

When we came back from our Mexican vacation at the end of May in 1984, we found that our old dog, Skuffy, was in very bad shape. We had her for 15 years, and she had slowly become both blind and deaf. She could no longer control her bodily functions, and I painfully admit that I

92

had lost patience with taking care of her. After our return from Mexico, we found that we needed to put her to sleep at last. It was a sad moment, but also a relief to have it finally over with. Almost immediately, the boys were after me to get another dog, to which my reply was always, "No, no, no! I do not want another dog to clean up after!"

Not to be defeated, at Christmas the following year, they presented me with a package and mischievous smiles from ear to ear. It was apparent that they each could hardly contain their excitement. Upon opening their gaily-wrapped present, I found to my dismay, a battery operated cat! This cat was better behaved than most cats, and actually responded when we did the appropriate commands. Certain claps brought certain behaviors: one clap told it to go forward, two told it to go backward, six meant to go in circles, and when you rubbed its head, it actually purrrrred! I felt awful that they wanted a pet so badly that they had to go to this extreme. What kind of hardhearted woman was I? But, really, who would ever be nuts enough to invent this gimmick?

Right after the new year, some signs went up on the busy road at the bottom of our hill. A family had lost their beloved dog and was offering a reward for his return. After a few days, I spotted their dog running along the roadway and coaxed him into my car. We were delighted to call the family to let them know of our find and left a message on their machine. Well, this dog had some problems. To begin with, he kept falling down the stairs. Then he lifted his leg right on my planter box in the kitchen. Boy, was I glad he did not belong to me. "See, boys, this is exactly why we don't need another dog!"

After about an hour, we got a return call from the family who was missing their pet to find that this was definitely not their dog. Just great... There was no way I would put him back out on that busy roadway again. We called the vet who told us to bring him over and they would hold him until the owners came to claim him. After examination, he was sure that the dog had been hit by a car. This would certainly explain his instability and erratic behavior.

A couple of days later, with the matter well behind us, I received a call from the local dog pound. It seemed that the vet had finally turned the dog in because nobody had claimed him, and he gave the pound our name as the "last owner." I explained the situation and she informed me that the dog was going to be put to sleep the following day unless someone took him home. Of course the boys were pleading with me to go back and get him. None of us could stand the thought of him being killed, so on a rainy, cold afternoon in January we traipsed off to rescue this poor miserable beast.

Upon arriving at the pound, we were told that someone must have taken him because that particular dog was no longer there. *Oh brother!* Then the pleading began in earnest, "Pleeease, pleeease, Mom, can't we pleeease go look at the other dogs?"

Those boys knew just how to get to me. "Oh, all right!"

Once I was in that kennel, there was no turning back. We found a cute, little beige puppy with funny, Yoda-like ears that had been trampled on by all the other larger dogs in her cage. She was the last of her litter, the runt, and would soon meet her demise if not rescued. The card on her cage told us that she was a lab mix, approximately eight weeks old. On the way home, we stopped at the local market to get some dog food. While we were in the store, no more than a couple of minutes, she pooped on the floor of the car. *Not off to a good start,* I thought.

"Don't worry, Mom! We'll take care of it!"

Yeah! Right! I could see that I had been boon<u>dogg</u>led!

The first thing we did was to put our new puppy in the bathroom sink to wash off all that crusty, brown, smelly stuff and found that she did have quite a bit of white mixed in with the beige. We were all delighted with her; she did not seem to be the least bit timid, and loved romping and playing on the stairs in her newly found freedom. At bedtime, we decided to lock her in the downstairs bathroom just off the kitchen. We put a little water bowl, food, and a chew toy on some carefully spread out papers, with an old rug for her to sleep on during her first night in our home. Of course she cried and yelped for quite awhile but, with enough doors closed between us, we eventually got a few hours of sleep.

In the morning, I could hardly wait to go in and check on our little darling. What a rude awakening. She had turned over her water and food, totally saturating the newspapers, and then pooped and piddled over the whole mess making a wonderful paste to stick it all to the vinyl like a papier-mache' floor covering! The odor was an additional added attraction. She was very happy to get out of that mess as you can imagine. Of course the boys had to go to school so you already know who got to "bond" with our new addition by cleaning up after her. The next night was even more eventful when, in addition to the aforementioned delights, she ripped up our floor away from the corner and gnawed the pieces making it her newest little chew toy.

This was one tough dog. She just barreled through things as though they were not even there. Consequently, we gave her the name Bonzai, as in the cry Japanese fighter pilots used before they crashed into enemy ships. Even though she got off to a very rough start with me, I absolutely grew to love that dog. When we first took Bonzai to the vet and showed him her card that said "lab mix," he just laughed and said, "Well, mostly MIX."

Unfortunately, as she grew into her ears and feet, it became apparent that part of the mix was pit bull. No wonder she was not timid as a pup. She became very aggressive with strangers and one event almost landed her back at the pound.

Erik had a friend whose parents were divorced. We knew the boy's dad quite well but had never met his mother, although we had heard lots of horror stories about her through the grapevine. One day she came to pick up her son at our house. Bonzai, having never met the woman before, proceeded to growl and bark at her, chasing her right up onto the hood of her brand new car, in her high heels and miniskirt! What a site! Of course we were horrified that our Bonzai could do something like that, but the memory of the woman up on top of her car still brings a chuckle to the boys when they think about it.

My husband was <u>not</u> amused, however, and told the three of us that he was going to have Bonzai put to sleep unless some miracle transformation took place in her personality. We, of course, clutched our dog and promised we would watch her more closely. Our family just could not bear the thought of losing our beloved pooch.

The next day or so, Lindy came over for a visit. She had a special love for Bonzai as well. I related the story of our near disaster, wondering out loud what we were going to do to insure that she never did that to anyone again. She told me matter-of-factly that the Lord could change our girl with no trouble. All we had to do was ask. So I got some olive oil out of the pantry and we anointed her head, asking God to give Bonzai a renewing of her mind. After all, the Bible says in Romans 12:2, *"Do not conform any longer to the pattern of this world, but be transformed by the renewing of your mind."* We figured that, because God loved that dog, He could also transform her. Talk about childlike faith. Were we nuts or what?

From that day forward, however, she never attacked anyone in that manner again. Though she was still aggressive, after our prayer, she immediately became a new dog; the pit bull part of her personality became more dormant and the lab came to the surface. Hard to believe, isn't it?

We have such fond memories of Bonzai chasing and yelping after the boys as they rode their bicycles and motorbikes all over our yard and through the neighborhood. She brought many smiles to peoples' faces when they saw her pulling Chris or Erik down the street at breakneck speed on their skateboards. She actually thought she was a family member as depicted by her wheedling her way up on the end of the couch, casually draping herself along the back so that she could be in contact with each of us as we sat together watching television. Yes, we let her get away with a lot. She was such good company for me; in fact, I am sure she helped me refocus and brought a little bit of sanity back into my stress-filled life.

✝ Complete Repentance

Acts 19:18,19 *Many of those who believed now came and openly confessed their evil deeds. A number who had practiced sorcery brought their scrolls together and burned them publicly. When they calculated the value of the scrolls, the total came to fifty thousand drachmas (drachma = 1 day's wages).*

Complete repentance---they turned away from their past and even destroyed the tools of their trade so that nobody else could use them, at great cost to themselves.

This made a huge statement to everyone, believers and non-believers alike. They completely gave up their past and their livelihood to go forward with Christ. I actually saw this happen once.

A known witch came to a large gathering of believers for a prayer service on Halloween in San Francisco. He got saved after hearing the message. His appearance changed from the very moment of salvation, and I learned later that he burned all his Wicca books and materials. He gave it <u>all</u> up and went on with Christ. You cannot simply add Jesus to your old life; you must put away everything unlike Him. Start fresh with Him at the center of your life, regardless of the cost.

We had been praying in the car on our way to this event and asked for God's protection because we knew it could be dangerous. Someone was given a prophetic picture that gave all of us great encouragement. She saw one lighted match in the darkness, then another, and another. These little lights, representing God's presence, were coming from all over the Bay Area to the center of the witchcraft gathering on that particular night. As the lights came together in all that darkness, they became one big torch to extinguish the evil presence that normally existed there on Halloween. It was the presence of God that drew this witch away from his demonic activity and to the Lord Jesus Christ.

Lord, thank You for the salvation of this high priest of Wicca. Thank You for the salvation of the sorcerers mentioned in Acts. You have great power, greater than any witchcraft. And, thank You for bringing me out of my past! God, though I wasn't involved in witchcraft, You have so changed me. I give You praise and honor.

⊥ Never Give Up

Hebrews 11:13,14 *All these people were still living by faith when they died. They did not receive the things promised; they only saw them and welcomed them from a distance. They admitted that they were aliens and strangers on earth. People who say such things show that they are looking for a country of their own.*

We continue to pray for the desires of our hearts right up to the point of our death here on earth.

We are aliens living in a foreign land. Our real home is in heaven. Our prayers seem fruitless at times as we wonder if they will ever be answered. Even these great saints of old did not see all the answers, though they were devoted in their prayers. God did answer, yet not in their time frame, and often not in their way. He is faithful.

Thank You, Lord, that we can trust You, and not ourselves, to bring about the answers. You will answer in Your time, in Your way.

Obedience Is The Key

Acts 13:22 *After removing Saul, God made David their king. He testified concerning him: "I have found David son* *of Jesse a man after my own heart; he will do everything I want him to do."*

Again, God removes those people who do not follow Him, replacing them with people who do follow after Him.

David made a lot of mistakes but his heart was sold out to God. He always sought out God's forgiveness and had a desire to be obedient. God knew, overall, that He could trust David to do what He was asking him to do.

Lord, give us a heart of obedience. We thank You that You don't expect perfection of us, and that you do continue to love us even when we make mistakes. But, please help us to stay on track!

Bitterness Takes Us Captive

Acts 8:21-23 *You have no part or share in this ministry, because your heart is not right before God. Repent of this wickedness and pray to the Lord. Perhaps he will forgive you for having such a thought in your heart. For I see that you are full of bitterness and captive to sin.*

God looks at the heart to determine a man's worth. He knows who is with Him, and who is out for his own gain.

How is my heart? I do a lot of things in and around the church, but if my heart falls short, God is not pleased. My attitude fails, at times, to meet God's standard if I operate in hypocrisy, pride, judgmental attitudes, or anger. I constantly need His conviction of the Spirit so that I can be pleasing to Him. The word "hypocrite" originated in Greece. The term was used for a one-man theatre performance. He would don various masks to represent each person he was portraying. Interesting, isn't it?

Psalm 19:14 *May the words of my mouth and the meditations of my heart be pleasing to You, my Lord, my God and my Redeemer.*

 Isolation

Hebrews 10:24,25 *And let us consider how we may spur one another on toward love and good deeds. Let us not give up meeting together, as some are in the habit of doing, but let us encourage one another---and all the more as you see the Day approaching.*

Isolation brings destruction.

There was a period in the middle of our financial trials that I succumbed to isolationism. I would get up extremely early in the morning to spend time with the Lord. Then I remained alone all day long, only leaving the house when I absolutely had to, to pick up the boys from school or to get groceries. It was a very solitary, depressing time. I *thought* I was handling it well. Isolation began ruling me, however, and it was then that I realized how harmful seclusion was to my well-being.

Because we were building houses on steep hillsides which required many stairs, it was mostly professional athletes who bought them. Consequently, we were given four tickets to an Oakland A's game by one of the pitchers. We brought our good friends and were having a wonderful time.

During the course of the evening, I uttered the words, "Wow! It's so great to talk to people I can actually see!" In return, I got quizzical stares, and realized how messed up I had become. It shook me to realize how strange it sounded. I was so bent on being super-spiritual during our great trials that I was on the verge of losing my credibility.

The enemy of my soul had succeeded in keeping me away from friends and family who would have held me accountable. Once I realized what had happened, I made sure to become more social again, plugging into various activities, until that extremely stressful period of life was behind me. We must continue to meet with other believers for the good of the entire body, both them and us.

A Critical Spirit

Acts 11:18 *When they heard this, they had no further objections and praised God, saying, "So then, God has granted even the Gentiles repentance unto life."*

They previously criticized without knowing all the details.

There have been times when I was critical of others, even trusted leaders or friends. I questioned something they did

103

or said without having all the facts. That critical spirit needs to cease! It is destructive, divisive, and brings bad fruit. Then, when all the facts are known, I am very humbled to have to admit my error.

Lord, help me to have a gentle attitude toward everyone and to always think the best. Then, if I need to question someone, I can do it in love without criticism, the way You would have me do it.

 Clean Hands And A Pure Heart

Psalm 15:1-3 *Lord, who may dwell in your sanctuary? Who may live on your holy hill? He whose walk is blameless and who does what is righteous, who speaks the truth from his heart and has no slander on his tongue, who does his neighbor no wrong and casts no slur on his fellow man.*

God loves His people who walk and talk in obedience to His desires. Their lives are centered on Him.

Again, having a pure heart without criticism of others is essential to our relationship with God. My words must be truthful and sincere, without malice toward anyone. I may not have all the details of a situation, and my interpretation may be in error. It is bad enough to think unkindly of someone much less to speak it.

Lord, cleanse my mind and my tongue with Your Holy Spirit. Create in me a pure heart.

104

<u>You Are All I Need</u>

<u>Psalm 16:5,6</u> *Lord, you have assigned me my portion and my cup; you have made my lot secure. The boundary lines have fallen for me in pleasant places; surely I have a delightful inheritance.*

God gives us good gifts; He is all we need. He gives us life and He knows our future.

Lord, the life You have given me is more abundant than I ever imagined. You have turned my life right side up, from the time I fully came to You until now. You shook out all the bad stuff and filled me with Yourself and the gifts that are so abundant in You. You have given me a desire to write again, but with a purpose; You have given me a desire to worship You again with my instrument. My purpose in life is to serve You and to bring You glory.

Oh, Father, I pray that You would bless and encourage the readers of my writings to use their gifts. Whatever blessings You have poured out upon them need to be used, both to minister to others and to bring You glory.

<u>A Special Touch</u>

Very early on in my walk with Jesus, a group of ladies was going down to a seminar featuring James Robison one evening in San Jose. They were women from Lindy's church that I had not met before, but I was always willing to take off and have fun, fun, fun! Little did I know that *fun* was not what was in store for me that night.

One of our entourage was in a wheelchair, allowing us to sit in the very front row of the auditorium. Because I did not go to their church, I had not experienced the movement of the Holy Spirit in the way they had. The ladies seemed a little concerned over how I would respond to this new style of teaching and worship. They did not need to worry; I absolutely loved both of these new opportunities. I remember that the teaching dealt with fear, which was something that immediately got my attention. The Scripture reference he used was from Deuteronomy 6:23, as he taught that "God brought you out to bring you in," into a new experience, into a new life, away from the bondage of your past life, into the new life He is giving you.

At the very end there was an altar call for those who wanted to be set free from fear. Because we were already in the front row, it was almost as if my feet had a mind of their own. My body was still in the seat but my legs were leading me forward. As Pastor Robison began praying for people, some of them fell down to the ground. Looking around me, I wondered what in the world was going on. I prayed, *"Oh, Lord, please don't do that to me; I'm a Presbyterian!"* God honored my cry as He also set me free from the spirit of fear. Though fear could not live in me, it seemed to always be around to harass whenever possible.

The next day, while working in my yard using a weed trimmer, the long grass kept getting tangled up on the blade. I would have to stop periodically to remove all the debris so that it would work properly. I felt the Lord speak to my heart. *"Sometimes it takes a special touch to free <u>you</u> from the things that bind, just like this weed trimmer."*

God certainly did untangle me from fear that night. I am forever grateful for His goodness to me.

Receive The Truth Gladly

<u>Acts 17:11</u> *Now the Bereans were of more noble character than the Thessalonians, for they received the message with great eagerness and examined the Scriptures every day to see if what Paul said was true.*

They examined the Scriptures, testing Paul and Silas to see if they were telling the truth.

So often today people are too lazy to do this. They are like baby birds with their mouths open receiving whatever their mother drops in. This is how people get led astray, by believing what false teachers are delivering to their eager ears, without ever checking the Scriptures. Thankfully, the Bereans received truth with examination and eagerness. Oh, that we could all follow this example!

Father, help us to look things up and check for correctness in what we believe. We're eager to know the truth and to know You on a deeper level. We don't want to be led astray by false teachers.

The Joy Of My Salvation

Acts 16:34 *The jailor brought them into his house and set a meal before them; he was filled with joy because he had come to believe in God---he and his whole family.*

Oh, the joy that salvation brings.

The longer I walk with the Lord, the farther I come away from my old days. At first I was excited and joyful because my life was so different and the presence of the Holy Spirit was completely new to me. Now, as in a marriage, this relationship is comfortable in that I sometimes forget how miserable I was before. I take for granted the love that is continuously poured out on me and the help I receive on a daily basis, both in the physical and spiritual realms. His presence is here with me always when I put aside my prior life. As Jesus brings me into His kingdom, the darkness that hung over me is no longer here; the curtain has been torn in two.

Lord, God in heaven, pour out Your Spirit on us, bringing us the joy of Your salvation once again. We don't want to forget what it was like without You. Thank You for Your free gift (though it was anything but free for You); help us always to remember the depth of pain and loneliness we (and You) once felt so that we can fully appreciate the joy we have now and share it with others.

Receive A Gift With Godly Wisdom

1 Samuel 18:21 *"I will give her to him," he thought, "so that she may be a snare to him and so that the hand of the Philistines may be against him."*

1 Chronicles 15:29 *As the ark of the covenant of the Lord was entering the City of David, Michal daughter of Saul watched from a window. And when she saw King David dancing and celebrating, she despised him in her heart.*

A gift may not always be as it seems.

If I receive a gift from someone who usually has not been very kind, I need to see what the intent of the present is.

Saul hated David because he was full of jealousy and fear of him. Why, then, would he want to give his daughter, Michal, to David? I suggest that he hoped that Michal would drag him down. Sometime after receiving this "gift" from his enemy, David danced before the Lord, which brought disdain from his wife. She, obviously, did not walk in the same faith as her husband, hating him because he loved the Lord. Evidently she walked in the same jealousy and fears that her father did, rejecting her spouse along with his God.

Lord, help us to see with Your eyes when someone offers something that is highly unusual. Help us to see the intent of their heart. Give us Your wisdom to see if the gift is being used for good or for evil. Will it be a stumbling block?

Are You Prepared To Leave Everything?

Matthew 4:21,22 *Going on from there, he saw two other brothers, James son of Zebedee, and his brother John. They were in a boat with their father Zebedee, preparing their nets. Jesus called them, and immediately they left the boat and their father and followed him.*

They left everything familiar: employment, family, and homes, to follow after Jesus. They left their dad standing in the waves.

When we come to Jesus, we should expect that we could lose everything. I should not be surprised that light and darkness could not dwell together under the same roof. I, thankfully, have changed since I came to the Lord. He has remolded and shaped me into a new vessel, fit for His use.

Thank You, Jesus, for calling me to serve You. I left my old life behind. Now, help me to quit grumbling about the losses that You told me I could expect.

Holy Conviction Killed Stephen

Acts 7:51 *"You stiff-necked people, with uncircumcised hearts and ears! You are just like your fathers: You always resist the Holy Spirit!" – Stephen*

Stephen hit too close to home on that one.

Stephen had recounted Exodus, and the Pharisees were happily hearing what he had to say… so long as it was just a commentary on their history. But, as soon as he spoke truth into their own lives, they could not take it. They stoned him to death. It is pretty much like that today. Where is the challenge to repent, to pray, to read, to die to self, and live in Jesus? We must hear the whole truth in order to grow.

Thank You, Father, for truth being taught in some of our churches. Thank You for encouraging us to grow strong in the Holy Spirit and to cling to Your Word. Give us strength to finish the race.

✃ <u>Just A Touch Of Holiness</u>

<u>Exodus 32:5,6</u> *When Aaron saw this, he built an altar in front of the calf and announced, "Tomorrow there will be a festival to the Lord." So the next day the people rose early and sacrificed burnt offerings and presented fellowship offerings. Afterward they sat down to eat and drink and got up to indulge in revelry.*

Add a little religion to our paganism and that will make it okay.

Aaron let them make a calf, then he blessed it by adding just a touch of religion, enough to make it more holy to God and yet acceptable to the people. Moses had gotten the people out of Egypt, but had not yet gotten Egypt out of the people. There he was, up on the mountain with God, meeting with Him for direction and guidance. Meanwhile, the man he was trusting to speak for him was too weak to stand against the wickedness of the crowds.

Lord, please purify Your church. Don't let the world sneak through the cracks in our armor. God, give us strength and wisdom to hold to the truth, and to push the evil things away.

<u>Love Your Enemies</u>

<u>Matthew 5:44,45</u> *But I tell you: Love your enemies and pray for those who persecute you, that you may be sons of your Father in heaven.*

Love your enemies by praying for them? That is a tough one!

This does not mean that we need to subject ourselves to them or their bad behavior. We can love them at a distance while we pray for them. We do want to be children of our Heavenly Father, so we must also be obedient to what He asks of us. Therefore, let us pray for our enemies that their lives may be changed.

Father, I do pray for those who have persecuted me in the past. I have distanced myself from them so as to avoid further hurt. I pray that You will give me the grace to meet them once again. I can let Your love flow through me to them. I confess that sometimes I don't have any love of my own. Please give me the supernatural gift of love, even for my enemies.

God Gives Victory

Psalm 31:8 *You have not handed me over to the enemy but have set my feet in a spacious place.*

Psalm 54:7 *For he has delivered me from all my troubles and my eyes have looked in triumph on my foes.*

God gives victory. He delivers us from our troubles, and gives us a beautiful place to rest our feet.

There were many years that I read these psalms looking for vindication, destruction of my enemy's tactic, hope for the future, etc. Here I sit in victory, happy in a new life, my enemies far from my presence. Life is not exactly mint juleps on the veranda, but it is wonderful to see how far we have come!

Thank You, Lord, for bringing me through those awful years of struggle, for grounding me in You with deep roots and a thankful heart of praise. Thank You for growing me up and putting balance in my life, for refocusing my thoughts on You and what You were doing, rather than on what man meant for evil.

Coming Of Age, Part 1

I will never forget the day Chris got his driver's license. There happened to be a dance that night; he was the first of his buddies to get to drive, and he had an old, "middle-of-the-road" gold colored VW Rabbit to chauffeur them in. He was polishing and cleaning up our old castoff when he saw me approaching the driveway from his rearview mirror. Not wanting to hold me up from entering my side of the garage, he backed out quickly... with his driver's door open. The car door caught on the edge of the garage and came crashing down to the floor in one quick catastrophe. Looking in disbelief and horror, his face drained of color.

Feeling sorry for him, I decided to lend him my Mustang to drive his buddies to the dance. Later that night he came in chagrined that he had ruined the rim and tire "avoiding a possum that ran into the road." To this day I will never know what really happened that night while he operated my car. It is true about guys and duct tape, though. He drove that old Rabbit with the driver's door taped shut for quite some time.

 ## Coming Of Age, Part 2

When Chris was about 19, he finally had a car he really liked. It was an old classic, four-wheel drive, red Land Cruiser that rumbled and rattled along. He was very proud of his wheels. One evening I got a phone call from the police. "Your son has been arrested because he had beer in the back seat of his vehicle. We have him at the station. Do you want to come down to get him?"

In other words, it was the phone call every parent dreads. I answered, "You keep him in there for awhile and we'll come down later to get him, after he's had a good scare."

We showed up around 11:00 and he tried to bluster his way through, saying that he didn't even know the beer was there. *Yea, right!*

Eventually, he had a court hearing that I was required to attend. Taking time off from work, I met him at the courthouse. He was pretty scared but tried to act self-assured. Eventually, he was called up on the stand. The judge had Chris tell his side of the story about two girls needing a ride, him letting them into the backseat, then arriving at their destination and hopping out, accidentally leaving their beer without his knowledge.

Abruptly, the judge turned to me and asked, "Mom, do you believe this story?"

I was so shocked when he addressed me, I just sat there dumbfounded.

The judge responded, "See, even his own mother doesn't believe him!"

The entire courtroom broke out into laughter. When the judge turned back to Chris, my son responded, "I swore on a Bible, didn't I?"

The judge, now somewhat astounded himself, quickly brought the gavel down with a sharp rap saying, "Case dismissed."

I am sure Chris is still retelling the story about how he finagled his way out of that one.

Father, I pray that you will use these things in my son's life to remind him of Your goodness to him. Years have passed and he's a grown man now. Show him how much You have never given up on him.

Enter Through The Narrow Gate

Matthew 7:13,14 *"Enter through the narrow gate. For wide is the gate and broad is the road that leads to destruction, and many enter through it. But small is the gate and narrow the road that leads to life, and only a few find it."*

115

Most of the world flocks through the wide gate seeking pleasures, palaces, money, fame, and fortune. They do what they can to make themselves happy. Usually their efforts are fruitless, empty, and only temporary.

Christianity is a much simpler life. We seek after the Lord, doing the things He lays on our hearts. He rewards us with good gifts, things we probably never would have acquired, or even wanted, on our own. He gives us joy, peace, and contentment. But that is not all; He also gives us eternal life.

Thank You, Lord, for showing us the narrow road, the path You planned out for us. It is often not an easy trail, but it is far more fruitful than where we were headed.

 ## Head Knowledge Isn't Enough

Acts 18:24,25   *...Apollos, a learned Jew, with a thorough knowledge of the Scriptures. He had been instructed in the way of the Lord and he spoke with great fervor and taught about Jesus accurately, though he knew only the baptism of John.*

Head knowledge is not adequate for the kingdom of God.

Apollos was a great teacher, had a lot of enthusiasm, and some instruction, though he was not Spirit filled. He had only received a spirit of repentance, but had not yet believed in Jesus fully as Lord of his life. That did not stop him from teaching what he <u>did</u> know. Fortunately, Priscilla and Aquila took him aside and gave him the full truth, where I am sure he met his Savior. It is not enough to have head knowledge; we must be filled to overflowing with the Spirit. We need our brothers and sisters in Christ to keep us on track and accountable.

Lord, I thank You for other believers and for our dear friends that You've given us. Let us all be bold with one another when we see error. Help us all to be ready for correction when needed.

The Lord, Our Victory

Joshua 24:12,13 *I sent the hornet ahead of you, which drove them out before you---also the two Amorite kings. You did not do it with your own sword and bow. So I gave you a land on which you did not toil and cities you did not build; and you live in them and eat from vineyards and olive groves that you did not plant.*

It was not you; it was God.

Oh, foolish Israelites. Did you think you won the victory and took the spoils on your own? Surely not. The God of the universe declared victory for you, and He gave you this beautiful gift. Yet you refuse to bend your knee; you have hardened your hearts, and neglect to see that you are highly favored. You will not look up to give thanks to your God. How like the world.

Oh, my Lord, I recognize that You are the One who gave us favor with my family. You are the One who opens doors to us. You are the One who gave me a blessed life and have shown me favor throughout my days. Thank You for Your wonderful hand of covering and blessing. Don't let my eyes be blinded to Your goodness.

The Gifts Of The Holy Spirit

1 Corinthians 12:7-11 *Now to each one the manifestation of the Spirit is given for the common good... wisdom, knowledge, faith, healing, miracles, prophecy, discernment, tongues, and interpretation... All these are the work of one and the same Spirit and he gives them to each one, just as he determines.* [abbreviated]

The same Holy Spirit works differently in all of us who believe.

He is the Giver of Gifts. He chooses who He wants to receive the various gifts He has to distribute. Since God created us and knew us before we were even born, He also knows what gifts work best for each individual. Then there are gifts which are really on loan for a special occasion. We might require a certain gift for a one-time event, so the Holy Spirit distributes it for that time only.

Thank You, Lord, for pouring out Your gifts as we need them. It's awesome to experience Your powerful love flowing through us to help others who are struggling.

118

Kingdom Of Heaven/God

Daniel 2:44 *In the time of those kings, the God of heaven will set up a kingdom that will never be destroyed, nor will it be left to another people. It will crush all those kingdoms and bring them to an end, but it will itself endure forever.*

To me this speaks of an eternal, heavenly kingdom.

The evil of this world will pass away. We, who have asked Jesus to be Lord over our lives, will live in this eternal kingdom. However, prior to this, we have received eternal life. The Kingdom of God lives within us (Luke 17:21); the temple is our own body bought with a price, the temple of the Holy Spirit. In other words, we need to live believing that our eternal life has already begun, because it actually has. I visualize us with our heads and hearts in the clouds with Jesus, while our feet are reaching down to the ground, living out the life He has given us on earth. [Notice the cover of this book as a picture of this thought.]

Jesus, this is a hard concept. I know that I belong to You right now, but to imagine that my eternity began the moment I asked You into my heart is a difficult one to grasp.

 ## Love With Wisdom And Knowledge

Philippians 1:9,10 *And this is my prayer: that your love may abound more and more in knowledge and depth of insight, so that you may be able to discern what is best and may be pure and blameless until the day of Christ.*

119

Love is not just a syrupy feeling that we get; it is a commitment.

Love covers a multitude of sins. The love that God gives us also includes His knowledge, insight, and discernment. We are called to love our brothers and sisters in Christ, but that does not mean we allow them to stay in their old, bad habits and sinful lifestyles. God shows us how to pray for them and how to care for them, to help them mature and be the best He created them to be. They, likewise, help us in our weak areas. The stronger, more mature believer exhorts and sets the example for the weaker believer to follow.

Lord, I certainly don't see myself as "pure and blameless," but thanks to the blood that covers my sins, You see me that way. Thank You for bringing me this far, and thank You, also, for my brothers and sisters in Christ who help keep me accountable.

✝ Transportation Troubles

In the fall of 1982 I began working for a man who was a property manager and Realtor in town. He was also head of the Salvation Army there in the Walnut Creek branch. Because of his affiliation with Salvation Army, I would have the opportunity to help people get assistance with vouchers for places to stay, transportation, or meals. We also gave them assistance with their electric bills in the event that they were about to be disconnected.

I had been riding the bus to work for several weeks because our car needed some repairs. Somehow, riding the bus was very difficult and I would inevitably be on the wrong side of the street, or had the wrong schedule, or missed the bus due to one problem or another. I just did not get it. I know people who use public transportation all the time and do just fine, but its usefulness escaped me.

One dreary, wet afternoon I was thinking about having to catch the bus to get home and decided to pray that the Lord would provide a way for me without having to stand out in the rain. The telephone rang shortly before it was time for me to get off work. It was a young woman named Angela who needed to have a voucher for her electric bill. Not wanting to mess with it that late in the day, I referred her to another number at PG&E, hoping they would handle the situation for her. As soon as I hung up that phone, I realized she was God's answer to my prayer. *Oh, Lord! I am sorry. That was so selfish of me. Please have her call back.*

Within a matter of a few minutes, the phone rang again and Angela explained that there was no answer to her PG&E call. I told her to come down to the office so I could get her a voucher right away. In filling out the paperwork, I realized that she lived only a couple of blocks from me. She was delighted to give me a ride home, and it turned out that she was a Christian looking for a good church in town as well. In addition to that, she was going to a special baby dedication for her sister but did not have the money for a gift. Erik had a new toy he got at a raffle, a soft stuffed animal that played "Fleur de Elise." Of course he was too old for it, so was happy to contribute it for the baby.

I told Angela about Zion Fellowship. She began attending there, where I often introduced her as the "angel" that God sent to give me a ride home in the rain. Isn't it wonderful how the Lord knits his body together to meet each other's needs?

Another bus story: On a day that I actually managed to board the bus, I was reading a nice, little Christian book when a peculiar, noisy, slightly intoxicated man sat down next to me.

Looking over my shoulder to see what I was reading, he expressed his views in a loud voice, "I believe in God too!"

"That's wonderful," I replied quietly.

After several more boisterous comments, he asked, "I believe God is the God of <u>all</u> religions, don't you?"

Oh, Lord, help! To my surprise came the most beautiful response, "Unless your God sent His Son to die for your sins, he's not the real God."

The bus driver cheered and yelled, "Amen, sister!"

The strange man became very agitated and got off at the next stop, but I believe a lot of people heard that simple exchange and, hopefully, it helped them to think about the truth as well.

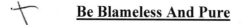 **Be Blameless And Pure**

Philippians 2:14,15 *Do everything without complaining or arguing, so that you may become blameless and pure, children of God without fault in a crooked and depraved*

generation, in which you shine like the stars in the universe.

There is that "blameless and pure" again.

We must guard our tongues and our hearts to keep from complaining and arguing. My thought life is as important as my speech in this respect. In order to be pure, I must dwell on the positive, not even thinking unkind things. The world is depraved, crooked, and getting more so very quickly. We must shine and make a difference in the darkness of this perverse generation.

Lord, in order to do this, we need more of Your Spirit to fill us and convict us when we are going the way of this world. We want to make a difference where You've placed us.

 ## Standing With Jesus

Hebrews 11:33,34 *Sometimes you were publicly exposed to insult and persecution; at other times you stood side by side with those who were so treated. You sympathized with those in prison and joyfully accepted the confiscation of your property because you knew that you yourselves had better and lasting possessions.*

We must stand with Jesus, no matter how the persecution presents itself.

When I first came to Jesus, I was attacked for my faith but knew that He is far more important than anything my attackers could come up with. My husband left in 1987 blaming my six-year relationship with Jesus. I lost my home in the divorce. I know that that home was a "god" of sorts in our life, so it actually was for my best. My eternal home is in heaven and nobody can take it from me. Though it was extremely difficult at the time, I had to keep an eternal perspective in order to, not only survive, but thrive, in the heartbreak.

Oh, my Lord, You are central to my life, hopes, and dreams. I stand with You. Give me the strength and wisdom for every circumstance. Our home is not of this world; we have a heavenly calling that far outweighs any disappointments here. Help that to always be our focus.

My Sheep Listen And Follow

John 10:26-28 *...but you do not believe because you are not my sheep. My sheep listen to my voice; I know them and they follow me. I give them eternal life, and they shall never perish; no one can snatch them out of my hand.*

Those who do not believe and obey are not His.

Do I hear the Lord's voice? Do I listen and pay attention to what He says through the Holy Spirit to me? Am I attentive, or am I doing my own thing, busy in my own, self-imposed works? I love to write, and sense that it is a gift He's given me. Yet how often do I actually put pen to paper? I know that I will spend eternity with Him, and that I will not die because of His gift of eternal life. But what about the gifts He's given me for <u>this</u> life? Am I using them or wasting them?

Lord, help us to set priorities. Help us not to waste our time. The clock is ticking. You have a purpose and a plan that we need to be aware of.

Praise His Name

Psalm 96:2,3 *Sing to the Lord, praise his name; proclaim his salvation day after day. Declare his glory among the nations, his marvelous deeds among all peoples.*

Sing praises to the Lord every day with a thankful heart.

As we declare the glory of the Lord wherever we go, be it here in Redding or to the uttermost parts of the earth, people will come to know Him. Praise Him for His goodness in the presence of your enemies. Live for Him among <u>all</u> peoples. He deserves our praise. Praise Him when you rise; praise Him when you lie down; praise Him at all times in between. He has done such marvelous deeds on the earth for all mankind and in our own daily lives; how can we help but to thank and worship Him?

Lord, we choose to praise You. You are our Creator, Savior, Lord, and King! We will praise You wherever You take us.

Office Services To Go

I began having some difficulties with working at the Realtor's office about the beginning of summer 1985, while

125

the boys were out of school. King and Carol had really helped us during the years that I worked there. I was grateful for that, but felt that it was time to move on.

My husband suggested that I take the rest of the summer off, preparing to go back to work elsewhere when the boys returned to school. It was with some sadness that I handed King my two-week notice the following morning, but I really looked forward to having six weeks off with my boys.

Within a week, I was asked by one of the guys I had met at King's office if I might want some part-time work from him in the fall. I did not really want to work in that particular atmosphere, amid several fierce salesmen who were avid sportsmen and heavy drinkers, but thought I could put it on the back burner in case nothing else came up. I had a nagging thought in the back of my mind that perhaps I should start my own bookkeeping and word processing business.

At that time, my sons began attending a new center that a friend and neighbor of mine had started about nine months before, "The Reading Game," in Pleasanton. Chris and Erik needed some help with their reading skills, and Linda suggested we could barter bookkeeping for tutoring. During the times that they were in class, I began organizing her bookwork. She had not had a bookkeeper since the inception of her business so it truly was in disarray. I brought some of the bookkeeping home in addition to what I was doing there at the center. That worked really well between us. We certainly helped each other out during the rest of the summer.

The thought of starting my own business would not leave me, and I began asking the Lord to bring me some clients if He was the originator of the idea. Four days before my deadline for starting a new job, Linda asked if she could be my first client. I was thrilled beyond belief. I designed some business cards with a dove carrying a scroll trailing out of its mouth with my new name, "Office Services to Go," inscribed on the front.

After working for Linda a couple of months, I realized that I was getting her caught up, and then I would need more clients. *Lord, could you please bring me another job?* Meanwhile a nice couple, Gil and Barbara, became our sponsors at the church we were attending. As we were visiting with them one afternoon, I explained about the desire for my own business and the need for a new client. Gil, a very kindly, well-respected businessman, told me that he and a partner were in property management and in desperate need of a bookkeeper, just one day per week. Would I like to give it a try? Would I! Observing that I only had a hand-held calculator, he gave me a 10-key and I began working with him right away. I had quite a hard time at first, learning what he needed me to do but, with a lot of patience, he helped me to understand my duties. *Thank you, Lord!*

Within a short period of time, one of the teachers at "The Reading Game" told me that her husband, Ron, needed someone to type his engineering reports. Could he contact me? At first I said that would be fine, but realized that I did not want another client in Pleasanton with a half-hour commute. Oh well, it would not hurt to talk to him. Ron called one afternoon to explain the nature of his engineering business. When I made it clear that I did not relish the drive to Pleasanton several times a week, he quickly replied that his office was in Walnut Creek. Terrific! Not only that, I could work out of my home on a computer that he provided. He dictated his reports onto a Dictaphone™ that he also gave me to use at home. It could not have worked out any better.

With these three steady clients, my work dovetailed to the Lord's orchestration. When we needed the extra money, my workload would increase; when I needed a break, the time would be allotted for it. I was able to be home for my family, while making much more money than I would have working for one employer. It was a wonderful opportunity that afforded me a diversity of experiences over the 13 years that I was in business for myself.

Through Gil's C.P.A., I learned a lot about running my own business. She gave me much advice over the years, thus building my confidence. I had many other clients that came and went during that time. One in particular comes to mind. I needed a new look, some new clothes, and a general makeover, but also did not want to spend the money on such extravagance. A woman that went to my church lived just a few blocks from me. Her business involved a line of clothing and accessories, makeup, and color coordination. She asked if we could barter, and, of course, my positive

response was instantaneous. We worked together successfully for over three years. I also bartered with my hairdres-
ser for a couple of years.

The Lord blessed me so abundantly through that business,
and I sensed His provision on a daily basis. When one
client was getting ready to close his doors to leave the area,
the Lord brought me a new client to take his place. It was
incredible how He worked things out. I really learned how
to trust Him through this business that He created.

God Is In Control

Jeremiah 45:4,5 *The Lord said, "Say this to him: 'This is
what the Lord says: I will overthrow what I have built and
uproot what I have planted, throughout the land. Should
you then seek great things for yourself? Seek them not. For
I will bring disaster on all people, declares the Lord, but
wherever you go I will let you escape with your life.'"*

God is in control. Seek Him for everything.

Time is getting shorter, and eventually disaster will come
upon the earth. If I am here to build my own little kingdom,
I am missing the boat (ark!). He says He is going to bring
calamity on every living thing. But, because we love Him
and trust Him, we will escape with our very lives if nothing
else. We must sit at His feet and wait for direction so that
we can draw near and hear His leading. Everything that is

done with an impure motive will burn. Where is my heart? Where is yours?

Lord, I trust You; I love You. Give me attentive ears to hear and follow You. Make me aware of my selfish motives that will only bring destruction.

The Redeeming Blood

Psalm 139:16,19-20 *All the days ordained for me were written in your book before one of them came to be... If only you would slay the wicked, O God! Away from me, you bloodthirsty men! They speak of you with evil intent; your adversaries misuse your name.*

Just think, the Lord knew my whole life story before I was even born.

He knew the depravity of my heart, and yet He knew that I would give that same wicked heart to Him, finally, in 1981. In giving my life to Him, my entire personality has changed over the years. I was no longer a pleasure to my husband but a stench to his nose. How can light and darkness dwell together? He chose to separate from me, the darkest days of my life. But God has redeemed those darkest of days for His glory, to help others know His love and forgiveness.

Thank You, Lord, for Your redeeming blood. I didn't think I could live through divorce. You gave me strength and courage I didn't have on my own. You knew the plans You had for me, to help strengthen others going through similar trials.

Courageous, Not Discouraged

<u>**Joshua 1:6,7,9,18**</u> *Be strong and courageous...Do not be terrified...or discouraged.*

Three times in one chapter, the Lord tells Joshua to be strong!

We know that, when something is repeated, God is making a huge point. These words spoke to me earlier in my life, and they spoke to me again today. He also says that He will give me every place I set my foot (verse 3). We believe we are about to embark on a new adventure and it is very exciting, but things have not started rolling yet. We will need to trust Him to give us the wisdom we need. We have been "making tents" here a long time and it is very comfortable, after all. I hope we won't need a jump start when it is time to get moving.

Lord, I noticed that <u>courage</u>ous and dis<u>courage</u>d are polar opposites with the same root word. We must choose which direction to go. I choose to be obedient to You and to <u>not</u> fear.

Prototype Congregation

<u>**Acts 2:42–47**</u> *They devoted themselves to the Apostle's teaching and to the fellowship, to the breaking of bread and to prayer... All the believers were together and had every-thing in common. Selling their possessions and goods, they gave to anyone who had need... They broke bread in their homes and ate together with glad and sincere hearts,*

131

praising God and enjoying the favor of all the people. And the Lord added to their number daily those who were being saved.

It is happening again in our day, and in our church.

I have always said, "I want to be a part of an Acts Chapter 2 church." This pretty well describes our fellowship. We need to be grateful for the people who want to share in our community, and in the Lord's goodness to all of us as family. The love He has given us for one another is evident. That love covers those quirky parts of our personalities, and the habits that could so easily entangle us in gossip and backbiting. We come together joyfully, with laughter, prayer for one another's needs, praising the Lord, and in sweet times of fellowship.

Lord, thank You for leading us and guiding us, keeping us, and providing for us to do what we love. Thank You for the beautiful church family in which You have placed us. Your name is being glorified as we share our lives, one with another. We are content and oh, so grateful.

Salvation Of His People

Zechariah 8:12,13 *Now they will sow in peace, the vine will give its fruit, the ground will produce its yield, the sky will give its dew, and I will cause the remnant of this people to possess all these things. House of Judah and House of Israel, just as you were formerly a curse among the nations, so now I will save you; and you will be a blessing. Don't be afraid, but take courage. [CJB]*

The Jews and all their brothers are the apple of God's eye. Nothing can change that.

Just as a good earthly father will need to punish his wayward son, so God must punish His children. It is for the good of the child, though it is painful for both the child and the parent. The punishment is necessary to bring them back into alignment. The Father does not love them any less. When the remnant once again comes under His covering, He will pour out blessing upon them.

Father, as we watch the world in these last days, we can expect to see Your divine intervention in behalf of Your people.

We Are The Temple

2 Chronicles 20:7–9 *"O our God, did you not drive out the inhabitants of this land before your people Israel and give it forever to the descendants of Abraham your friend? They have lived in it and have built in it a sanctuary for your Name, saying, 'If calamity comes upon us, whether the sword of judgment, or plague or famine, we will stand in your presence before this temple that bears your Name and will cry out to you in our distress, and you will hear and save us.'"*

The Lord spoke this to my heart right after we moved to Redding.

We live in a new "temple" wherever we are because the Holy Spirit dwells in us. We pray and fast when we are frightened; when the enemy attacks us, we seek God's guidance. We give Him praise for who He is. When He wants to move us into a new place (a home, a job, a church for example), He drives out the previous inhabitants to put in their place a people who would worship Him, who would honor Him in that location, people who would bring His Spirit to dwell in that land. They stand in their temples of the Holy Spirit and worship Him, praying to Him in their time of trouble. He then hears them and rescues them.

God wants us to inhabit these places in the world, to bring godliness and holiness, to bring the fruits of the Spirit there, to be a witness for Him wherever He has placed us. We are to be in the world but not of it; to change that place where we dwell into a place where it is fitting for Him to dwell. People can recognize that this is somewhere special, because God's peace is present. As we bring the temple of the Holy Spirit into a location, others will be drawn to God or, contrarily, we will be persecuted for our relationship with Him. Our job is to occupy the territory God has given us, and stand in the power of His Holy Spirit, waiting upon Him for direction, deliverance, and guidance.

Father, so many people tell us that they sense Your presence here in our home. Your peace dwells here, and they love to bask in it. Thank you for this place of rest that our friends and family can come to. We love sharing what You've given us.

<u>Prayer And Fasting Bring Fruit</u>

Though the previous writing comes from the 1990's, I felt strongly that I was to share it with our Church Council. We had been asked to pray and fast for a meeting they were going to have that very evening (June 27) and the original, handwritten version literally fell out of my Bible that morning. *Lord, are You sure?* I sat on it for several hours and finally decided to send it along to our friends who had asked for prayer, along with another short writing the Lord had put on my heart. I had no idea what their meeting was about, but was much encouraged when I heard a council member later that evening tell me how "right on" my email was. I was so delighted that the Lord used it, and very relieved that I was hearing Him correctly in the process.

You can imagine my surprise, only three days later, to walk into our church to find that many people were missing. The associate pastor (our music/youth leader) and his wife (our women's ministry leader), along with about 35 other people in their entourage, including the balance of the worship team, sound booth techs, and other key leaders in our community, were no longer there. It was devastating to our small church, which we had been attending for a year. Immediately, our pastor put Lindy and I in charge of Women's Ministries as he, Sean, and Rishaye, the church secretary, took over the Youth.

That first Sunday, worship did not go well at all. The following Sunday, worship was not any better. I heard in my spirit, *"Craig has a heart of worship."*

Lord, You Do It!

Hebrews 11:1 *Now faith is being sure of what we hope for and certain of what we do not see.*

The following Sunday my husband placed me in the sound booth along with him to help in the visuals in an emergency situation. I said yes, though my heart feared the worst. When I got there to find a totally different computer program, my heart panicked. I froze on the spot. It was a futile attempt at best. It was evident from the very start that I was not a help but a hindrance to the worship nightmare in which we found ourselves. There were many stumbles, but we finished the race.

Oh, Lord, I prayed that You would go before me. It was a disaster on my part, and it's just not my gifting. Lord, I pray that you would orchestrate the entire worship team and bring it together for us.

Holy Spirit, Is It You? (July 16)

Hebrews 11:1 *Now faith is being sure of what we hope for and certain of what we do not see.*

Last week when the worship was less than worshipful, I shot prayers up to the Lord. Those arrows seemed to momentarily pierce the darkness, and we got through it. Again, the thought came to mind, *"Craig has a heart of worship."* It reoccurred several times over as many days, so

I finally spoke it out loud to Dave on Wednesday. He pooh-poohed the thought with, "That's impossible. Craig and Judy are getting ready to buy a house in Denver. They're getting all settled in there. Besides, they wouldn't want to leave their kids."

Yet, that still, small whisper would not leave me, so on Friday I called Judy and left a message just to check in. On Sunday, the overhead portion of the teaching and worship got really bad (at least for me), with technical difficulties galore. I was so glad when it was over. That same afternoon we hosted a picture-perfect potluck barbecue at our home. Forty or fifty people from church came and it could not have gone any better. We needed time to bond, heal, and encourage one another. That is where we are gifted. And Dave is enjoying the yard work, happy to stay here if that is where the Lord wants us. *Thank You, Lord!*

Monday, I began washing the patio room floor on my hands and knees when I found a music binder laying underneath Dave's keyboards. I opened up this old binder to find a bulletin dated 1997 from a previous church and glanced through it, putting it away for later. Within an hour Judy called me back. I was so excited to hear her voice, and immediately spilled out to her about all that had transpired the last few weeks in our church. I did not even give her a chance to talk for the first couple of minutes. Looking back, that was rather odd. When I finished the story, I asked her what was going on with them. "We're moving back," was her response.

I could not believe my ears! Tears were my first response. Oh – my – goodness! Judy told me how they could not get used to Denver and felt strongly that the Lord was calling them home, though she could not explain why. They had already purchased a little fixer upper in Shingletown to live in, remodel and possibly flip when it is completed. Judy had told Craig that his construction work is just too hard on his body at his age and God maybe wants to provide for them in a different way. She had previously told him that she wanted to get really plugged into a church of their own choosing, no more following around after their kids. They will be back in two weeks.

Lord, I know in my spirit that this is You! I looked at the old bulletin from 1997 to find Craig mentioned in there as he was building the worship team. Lindy was also the contact for intercessory prayer and women's ministry. I called Pastor Jim and asked him to pray about Craig's role in worship. He, understandably, had reservations and did not ever want to go ahead of the Lord again. I had also continued praying that the Lord would hand pick his worship team. *Lord, are You bringing Craig all the way from Denver?*

I called Judy again the following day to see what they were thinking. When she told Craig what was going on, surprisingly, he did not say no.

His words were, "Hmmm. Well, maybe. We'll see what the Lord's doing."

She reiterated that I should talk to Pastor Jim to request more prayer. We all agreed that we did not want to MAKE this thing happen; we just wanted to be open to what the Lord was doing, if anything.

 ## God Hand Picks His Worship Team

Hebrews 11:1 *Now faith is being sure of what we hope for and certain of what we do not see.*

The worship continued to be less than worshipful. We had been praying about Craig and Judy being here, but did not know how to find them without their cell numbers. We had even driven around their area in Shingletown a week before to see if we could stumble across them. On Saturday, August 10, they finally called. I had a great visit with Craig. He asked about what was going on at Westside. That afternoon we dropped in on them in Shingletown to say "Hello, our friends, hello." It was so awesome to see them again.

Tuesday, August 13 – Women's Ministry had been studying about the Holy Spirit all summer, and He graced us with His presence at the final class. It was <u>delightful</u>! Lindy and I were still glorying in that after everyone else left when the phone rang. It was Pastor Jim. The bottom line details were: "Are your friends back from Denver? Can you call him to set up an appointment with the Church Council?"

Oh, Lord, You're doing it! It's so incredible to watch You pull the pieces together!

139

Craig and Judy came over on Wednesday so that he and Dave could drive to the church, and Craig could interview with the leadership. Dave later told me how beautiful it was, just simple and unassuming. We were all pleased that the first meeting went so well. Only time will tell if this is a good fit.

Oh, Lord, have Your way. Please pick every person You want on the team, in the sound, and doing the visuals. We want a "heart of worship" to permeate our sanctuary, nothing else.

✝ Beautiful Music...At Last (August 16)

Psalm 95:1,2 *Come let us sing for joy to the Lord; let us shout aloud to the Rock of our salvation. Let us come before him with thanksgiving and extol him with music and song.*

We will come before the Lord with beautiful music... at last.

Dave is playing his music as backup keyboard player with Craig on guitar this Sunday. Who would have thought it would be 13 years before they ever played together again? They loved playing together so many years before. Lord, help us to be faithful in our worship of You. Let them be a blessing in this church. God, I pray that You will fix the sound system so that it works perfectly on Sunday. Help our hearts to make music to You with a joyful noise in the heavenlies. We want to worship You in spirit and in truth.

During the three awful weeks that I tried to do the visuals, I was all but in tears. It was very apparent that this was not my gift. Fortunately, everyone else knew it too, and my friend, Carrie, stepped up to do the announcements and worship lyrics the following week. Her husband, Frank, along with others, also stepped in a few weeks after that to help with the sound. I was working with sound as well (and doing better at that, by the way). When Frank learned that I had played clarinet in the past, he encouraged me to leave the sound booth and play at rehearsal one night after Craig was feeling more comfortable. Craig also encouraged me to give it a try. The story is still being written but I am enjoying playing my instrument again after 10 dry years. Dave is enjoying being creative, and Craig is so gifted to lead worship at this church. One of the mainstays of about 20 years even mentioned that he was "a perfect fit for Westside."

Lord, You knew it all along, didn't You? And I never dreamed that I would get to be one of the ones included in Your handpicking of the worship team. It's so wonderful to see how you have worked out all of the details. I'm forever grateful!

[Craig led worship for almost a year, when he suddenly needed to leave the area to find more work. He gave his notice, expressing his regrets to our pastor. The Lord, true to form, had already brought someone to the surface who our church had wanted for worship pastor a few years before. We only went about six weeks without a leader, and the church family all pulled together in the interim to make it happen. Dave and I personally miss Craig and Judy, but we know that we'll maintain our relationship no matter where they are or what they're doing... and then there's always eternity!]

✝ Are You Willing To Be Willing?

Thanksgiving 1984 was approaching and a certain in-law planned on coming up to our home in Walnut Creek for the holiday. This was something I had come to dread. This person was an alcoholic, incessant talker, and literally made me ill from being around her. I was visiting with Lindy a couple of days before her arrival and explained the situation. "I just can't stand her! Janell [name changed] has never really accepted me and I hate her! I'll never forgive all the things she's done to me over the years!"

Of course, Lindy, ever the spiritual big sister, asked, "Well, are you willing to be willing to forgive her?"

Hmmm. "That's a very small step. Maybe I can go that far."

She gave me Scriptures that pertain to loving your enemy, forgiveness, Jesus not forgiving me if I do not forgive, etc. You know the ones. Finally, we prayed together. She had me profess that I was "willing to be willing" to forgive and love this woman. I asked the Lord to make it real in my heart, though the words were just words at the moment.

Thanksgiving Day soon arrived. I was bustling about the kitchen preparing a great meal that might even please my relative. The house was spotless and the guest room was all freshened up for their arrival. They pulled in around 1:00. I found, to my surprise, that I was seeing her in a different light. The Lord had truly changed my heart. He had to have done it because I never could have done it on my own. We had a very nice weekend, and I think she may have enjoyed herself as well. It did not seem like as much alcohol was consumed as in the past. That was a turning point in our relationship. One small step for Jesus, one large step for womankind!

Who is that person in your life? Are you willing to be willing?

Father, thank You for helping me through this battle. May Your will be done for others as it was done for me. What a relief to not feel dread in seeing her!

God Is Our Refuge

Psalm 46:1-3 *God is our refuge and strength, an ever-present help in trouble. Therefore we will not fear, though the earth give way and the mountains fall into the heart of the sea, though its waters roar and foam and the mountains quake with their surging.*

The world is liable to fall around us, yet we can look to God for strength.

Calamities can occur at any moment, be they natural or man-made disasters. God is our only constant hope. Though a thousand may fall at our side, He is with us. Fear comes from a lack of faith in our Creator. His perfect love will cast out that fear as we look to Him in every situation, be it financial, physical, emotional, or a natural adversity.

Oh, Lord, when I am fearful, remind me that Your perfect love casts out fear. Help me turn to You in times of trouble. Fear cannot dwell in me when I am filled with Your love.

God Gives Us Everything We Need

Mark 13:22,23 *For false christs and false prophets will appear and perform signs and miracles to deceive the elect---if that were possible. So be on your guard; I have told you everything ahead of time.*

He has told us _everything_ ahead of time to prepare us.

We must be on our guard, not in fear, but in wisdom. As we watch the fig tree (verses 28-31), we recognize that the end is near. The Word has warned us; the Holy Spirit within us highlights events we see on the news or read on the internet. We are seeing things come to pass quickly in these days. We need to stay close to the Lord to recognize His voice and urgings. Then we must be obedient to the point of sacrifice.

Lord, I pray that You will continue to warn us and highlight those things You want us to pay attention to. I will focus on You and not the events because, one way or another, You will bring us through those events.

Friendly Persecution

1 Peter 4:3,4 *For you have spent enough time in the past doing what pagans choose to do---living in debauchery, lust, drunkenness, orgies, carousing and detestable idolatry. They think it strange that you do not plunge with them into the same flood of dissipation, and they heap abuse on you.*

Those that are still walking in the old life may turn against you.

I experienced this with a friend coming against me at my own birthday gathering. He is a Christian, but is not totally sold out to the Lord. He is walking on the fence. Even though I do not normally talk about my faith in Jesus in that crowd, the anti-Christ spirit rises up against me anyway. This "friend" comes out with little jabs laced in humor, especially when he is drinking.

Lord, I pray that Your Holy Spirit will convict him. Bring him into that tight walk with You that will change his behavior and thinking. Lord, I sense his unhappiness and know he's walking in guilt. Please bring him and his entire family to the foot of Your cross, and into a spirit of repentance.

Judge Nothing Before The Appointed Time

1 Corinthians 4:5 *Therefore judge nothing before the appointed time; wait till the Lord comes. He will bring to light what is hidden in darkness and will expose the motives*

145

of men's hearts. At that time each will receive his praise from God.

Only God knows the true motive and intent of the heart.

We will probably be very surprised when we get to heaven. Those that looked so good on the outside by all their activities in church may not know Jesus at all. They will not have a home in heaven because they never made their commitment to Christ. The Lord will shine His light on those darkened souls, exposing the true motives of their hearts. Likewise, people that seemed so lifeless on the outside may be full of a prayer life with Jesus on the inside. Sometimes you just never know. This is the reason we are told not to judge others, but to judge the fruit.

Lord, I pray that You will purify my heart, by giving right motives. Change me, oh God! I know how ugly some of my thoughts are, and many of my motives are less than pure. I need Your holy conviction in my life.

✝ __Be Kind To One Another__

__1 Peter 3:8,9__ *Finally, all of you, live in harmony with one another; be sympathetic, love as brothers, be compassionate and humble. Do not repay evil with evil or insult with insult, but with blessing, because to this you were called so that you may inherit a blessing.*

Be kind to one another. Do not live like you did in the past, to get even.

We have been called <u>out</u> of darkness. God has a higher calling for us. We must respond in a way that is pleasing to Him, and not the way our flesh would want us to, like we did before we knew Christ. When we live the way God commands us to, we will be blessed eternally. This time on earth is short compared to the rest of our eternal life; make the best of it.

Father, these words are easy when life is going smoothly. Help us to live them out when the stress of living comes in and tries to take over. It's only You in us that will give the success we need.

 ## Now Be Kind To Your Husband

2 Timothy 2:1 *You then, my son [daughter], be strong in the grace that is in Christ Jesus.*

I need to extend <u>lots</u> of grace today.

Dave had knee replacement surgery yesterday; I know I will need to give him more grace and kindness than I have available on my own. When we married, a part of our vows was to always be kind to one another. It is hard to fulfill that vow at the moment. This is one of those "in sickness and in health" times that seemed so far away when we were standing on a cliff holding hands at a sunset wedding. Everything was so blissful then, though the winds of adversity were blowing against us pretty hard as I recall.... The ocean breezes were so blustery, we cannot hear our voices over the microphone in the video. Life has its ups and downs as the years go by. Now is definitely one of the low points.

Thank You, Lord, for Your goodness and mercy to us. I lift my husband up to You right now and ask that You will relieve the nausea and pain for him to be able to come home. Then, Lord, please keep him in a peaceful state of mind. And, Father, please pour Your grace through me in a miraculous way. Help me to be the wife I promised to be.

Rely On God

2 Corinthians 1:9 *Indeed, in our hearts we felt the sentence of death. But this happened so that we might not rely on ourselves but on God, who raises the dead.*

We must trust God as we go through those trials of life.

So often when trials hit, we ask, "Why, God?"

But it is for our strength and endurance. Our ability to make it through comes from Him. We know we cannot do it on our own and that is when He draws us to Himself so that we learn to let Him carry us. I think of the shepherd carrying a lamb upon his shoulders. He might have had to break the leg of that wayward baby in order to keep the lamb dependent upon him until he heals. After that, the lamb will not leave his side. And, imagine! I did not even think about Dave's "broken leg" when I started this writing.

Lord, I don't need a broken leg to stay close to You. You are the strength of my life. You are the wisdom and endurance I need for every minute of every day. Thank You for this trial to draw us near and for the healing time we're in with this knee surgery.

Be Merciful To Those Who Doubt

Jude 22,23 *Be merciful to those who doubt, snatch others from the fire and save them; to others show mercy mixed with fear---hating even the clothing stained by corrupted flesh.*

My heart cried out for mercy for my father. *Lord, please bring Dad to Yourself before he dies. I pray that You will even heal him to show Your love and presence.*

God, full of mercy and grace, did miracles to show Dad His love and restoration. The bone cancer in his rib was causing so much pain that he could only be comfortable in his special chair. This is the chair we kids gave him four years before, on his 80th birthday. He was even sleeping in it during the night. Hospitalized on Easter, and then again on Mother's Day for a twisted hernia, the pain subsided somewhat. Then suddenly the ache was gone. We were not sure why; even his doctors could not explain it. They decided to do another round of radiation, which he went through. After that was completed, they took a new X-ray of his cancerous areas. The lymph node that was full of cancer was now clear. They did not think the radiation would do much for that, but it did. The rib that was causing so much pain because of the cancer was <u>gone</u>; not just the cancer, but the entire rib. Amazing! The doctor's comment was, "You must have had a lot of people praying for you. That is about the only thing that would explain what has happened."

Does my father see this? Is he turning his heart to Jesus? What is he doing with this miraculous move of God on his behalf? Our prayers were answered and I am so grateful, but will it make a difference in the eternal destiny of my father and the rest of my unsaved family members? I pray that they will respond to this extension of Dad's life and see it as the Lord of the universe giving a second chance for eternity with Him and with us. I <u>want</u> to spend eternity with Dad. That in itself is a prior wonder. God gave me love for my father when I had no love of my own. I had no feelings at all until the Lover of my soul poured out His love into my heart. Now, two decades later, my heart is hurting that this might be a wasted miracle. This healing of disease, though it may be temporary, gave him more time.

During the very roughest moments, I spoke words that I personally had not heard from Dad in my own life, "I love you."

At first, his response was just a grunt or an embarrassed, "Thanks."

He had never heard those words from his own father; what did I expect? But I, and others of our family, would persevere with telling him we loved him. Eventually, over the months that we thought were his last, he began to initiate with, "I love you, hon." Or "I love you, baby." My heart melted to hear him tell me. I knew he loved me; I could tell by his actions, but those words would be a memory that will live forever in my soul. God spared his life for this season, though he is kind of back to his old hardheaded ways. It breaks my heart. But I am bolder in talking about his miracle and telling him that God loves him very much.

Oh, Father, I continue to cry out for salvation and everlasting life for my family. I pray that You will break down those walls as we celebrate the birth of Jesus again this year. He came to die for us; His gift for us was His life given to set us free from eternal pain and death.

Write In A Book

Jeremiah 30:1,2 *This is the word that came to Jeremiah from the Lord: "This is what the Lord, the God of Israel, says: Write in a book all the words I have spoken to you."*

The Lord speaks to us as well.

Those impressions in our hearts, when we cannot say we have actually heard a voice, are often the Holy Spirit within nudging us with His promptings. We do not even recognize Him most of the time. We might mistakenly think they are our own thoughts. But, if we write those things down, we will see a pattern of godly wisdom and direction for our lives that only our Creator can give. We need to record those times when we see God's intervention so that they will not be forgotten by us or others important to us.

Lord, thank You for showing me again the importance of putting things on paper. You direct my path and I joyfully obey. I love to write what You've shown me.

Gratefulness

Psalm 118:19,21,24 *I will enter and give thanks to the Lord... I will give you thanks, for you answered me; you have become my salvation ...This is the day the Lord has made; let us rejoice and be glad in it.*

The Lord loves a grateful heart.

How many times have I prayed about something, the Lord answered favorably, and I did not just stop everything to acknowledge Him in gratefulness? How can I be so self-centered, so "I" focused?

Lord, forgive us! You are so awesome and yet You care about even the smallest details of life. Thank You, Father, for sending the Holy Spirit to complete the tasks You want done. You know we could never do them if left to our own devices. We are weak and helpless, and we need more and more of You on a daily basis. It's <u>not</u> about us. How many times have I said it? Now I must believe it. It's You that I long for, You that I need.

A Grateful Heart

Psalm 118:28,29 *You are my God and I will give you thanks; you are my God and I will exalt you. Give thanks to the Lord, for he is good; his love endures forever.*

He is God from everlasting to everlasting.

I will be praising my God throughout eternity. I am grateful for the free gift of salvation that He gave me. There are too many things to list on paper: salvation of family members; health; a new life; move to Redding; a wonderful husband; a blessed ministry; joy every day; a promise of a closer relationship with my children and their children, and on and on it goes. Of course, the gift of Himself tops the list.

Oh, Lord, my heart melts with gratefulness to You and Your orchestration of life. Even as Dave is reading about the life cycles of Your body of believers, I know there are life cycles going on right now, right here. As we watch history unfold before our eyes, You are the Writer of time and the Book that tells it all!

Natural Consequences

Jeremiah 11:14,15 *"So you, Jeremiah, don't pray for this people! Don't cry or pray on their behalf, because I won't listen to them when they cry to me because of their troubles. What right does my beloved have to be in my house, when she has behaved so shamelessly with so many? Offerings of consecrated meat can no longer help, because it is when you are doing evil that you are happy."* [CJB]

153

Let pride and arrogance have their way in the evil lives of those people.

There are natural consequences for people who call themselves Christians but who are disobedient to the Lord's calling on their lives. They are intent on doing evil, and yet cry out to anyone who will listen to all their woes. They never grow; they never change. It seems like we are always starting from square one every time they want to meet. God says to not even pray for them. It may seem hardhearted on His part, but I think He is saying, "Do not waste your time; I have plenty of other work for you to do."

Lord, I need to be careful or I could fall into that camp as well. It is not about committing the sin for me, but not *doing what You have called me to do. Again, what am I doing with the writing gift You have given me?*

  ## Spiritual Rebirth

James 1:18 *He chose to give us birth through the Word of Truth, that we might be a kind of first-fruits of all he created.*

This birth is a Spiritual birth.

Believers are the first-fruits because their eternal destination changed from the moment they accepted Jesus into their hearts. Jesus was the very first "first fruit" and He changed the course of direction for them. They find themselves suddenly headed a new way---away from the bars and crumby movies, away from drugs and promiscuity. They, naturally, bring others with them. Those that get angry over the changed life will walk away, but they will observe. They hope to see the believer stumble so they continue to watch with interest. Eventually, even those skeptics may have the desire for a changed life.

Lord, it's hard in the beginning to leave everything behind, but the reward is so much greater. Your life is so much fuller. Thank You for bringing us in.

My Daily Meeting With God

Isaiah 50:4 *The Sovereign Lord has given me an instructed tongue, to know the word that sustains the weary. He wakens me morning by morning, wakens my ear to listen like one being taught.*

God wants to meet with me first thing in the morning.

Am I excited to hear what the Lord wants to speak to me each and every morning? Do my eyes fly open with the expectation of meeting with my Heavenly Father? Sadly, usually not. As a pastor spoke recently, "If your devotional life isn't changing you, you need to change it."

Lord, I pray that You will awaken me morning by morning and give me the ear to hear Your voice beckoning me. I don't want to be lazy but I am... too lazy to be excited to hear from You. Oh, God, change me! Stretch and grow me as You speak daily through Your Word.

155

⊬ A New Journey With Jesus

Isaiah 50:5,7 *The Sovereign Lord has opened my ears, and I have not been rebellious; I have not drawn back. Because the Sovereign Lord helps me, I will not be disgraced. Therefore have I set my face like flint, and I know I will not be put to shame.*

I have gratitude that the Lord awakened me early this morning.

It was still very dark so I lay there quietly listening to the chiming of the clock, trying to figure out the time. *Is that You, Lord?* I guess so. I was excited to see what He would give me for today. My face is toward God, my ears are awakened for our meeting. Shame is not for me because I trust in the Lord. He is showing me my <u>spiritual</u> family, those that also belong to Him.

Yes, Lord, I have gratitude and much thanksgiving at this Thanksgiving time of year! Thank you for my husband, my Redding sister and brother-in-law, and our church family into which we've been adopted. "Though my father and mother forsake me, the Lord will receive me." (Psalm 27:10)

⊽ Trust In God, Even In The Dark

Isaiah 50:10 *Who among you fears the Lord and obeys the word of his servant? Let him who walks in the dark, who has no light, trust in the name of the Lord and rely on his God.*

156

Trust in God, even when the times are dark.

The Thanksgiving and Christmas time of year can tend to bring people down. Grief over the loss of close relationships with persons we love can weigh on us like a wet, heavy blanket. Rejection is always a hard one but, when it is family, it is especially difficult. The holidays seem to bring out the glaring reality that our interactions are not what we have longed for. Some relationships are strained, ugly, or totally absent, and no amount of gift wrapping can make them any prettier.

Lord, my heart is broken because our families are broken. You have given me a new family, people who love You and serve You with a whole heart, yet they like to have fun and laugh as well. For the moment, I'm emotionally breaking those old family ties---again. They do not want a relationship or they would be here. Thank You Father, for Your love and forgiveness. You accepted me right where I was and have been gradually changing my heart. I don't want to be stubborn anymore. Help me to love them just as they are. But, Lord, please change their hearts as well.

I wrote this the day before Thanksgiving. I felt so victorious over the past at the time these words were put on paper, but on Thanksgiving Day my heart and emotions took the usual nosedive. You know, it is a choice. We have to choose to keep our focus on the good and not the disappointments. Self-pity can come in and take over if we let it; it is our decision to walk with the joy of the Lord every day, no matter what time of the year it is.

Can A Mother Forget Her Child?

Isaiah 49:14,15 *But Zion said, "The Lord has forsaken me, the Lord has forgotten me." Can a mother forget the baby at her breast and have no compassion on the child she has borne? Though she may forget, I will not forget you!*

I forgot my child for a moment, but, thankfully, the Lord will not forget me!

There was a party when Chris was only a few weeks old. We were having fun and laughing. I had been <u>so</u> sick during the entire nine months of my pregnancy; it felt good to have fun once again. But someone hollered out, "There's a baby crying in here!"

My response was, "Oh my goodness! My poor little guy!"

We all laughed as I rushed back to pick up my son. At that point, I realized it's not all about me! It is good to know that our Heavenly Father does not forget about us like that.

Oh, Father, I wish I hadn't been so selfish as a young mother. The world revolved around me in my youth, sad to say. Again, I want to grow into the woman and mother You created me to be. Teach me, Lord, even at this late date.

A Word Of Encouragement

Isaiah 49:16-18 *See, I have engraved you on the palms of my hands; your walls are ever before me. Your sons hasten back, and those who laid you waste depart from you. "As* *surely as I live," declares the Lord, "you will wear them all as ornaments; you will put them on like a bride."*

This is a word spoken over me by our dear friends, Dave and Phyllis, a few years ago. They pray for our kids often, as we do theirs.

God says, "As surely as I live," you will have your sons as ornaments as close as your own skin. It is a hope of mine that this word would come to pass like Jeremiah 31 did, that our families would become an even closer part of our lives, that we would spend many more good times together. There are so many families that find themselves in this situation. I know I am not alone, and hope that these words of encouragement might minister to others as well.

Lord, I believe this promise to be true. We have seen such healing in recent years. I hope that more is yet to come. You are the focus and You are the answer.

The Lord, Our Vindication

Isaiah 50:8,9 *He who vindicates me is near. Who then will bring charges against me? Let us face each other! Who is my accuser? Let him confront me! It is the Sovereign Lord who helps me. Who is he that will condemn me? They will all wear out like a garment; the moths will eat them up.*

The Lord is our vindication.

The Lord will handle those that hate us. He does a much better job than we ever could. He is the One who can orchestrate the circumstances and bring humility to those that would try to condemn us. It is amazing to watch Him work. Truth will come out in the end. Lies that have been proclaimed from the rooftops will be thrown down and trampled underfoot in the alleyways.

Lord, I thank You that I don't need to think about these things or even try to figure them out, much less orchestrate the circumstances to make them happen. Just because You love us, You give us favor. I'm so grateful for Your unending love.

⸞ The Lord Is My Vindication

My high school was having a multi-class reunion around the year 2000 and I had already decided not to attend. However, a friend contacted me, urging me to go since we had not seen each other for about 35 years. We had been such good friends in high school, and it seemed a shame that we had lost touch for so long. I had not wanted to attend any class reunions because I had a falling out some time before with a couple of graduates who might also be there. But I bought a new dress for the occasion and worked up my courage to enjoy everyone else I knew, especially my friend, Christie. Dave thought it would be fun to tag along to find out more about my growing up years, so we headed down to Lompoc, my alma mater.

We went to Christie's hotel room to get her and it was so much fun catching up, laughing and talking about the old times. We got to the reunion and, to my dismay, the dress I so carefully purchased was all wrong. Oh well. There were a couple of others who were overdressed as well. Fortunately, we all had name tags with our high school pictures on them or I would have never recognized any of these people. The couple I did not want to see arrived but, rather than being overdressed, they were dressed like the 60's, meaning they looked a little out of place as well. What a relief that was. Dave and I danced and had fun but, I have to admit, I just was not interested in hanging out with most of the people there. We had all changed so much, and there really was not anything in common anymore.

As the evening wore on, and we carefully avoided contact with the dreaded couple, we decided to leave a little early so Christie and I could visit in a more quiet location. Dave only had one more photo on our camera, so he turned around and flashed a picture into the middle of the dimly lit dance floor as we were leaving. To his horror, this particular pair was in the center of the image. We visited a few more friends on the way out, and then the three of us piled into our car and headed back towards Christie's hotel.

On our way, we decided to stop at a local restaurant for some coffee. The place appeared deserted except for two people in the far corner. The hostess seated us at a table next to a 4-1/2 foot high dividing wall, and we began reminiscing with delight. Christie eventually asked some pointed questions about the couple, which got us started on a rather lengthy conversation. Dave and I talked about what had transpired between us to cause all the problems. I had a real sense to be gracious and not bitter as my flesh would have wanted to do. I told her how foolish it was to have this

161

falling out and explained that, no matter how we tried, these two were so nasty and vindictive, it became impossible to have a relationship. Christie, at one point, commented that she would not even recognize them at the reunion if she saw them.

Suddenly, a man and woman on the opposite side of the short wall between us stood up to leave. By this time there were only two occupied tables in the entire restaurant. I glanced over to see that it was the same couple we had been talking about all this time! I could not believe it! How could they have arrived there before us? After all, we took a picture of them on the dance floor as we left. They were alone and had to have heard every single word we said. I was so grateful that the Lord put a check on my tongue and that I did not lash out in anger, but only because I did not want to be a gossip to my friend after all these years.

It was a beautiful experience. I had gotten to say absolutely everything I had ever wanted to say to them but was never given the opportunity. The Lord defended me, and I did not even realize it until I saw them slinking out the door. What a memorable encounter and a perfect story to illustrate that the <u>Lord</u> is our vindication.

<u>Those Stubborn Ones</u>

<u>Isaiah 30:1</u> *"Woe to the obstinate children," declares the Lord, "to those who carry out plans that are not mine,*

forming an alliance, but not by my Spirit, heaping sin upon sin."

There are stubborn children from generation to generation.

This Scripture is speaking, in particular, about Israel and that obstinate nation aligning with Egypt. They looked for protection in the wrong place; they did not run to their Heavenly Father for covering. Instead, they looked to man for wisdom. Consequently their hearts became hard and full of sinful desires. It was a shameful situation, but this Scripture is as much for today as it was in 700 B.C. In fact, I am sure it speaks to every generation in one form or another. There will always be stiff-necked people to deal with.

Father, help me personally to always seek Your wisdom and guidance. I do look for confirmation from others, but the bottom line should be Your approval and direction. Thank You for speaking to my heart today.

Godly Wisdom, Part 1

James 3:13 *Who is wise and understanding among you? Let him show it by his good life, by deeds done in the humility that comes from wisdom.*

We must be wise in what God is showing us to do.

Humility is the key to this verse. As we sit with the Lord, He will show us the deeds He wants us to be involved in. If we are doing something for someone in need and do not have a right attitude, it will not last. God will give us the wisdom as we bow before Him. We must know that He is doing the giving; we are merely His instrument. I see a pitcher being poured out on a dehydrated man. The pitcher only <u>contains</u> the gift; the gift is the Living Water giving life to the thirsty.

Lord, You are the Gift and the Gift Giver; I am merely the instrument that You use to impart Yourself to others. I am dispensable; if I won't obey, You will use someone else. Thank You for this humbling thought. I am nothing---You are everything!

Godly Wisdom, Part 2

James 3:13 *Who is wise and understanding among you? Let him show it by his good life, by deeds done in the humility that comes from wisdom.*

Additional thoughts on this subject: The Living Water being poured out on a thirsty man requires the recipient to do something as well. He must open his mouth to receive. To me this is a picture of a dying man swimming in the abundance that the Spirit has to offer rather than drinking in what the Spirit is giving. We must open our mouths to let the water fill us to the brim. Likewise we must open our hearts to the Spirit and be filled by Him so that we, too, can give those gifts away as the Spirit leads. Many people are content to receive from others---their wisdom, their prayers, their attention, but they never learn to receive from God on their own. They never grow beyond the "baby bird" stage.

Again, Lord, I need Your wisdom. I don't want to waste my time on those that don't truly want You and what You have to offer.

✓ Life Application...Many Years Later

I was taking a hot bath this morning and, afterwards, the Lord met me in a profound way. When I got out of the tub, while drying myself off, I became very woozy and light-headed. After sitting in a recliner with my feet up, the thoughts came that this is a perfect reflection of the water of the Holy Spirit. I was surrounded by water, but I had not really drunk any water today. I needed to take in the water, to be refreshed by it. My body was parched and I had nothing left to run on.

Our spirits are like that as well. We can be in the Word, in a church surrounded by other Spirit-filled people, or even worshiping the Lord, but unless the Holy Spirit has filled us and equipped us, empowering our lives, we are as a dry, crusty sponge. Sitting on the counter, we are of little use to the whole body, or even ourselves, without the Living Water filling us. Drink in the Living Water and let your life be squeezed by the Lord so that the same water can replenish others in the process. For instance, this was written after the large pitcher of water replenished my dehydrated mind.

Demonic "Wisdom"

James 3:14,15 *But if you harbor bitter envy and selfish ambition in your hearts, do not boast about it or deny the truth. Such "wisdom" does not come down from heaven but is earthly, unspiritual, of the devil.*

Demonic "wisdom" puffs up and is a counterfeit to godly wisdom.

You can see it with your spiritual eye of understanding. You know your motives and I know mine. We must get rid of those selfish ambitions. Am I typing my journal to bring glory to myself, or to help others grow in the Lord right along with me? Am I out to get rich and famous (hardly!), or am I being teachable so that God can also reach others?

Lord, I want You to be poured out because I have no wisdom of my own. It's only Your gift that will last. Do I want to be a plastic pitcher that will melt in the heat of the flame, or a crystal one that has been refined by the fires of life?

Selfish Ambition Brings Disorder

James 3:16 *For where you have envy and selfish ambition, there you find disorder and every evil practice.*

If self is on the throne of life, all manner of sin and deceit enter in to take over.

I was at a Bible study this week and we talked about this verse in James. There are two kinds of wisdom: godly and

166

evil. Wisdom that comes from self is full of the kind of fruit we <u>don't</u> want. There you will find a life of disorder, chaos, and confusion. Selfishness leads to depravity, jealousy, and strife. Godly wisdom, on the other hand, brings His fruitfulness into our lives. His fruits are love, joy, peace, patience, kindness, goodness, faithfulness, gentleness and self-control (Galatians 5:22).

Oh, my Lord, I see very clearly how I can get off track before I even realize it. The evilness of my heart before I knew You shows me my own depravity and capability of selfishness if left to my own devices. Please convict me when I start wandering in that direction again. You have the wisdom I need in my life.

The Fruit Of Godly Wisdom

James 3:17,18 *But the wisdom that comes from heaven is first of all pure; then peace-loving, considerate, submissive, full of mercy and good fruit, impartial and sincere. Peacemakers who sow in peace raise a harvest of righteousness.*

The fruit of godly wisdom is evident, in our inner man and to others.

When we are operating in His wisdom, we know it. Our lives reflect His peace, mercy and righteousness. We will still be under fire from the enemy of our souls and those he operates through. But we will have wisdom about how and when to respond. That turmoil that used to run (and ruin)

167

our lives will no longer be there. Peace, submission to God, and mercy will prevail in trying times.

Oh, Jesus, thank You for dying on the cross so that the Holy Spirit could come and indwell us. You have given the gift of wisdom among so many other gifts. We need all that You have to offer us to live during these chaotic times.

Do Not Go By Appearances

James 2:1-4 *My brothers, as believers in our glorious Lord Jesus Christ, don't show favoritism. Suppose a man comes into your meeting wearing a gold ring and fine clothes, and a poor man in shabby clothes also comes in. If you show special attention to the man wearing fine clothes..., have you not discriminated among yourselves and become judges with evil thoughts?*

This is the first verse where God spoke to my heart, on the very day I got saved.

What a perfect picture of our previous church! We offered so much to anyone who walked through our doors. It was a very grand facility and many of the people who attended would not be able to afford coming to that venue if we had not offered it freely. But did they feel welcomed? Did they sense God's presence by those of us who ministered to them on a weekly basis? And, most of all, were their spiritual needs being met; were they growing spiritually in the process?

Lord, You helped me to love each person that came, regardless of their appearance. You gave me Your love and heart for them, but You also gave me discernment. It was a difficult assignment for those last five years that we were there, but we made the best of it. Many who came just wanted more, not appreciating what we already did for them. Thank You for Your covering in those difficult circumstances.

Keep An Eternal Perspective

James 1:12 *Blessed is the man who perseveres under trial, because when he has stood the test, he will receive the crown of life that God has promised to those who love him.*

Perseverance---going the whole distance.

Sometimes trials come that seem like they will never end. We think we cannot go on another moment and yet, if we are in Jesus, He gives us the strength, day by day, minute by minute. Some people choose to fall away saying that it is just not worth it. We cling all the harder to the Lord knowing that He will bring us through with victory on our lips. The reward is so great, both on earth and in heaven. Though the trial seems like it lasts forever, it is but a blink of an eye compared to the eternal blessings that await us.

Though the answers didn't always come my way in my time, You had the better plan, both for me and for Your kingdom.

169

Persevere Through The Pain

James 1:14,15 *...but each one is tempted when, by his own evil desire, he is dragged away and enticed. Then, after desire has conceived, it gives birth to sin; and sin, when it is full-grown, gives birth to death.*

The non-persevering person dies spiritually.

Those that choose to walk away from the Lord in their trials will, again, take things into their own hands. Their desires overwhelm them, and the enemy of our souls will dangle a worm-shaped temptation right in front of them to entice them away from God's purpose. Once that desire has been satisfied, the hook has been set and, instead of being the fishers of men that Jesus talks about, we become the fish. We get devoured by Satan and his plan.

Father, how do I know this? Because I lived it. Years ago I couldn't wait for the man You had for me; I thought I knew better and almost made a Titanic out of my life. Thank You for snatching me out of the breakers once again. Thank You for giving me the husband You handpicked just for me.

 ## Wait Upon The Lord

James 1:16,17 *Don't be deceived, my dear brothers. Every good and perfect gift is from above, coming down from the Father of the heavenly lights, who does not change like shifting shadows.*

Wait upon the Lord---persevere in His strength.

Deception seems sweet, but it is like shifting shadows. It is never satisfying for long. We get drawn into the darkness and, as the light shifts, we go deeper and deeper into sin. It is a trap set for us by the expert trapper. Contrarily, our Heavenly Father turns on the lights; He gives the good and perfect gifts that we need to nourish us, to grow us up in Him. He shows us our sinful patterns, and then helps us to be overcomers in those areas. He wants only good for us, now and forever.

Oh, Father, thank You for Your gifts. Thank You for strengthening us in the hard times to be able to hang onto You and Your plans for our lives. You give us what we need for now and in the future.

Sin Separates

Genesis 3:8 *Then the man and his wife heard the sound of the Lord God as he was walking in the garden in the cool of the day, and they hid from him among the trees in the garden.*

Sin separates us from God.

When we sin against God and man, we want to hide. We do not want Him, or others, to know what we have done. The trouble is, we cannot hide from God. He knows everything. Our trying to hide just brings a chasm between us and Him. Sin has its way by causing us to withdraw from the only One who can cover our sin and bring us back into right standing with God. Isolation from man also allows Satan to have his way in our thought life and actions. We lose accountability to the believers God has placed in our lives and we get bogged down in the quagmire of our sinful nature. Thus Satan has his way.

Lord, help me to be quick to repent! Thank you for saving me from myself.

Be A Light That Draws

Luke 8:16 *No one lights a lamp and hides it in a jar or puts it under a bed. Instead, he puts it on a stand, so that those who come in can see the light.*

God has put us, His believers, as lights to the nations.

Do not let your light go dim, or hide it from those who do not understand. Little flickers of light at appropriate moments in their darkness are all that they can tolerate. New believers will often blast the eyes of their friends and family with headlights like a car rather than lighting a candle in their darkened souls. That dim light would draw them to Christ instead of repulsing them, as is often the case when given too much at one time. Let the Holy Spirit lead the way and do not do anything with ulterior motives. They see right through your calculating thoughts.

My 84 year old father is dying once again. His cancer has moved back into his bones now and we do not know how long he has with us. We went down to a conference in Southern California and stopped in Lompoc to spend a couple of days with he and my stepmom. I had hoped that the Lord would give us a special time with them but, after 1-1/2 days, Dave and I decided that there were no spiritual openings and that God probably was just giving us opportunity to show our love for them.

Our last night there, the Lord woke me up at 2:00 with a multitude of thoughts rolling around in my head. It became apparent that He wanted me to write them down in a letter to my dad. I wrote until 3:30. The Lord enabled me to intertwine the things we had been talking about (the sad state of the world; sexual perversion; economy; rebellion of children; a book written by my stepmom's father; a train ride to our home) with the gospel message and Jesus' love, as well as my love, for them. It was incredible. I read it to them the next morning with laughter and tears, and promised to mail a copy for them to keep. It was written in a journal that has quotes from Christian authors, as well as Scripture that was also pertinent, on the borders of my handwritten pages. I pray that God will use it to bring them to Himself.

Lord, help me to know when to share and what to share so that I may be a sweet smelling savor and not a stench to those you've placed in my path.

God Knows Our Hearts

Psalm 7:9 *O righteous God, who searches minds and hearts, bring to an end the violence of the wicked and make the righteous secure.*

Everyone gets their just reward.

As God tests the hearts and minds of men, He knows what resides there. People are not always who they appear to be... including me! A total stranger showed up while I was

173

church secretary, asking if I could give her a ride to her doctor's office. I said a quick prayer and, contrary to my normal reaction on such a busy day, agreed to escort her to the appointment. As we talked, I thought, *What on earth am I doing here? Lord, I thought I was hearing You.* This woman seemed totally out of touch with reality in some respects, but I kept trying to have a conversation while we waited for her time to go into her appointment. She had a nodding acquaintance with Jesus but had difficulty reading the Word. I suggested a church website where she could actually listen to the Bible being read to her.

Finally her turn came and, breathing a sigh of relief, I began to settle into my book. At that moment, a husband and wife who had been sitting across from us tapped me on the shoulder.

She began speaking, "We couldn't help hearing your conversation. Can you please give us that website you were talking about? My husband can't read because of impaired vision and I have to read to him all the time."

I gladly gave her the website and an invitation to our church.

"You know," she said, "what you're doing for that lady speaks volumes to the rest of us here."

I was immediately convicted about my inward thoughts. *If she only knew.*

Lord, my heart was anything but pure in my obedience to that still, small voice. I questioned You and thought I was on a wild goose chase with this strange woman you placed

174

in my path. I even questioned whether it was You who directed me that day. Thank you, Lord, for Your leading and faithfulness, even when I was inwardly grumbling. Though my heart was not pure, You showed me Your presence. Thank You for using me to reach others in the room, in spite of my self-centered attitude.

Flesh Overcomes The Spirit

Mark 14:38 *Watch and pray so that you will not fall into temptation. The spirit is willing, but the body is weak.*

Jesus found them sleeping when He needed their prayers so desperately.

I am in good company at least. There are so many times when my spirit wants to pray, praise, worship, or dance. Yet I, succumbing to my flesh, will take a nap, flip on television, or get busy doing a mindless project. Then I feel guilty as I look back at the wasted hours in my day. Isn't my heart full of joy when I spend time with Jesus? Of course the answer is yes, but I am living in a fallen world where any number of things, or people, are vying for my attention. However, there are no good excuses. It is all about choices.

Father, wake me up early to spend time with You in writing and prayer. May the Holy Spirit control my flesh, to give me the energy I need to do what You want me to do. Help me to die to self and to live for You.

The Foolish Things

1 Corinthians 1:21 *For God in his wisdom made it impossible for people to know him by means of their own wisdom. Instead, by means of the so-called "foolish" message we preach, God decided to save those who believe.*

It is true. He takes the foolish things of this world (like me) and gives them divine wisdom, by God who is alive within them, and not only in spiritual matters.

When the Lord gave me my bookkeeping business, I was so totally lost at times, not knowing what I was supposed to do, or how to do it. But I would turn to Him for wisdom and He showed me how to accomplish what I needed to do in order to get the correct numbers. Creative thoughts would come to mind that would bring the desired answer. He was my Teacher, even in bookkeeping.

Holy Spirit, You are here to guide us to know Jesus better, but You are also here to help us through all phases of life, the difficulties and trials along with the joys. You build our faith to believe for the impossible. Thank You!

He Is The Living Water

John 7:37,38 *On the last and greatest day of the Feast, Jesus stood and said in a loud voice, "If anyone is thirsty, let him come to me and drink. Whoever believes in me, as the Scripture has said, streams of living water will flow from within him."*

176

Jesus is the Living Water.

The fresh, pure water of the Holy Spirit will flow through us more and more as we open up to the cleansing and purification He provides in our lives. God uses things we can get a grasp of in the natural to describe the spiritual… air (breath), water, fire, bread.

Lord, I know You're teaching me a simple but powerful concept. You have more, and I'm searching for You in the process. You be my Bread, that natural food will lose its savor. You be the Air I breathe; light Your Fire in me.

$\downarrow$

God Breathes Life

Genesis 2:7 *The Lord God formed the man from the dust of the ground and breathed into his nostrils the breath of life.*

John 20:22 *And with that he breathed on them and said, "Receive the Holy Spirit."*

God is the forever Life-Giver!

He breathed life. The first time, God breathed life into Adam. It would have been eternal life had sin not entered the world. In John, He breathed and told them about the coming of the Holy Spirit which would also give eternal life to those who received Him. His breath is eternal; everything about Him is eternal. To think that the third party of the Godhead has left heaven to come live in us. He is here in these last days to breathe His life into ours… to gift us, draw us, teach us, hold us, and love us.

177

Thank You, Father, for the gift of the Holy Spirit. I sense His presence so strongly this morning. I know He will give more on this subject and I can't wait!

 **He Is The Vine**

John 15:1,2,4-6 *I am the true vine, and my Father is the gardener. He cuts off every branch in me that bears no fruit, while every branch that does bear fruit he prunes so that it will be even more fruitful... Remain in me, and I will remain in you. No branch can bear fruit by itself; it must remain in the vine; you are the branches. If a man remains in me and I in him, he will bear much fruit; apart from me you can do nothing. If anyone does not remain in me, he is like a branch that is thrown away and withers; such branches are picked up, thrown into the fire and burned.*

There is so much in these few verses!

Where do we begin? First of all, Jesus is the TRUE vine. He is the original, perfect One who stepped down from heaven to save us. There have been many counterfeits over the centuries, but He is the Way, the Truth and the Life. He comes from the Father. Jesus' roots go deep down into His Father. We, who branch off from Him, must bear fruit in order to be useful in His kingdom. God the Father will either cut off or prune those that are barren. Have you ever been so devastated by an event or person in your life that you wondered, "God, where are You? I can't take this another minute! I'm going to die unless you intervene."

Did you think He was cutting you off, throwing you into the fire? If you truly belong to Him, He would never do that. He loves you. So much so, in fact, that He trims off those unwanted, unfruitful areas of your life that are weighing you down, that are keeping you from a full walk with Him. It is painful for the moment, but so necessary for your growth and development.

In my personal testimony, God pruned off an unbelieving husband. God hates divorce but, by my husband's own actions, he was removed from my life. I was so completely destroyed, and thought I would never recover. I lost almost everything near and dear to my heart: my husband, my son Erik, my home that we had worked so hard for. Chris, thankfully, chose to stay with me. Everything that I feared came upon me (just like Job), but it all drew me ever closer to my Lord, Savior, Spiritual Husband, and Maker. I came to know Him in a deeply personal way, through the pain of hard pruning.

I chose to remain in Him, while the man I had been anchored to ran the other way. When the Lifter of my head came into our marriage, my husband grew jealous and did not like the woman I was becoming. Instead of this beautiful butterfly, he actually wanted the lowly worm that I had been, the one in the gutter when rain drenches the earth. That rain, in my case, was alcohol, where I was well on the road to addiction through depression. When Jesus came into my life, He became my habitation and set me free from that trap. Though I was devastated by the ripping and tearing of the loss of this marriage, over the years I have come to see the blessings that the Lord poured out upon me in the process.

Because I survived the severing and pain, the Lord has given me a very fruitful life, a desire to serve Him with a godly man who loves Jesus the way I do, a delightful home on a river, good health, and blessings beyond measure. I have always loved to write and now find myself recording all that He has accomplished in my life. *Thank You, Lord!*

Back to the Scripture... Because we are abiding in Him, our roots go all the way into the Father. The Holy Spirit comes to live in us, bringing many gifts with Him. I recently heard that He is our tool belt and gives us the proper tools at just the right times. We need a hearing ear and a soft heart so that He can use us. His still, small voice is imperceptible if we do not pull away from the hustle and bustle of life. We need to rest at His feet, drinking in His love letter written especially to us. If we love Him and serve Him, we need to love His Word as well. That is our "Western Garden Book" of Life. It tells us what conditions we grow best in, how much of His Living Water we need on a daily basis, and how much of his Son-light we require to thrive. You get the picture. If we are not growing in Him, we die and are burned in the fire of eternity. Choose eternal life, choose Christ.

Father, thank You for this gift You have given me this morning. I pray that You will use it in the lives of others that love and serve You. We need to be grounded in You as we are grafted into Your vine. I give You all the glory and praise, even in the pruning of my life.

The Fire Of The Holy Spirit

2 Timothy 1:6,7 *For this reason I remind you to fan into flame the gift of God, which is in you through the laying on of my hands. For God did not give us a spirit of timidity, but a spirit of power, of love and of self-discipline.*

The gift of the Holy Spirit far outweighs all others.

Paul laid hands on Timothy to pray that he be filled with the power of the Holy Spirit and love. Timothy only needed to receive God's gift to have the confidence he acquired, to complete the tasks that lay before him. So often we become fearful because, if done in our own strength, we know we will not succeed. We forget that it is not <u>our</u> strength, but God's strength, that will complete the task. The fire of the Holy Spirit that dwells in us will give us exactly what we need for the appointed time.

Father, I rely on the Holy Spirit for my life. I know I would fall flat on my face in ministry if I didn't have Him living within me to give wisdom, words, and mercy for others. Please keep His flame burning brightly within me.

 ## The Lord Covers My Fear

When my husband and I were separated, I knew he would be filing for divorce soon. Getting those papers was something I had come to dread and, whenever I saw him, I worried that this would be the time. My stomach churned and my knees felt like they would crumble at any moment. I heard in my spirit, *"When he wants to take you upstairs and is carrying his briefcase... that will be the time."* For several weeks, I remained calm in my husband's presence.

The fear was abated, at least for the moment. Then, one evening he came unannounced, carrying his briefcase. My heart sank. We chatted casually for a few moments and then he asked me to go upstairs with him. My knees started to give way. Again, I heard in my spirit, *"I have not given you a spirit of fear."* I obediently walked up those stairs with the Lord giving me the strength I needed. Jesus held me up as I signed the required paper stating that I had received my husband's unwanted gift.

Lord, I know my husband was totally unaware that there were actually three of us going up those stairs when I signed his paper. But I knew You were the One who was carrying me, enabling me to stand in his presence. Thank You! Oh, Father, as I am proofreading my stories, it is so painful to remember some of these things, like the end of a marriage that I never would have agreed to. All this looking back breaks my heart, though You've given me a new husband, a man I can respect and love, and who loves You like I do. Father, if this will help others who are going through that same painful process, it's worth it, but if not, please spare me the memories.

So Many Requests, So Little Time

Psalm 5:3 *In the morning, O Lord, you hear my voice; in the morning I lay my requests before you and wait in expectation.*

So many requests, so little time!

I have so many requests but do I wait for an answer? Or do I quickly throw them at my Heavenly Father's feet, and then run about doing my own business? He has got all the time in the world in eternity and yet He wants to spend some of those precious moments with us. What an awesome thought! He is our loving Father, nudging us to pay attention, highlighting areas of Scripture that He wants to speak to us, whispering ideas of how to bless others. What a wonderful Abba Father we serve, Holy God and Daddy all at the same time! What a pleasure to spend time with Him.

Oh, Abba, my heart cries out to You this morning. You love us dearly, and are training us and growing us into the people You want us to be. This spurs me on to live for You.

Following God Wholeheartedly

Joshua 14:8b,9 *I, however, followed the Lord my God wholeheartedly. So, on that day, Moses swore to me, "The land on which your feet have walked shall be your inheritance and that of your children forever, because you have followed the Lord my God wholeheartedly."*

Am I walking wholeheartedly with my God?

As we place our trust in God and spend valuable time with Him, He wants to give us our hearts' desire. But sometimes He changes that desire as we place our feet where He directs us to go. We find ourselves in places we never dreamed we would be. We must trust Him in the process and not listen to the bad reports others may give. If He has put something on our hearts, we must continue to pursue

Him and His plans for they are <u>good</u>. Watch for those confirmations that He will provide.

Father, thank You for putting those desires in us, for giving us hope and direction. Give us courage to forge ahead into what You're providing for us.

Jesus Prays For Us

John 17:20,21 *"My prayer is not for them alone. I pray also for those who will believe in me through their message, that all of them may be one, Father, just as you are in me and I am in you. May they also be in us so that the world may believe that you have sent me..."*

Way back then, Jesus actually prayed for you and for me. Imagine!

What an awesome thought. It so touches my heart to read those words and to know that I am referred to in them. But He wants us to be one, even as He and the Father are one. He wants us to love one another so that the world may see our love and come to know Him as well. As we connect under Jesus Christ and follow Him, the Father gives us His love and conforms us all into the likeness of His Son.

Father, let the love that flows through the blood of Your Son, Jesus Christ, flow through us to our family members in You. Give us love for one another.

A Much-Needed Reprieve

In August of 1988 my sister called to ask if I could possibly go to Ireland with her to escape from my life for awhile. After explaining to her that we did not have the money for that indulgence, she asked me to at least pray about it.

My sarcastic response was, "Right, I'm just sure that God wants me to go to Ireland."

But I did pray about it, and the answer came immediately. My income had been a steady $800 per month since my business first got off the ground. All of a sudden I was offered many extra hours and new clients. In one month, my income doubled, and the following month I made $1200. My entire trip was paid for before I left for the airport in October. An emotional basket case by that time, it was obvious, even to me, that God did want me to go to Ireland.

Fortunately, being an experienced flight attendant, Beth is well traveled because I had never gone anywhere without the covering of my husband. One of the experiences that had her laughing until the tears rolled down her cheeks was when we boarded the first plane. She took my garment bag with everything I owned for travel, and hung it by the door as we entered the aircraft. After we were settled into our seats and on our way to Atlanta, I looked at the closet where our bags were. Not only the bags, but the entire closet was gone! In great alarm, I cried out to Beth who patiently explained that they had gone up in an elevator inside the wall. Whew. That was a close one! We arrived in

Atlanta to meet Beth's friend, Norma Jean, a wonderful Christian girl who had fiery red, curly hair and really looked the part of an Irish lady. She was also a flight attendant so I let them take the lead during our entire trip.

Arriving in Shannon, our designated driver, Beth, was happy to discover that the vehicle we rented was exactly like hers at home, except, of course, that the steering wheel was on the right side. Not to worry. It was a little nerve-wracking at first to see busses whizzing by us to the right-hand side of the car on those little, narrow roads. Beth, however, was undaunted by this challenge. It did not take very long before she was right at home as our chauffer. Traveling through Ireland was, indeed, a glorious experience. We had our Christian music tapes playing while we sang out, making a joyful noise. We enjoyed the beauty of the emerald green countryside with white sheep dotting the pastures. We really felt as if we were blessing the land with the Lord's presence everywhere we traveled; He was certainly blessing us.

We had several experiences there that cannot go without mention. The first is the fact that Beth stopped at almost every available pay telephone to make calls to a particular church called the "Upper Room" somewhere in Cork. Tony Stone, a pastor she had heard about from a previous trip, had an especially fantastic fellowship. She really wanted to take us to meet the wonderful Christians there and to attend their services on Sunday. We had planned our entire trip around being in Cork on the weekend just for that reason. However, for three solid days, she could never connect with anyone. This was before the days of cell phones so, consequently, we have many memories and pictures of Beth at various telephone booths across Ireland.

Saturday morning, we arrived in Cork to find that it was the busiest shopping day of the month, when the stores are open longer and the sales are in full swing. We were hard pressed to even find a spot to park in all of the hubbub. Eventually, we found a place and shopped until we could no longer stand it, looking for a place to eat that would offer us a late lunch around 3:00. In exasperation, we found that all the restaurants were closed from 2:00 until 5:00. We finally did find an open Chinese café (of all things) that was on the second story overlooking the busiest street of that industrious city. It was so relaxing to sit and watch the traffic down below, which also included several wedding parades, just for our dining pleasure.

As we watched, a small band of people gathered across the street, handing out leaflets to the passersby. Soon some others joined in, and they brought a guitar, singing quietly as they passed out the flyers. After a few more moments, someone began reading from a book. Beth's curiosity proved too much for her, so she decided to go downstairs to check it out. Much to our surprise, the man reading a Bible was the pastor we had been calling from pay phones all over Ireland for the last three days! If we could not get a hold of him, the Lord brought the pastor to us. We did attend his church the following morning, and loved the people we met there.

Another precious moment happened in Belfast. We were a little nervous about traveling to Northern Ireland because of all the warfare that was going on at the time. Beth and Norma Jean particularly wanted to meet with some people they knew from Prison Fellowship.

We boarded a train in Dublin, stashing our bags overhead in the compartments. The trip seemed to be uneventful until the train stopped abruptly midway between two cities. As it turned out, the conductor was going through each car, matching luggage with the various travelers to make sure that there were no explosives on board. Now that was comforting. Upon arriving in Belfast, we were greeted by a representative of Prison Fellowship who took us over to the office to meet with the director. While traveling through the city, we saw several tanks and army personnel with their weapons. As I whipped out my camera for this wonderful photo opportunity, I was almost smashed to the floor by our driver. It turned out that I could have been jailed for taking such pictures there in that war-torn land. Now that I think of it, this would have been a great time for Prison Fellowship to show us what they could do for me while I was in jail.

The following day, Frank, the Director of Ireland's Prison Fellowship office, had some really wonderful news, but we did not have a clue as to what it meant. The conversation went something like this as he spoke with his secretary: "Patricia, I have talked to Bernadette and she's going to be in town today. She wants to come to lunch with our American visitors. Not only that, but Joan also called and, when she learned that Bernadette was going to be here, she requested that she get to come too."

At that, Patricia insisted that the office be closed for the afternoon so that she could join us as well. "Imagine! Both of these ladies at the same table."

As I said, we had no idea what was in store, but knew that it must be something spectacular.

Gathering in a private corner of the quaint restaurant, Frank introduced us to two women on opposite sides of the war in that country. Only the Holy Spirit could have brought us all together under one roof at this particular time to celebrate the love of Jesus in such a memorable way. His presence was very much there, and His peace permeated the entire building I am sure.

After the initial formalities, Frank asked Bernadette to tell us her story. She was the most beautiful, angelic looking little thing I had ever seen. Her curly brown hair topped off her delicate features perfectly, and her soft, Irish lilt belied the horror she had recently lived through. Her husband was a fine Catholic man who loved the Lord with all his heart. They had three small children and a very warm, close marriage. One morning as they were preparing for church, he put on a new hat and turned to her after looking at himself approvingly in the mirror, "Ye' got yur'self a fine one 'ere, ye' do!"

"Aye, I do! Ye' are definitely a handsome brute!" she replied with a laugh. They piled the children into the car

189

and, as he got in himself, a gunman fired shots at the vehicle and sped out of sight around the corner. One of her children was very seriously wounded but, worse, her beloved husband was killed instantly.

She went on to talk about the peace of the Lord during the days that followed, and how He had been there to comfort her during the most difficult times. While they were at the funeral, she turned to her brother seated beside her and asked, "Can ye' hear 'em?"

"Hear what?" he asked, puzzled.

"The angels! Can't ye' hear the angels singin'?"

As she told her story, we dabbed at our own tears along with her. Bernadette's husband had been a very active member of the IRA, representing one side of the centuries-old strife that continually tore Ireland apart. Apparently, the gunman belonged to the opposite side, the UDA. I do not know all the intricacies of this religious battle, but I do know that Jesus died for everyone.

After recovering from her moving testimony, Frank turned to Joan and asked her to relate her story. Joan's appearance was the opposite of Bernadette's. She was very hard looking with platinum blonde, short hair. The smell of cigarettes clung to her clothing, and her language was coarse.

She began by telling us that, seven years prior, her husband had been a guard for the prison. They were Protestants but not Christians. The IRA had killed him. After his murder, she "went off the deep end." Becoming a raging alcoholic, and suicidal to the point that her two small children were taken from her, she was institutionalized. While in the hospital, she tried to take her life four separate times. God spared her each time.

She continued, haltingly telling her story: After her release from the sanitarium, she was walking on the streets of Belfast when three men attacked and raped her. Allowing the pain of that experience to sink into our hearts, she continued by saying that she had finally accepted Jesus as her Savior two years before our meeting. Only through allowing Christ to work in her life had she been able to forgive the murderer of her husband, the three rapists, and all the other atrocities she had experienced previously. She cried out to us for help in getting her life together, and was afraid that sanity would slip through her fingers once again.

What an emotion-packed afternoon. We all rejoiced in the Lord after our luncheon. Joan and I spent a little time alone together, which gave me an opportunity to share a Scripture with her. I had only recently learned about, and desperately clung to, Isaiah 54:4–7: *"Do not be afraid; you will not suffer shame. Do not fear disgrace; you will not be humiliated. You will forget the shame of your youth and remember no more the reproach of your widowhood. For your Maker is your husband---the Lord Almighty is his name---the Holy One of Israel is your Redeemer; he is called the God of all the earth. The Lord will call you back as if you were a wife deserted and distressed in spirit---a wife who married young, only to be rejected," says your God. "For a brief moment I abandoned you, but with deep compassion I will bring you back."*

I was happy to see that this verse meant a lot to Joan as well. She seemed genuinely grateful that I took the time to share it with her, and we bonded during that brief time together in the Lord. As I was leaving, she took a fish pin off her coat and pinned it onto my lapel as a sign of her friendship to me. I treasure it to this day. It represents what only Christ can do in a person's life, if we will just let Him come in and live through us. He was so present that afternoon as these two women said good-bye to one another with warm hugs and tears. I am sure none of us have ever forgotten it.

We had so many memorable experiences in Ireland and, in spite of the pain in my own personal life, I knew the Lord was giving me a much needed refilling of the Holy Spirit as I went back into the trenches of divorce upon my return home.

 We Must Search For Wisdom

Proverbs 2:1–5 *...If you accept my words and store up my commands... turning your ear to wisdom and applying your heart to understanding, and if you call out for insight and cry aloud for understanding, and if you look for it as for silver and search for it as for hidden treasure, then you will understand the fear of the Lord and find the knowledge of God.* [Underscoring added.]

We do not become wise by accident.

God tells us to be diligent in our search for wisdom. We must read His Word and value wisdom more than all the riches the world has to offer. Only then can He teach us what we need as we cope with the challenges of this place. We look up to our Heavenly Father and listen intently for His instruction to know what to do during difficult days.

Father, thank You for Your protection and covering over us in perilous times. I'm so glad we are only passing through planet Earth on our way to our permanent home in heaven.

He Is Our Shield

Proverbs 2:7,8 *He holds victory in store for the upright, He is a shield to those whose walk is blameless, for he guards the course of the just and protects the way of his faithful ones.*

The Lord is our covering and our protection when we are walking with Him.

When the Word says "blameless," that does not mean perfect. We will never be perfect this side of heaven. It is talking about the intent of our hearts. Our lives need to be bent on God---He is our focus. We are faithful to Him and serve Him with a whole heart. When we do that, He is able to provide the protection we need and He guards our paths. We do not leave a window open for the enemy to come in and rob, kill, or destroy areas of our lives. When we sin, we are quick to repent.

193

Father, thank You that You do hold us in the palm of Your hand. I've said it before, but I need to repeat it to remember it. Nothing comes to us that doesn't pass through Your fingers first. When the tough times come, give me Your strength to endure.

Back To Reality

When I returned from Ireland, I found that my home had been put on the market while I was away, but at least it had been listed with a Christian couple I knew, liked and respected. My family had pretty well trashed my home while I was gone. Jet lag and all, I got up early the next morning to clean before the first open house that afternoon. I did not want anyone, much less my Realtor friends, to see it in the current state. During my cleaning frenzy, I prayed that the Lord would block anyone from coming through the house that absolutely did not need to be there. Of course, I also prayed that it would not sell, and that things would work out in our relationship.

My friends, Jim and Sue, arrived around noon and we sat in the conversation pit looking out over the valley. We all waited for the people to start coming through, in fact we waited all afternoon. At times, people would maneuver up the driveway but, strangely, they would back up again without getting out of their car.

Finally, after this happened a few more times, Jim verbalized their question. "This is certainly odd! What is going on here? Why hasn't anyone come into the house?"

I confessed that I had asked the Lord to block the doors and not let anyone in, to which they replied, "Well, quit it!"

We had a good laugh, but they were well aware of how miserable I was in this unwanted decision to leave my home. Toward the end of the day, a couple appeared who actually came inside. They took a long time, asking questions as they went through every room. I had a sinking feeling that they seemed a little too interested. I was right. Three days later, their Realtor was sitting at our kitchen table presenting their offer. My dream home was sold right out from under my breaking heart. Jim and Sue tried talking to my husband about his decision but, as far as he was concerned, there was no turning back.

The next night, Chris and I went for pizza and were talking about our future, our next possible home, etc. I explained that I had looked and looked, and could only come up with miserable, depressing fix-er-uppers that were in my budget in that pricey community. I certainly did not want to uproot him from his school and friends at this point; life was tough enough as it was. I told him about some condominiums I had driven by that might be a possibility, so we promptly went over there to investigate.

We drove down one street and then the next; there appeared to be several available in the area. At Chris' suggestion, I turned down the main road to find a short cul-de-sac that took me right back to Ireland. I could not believe this street. There were six brand new, two-story gray duplexes, with window boxes and bright green garage doors. They were absolutely charming, and both Chris and I got very excited.

195

There was a big sign at the beginning of the street revealing that there was still one unit available. The price on these places seemed much more in line with my budget than anything I had seen so far.

The next morning, I called the builder to inquire about that last unit. "Yes, it's still available," he responded. "In fact, my brother and I were going to keep it as a rental and just decided to go ahead and sell it after all."

I immediately made an appointment to go with my friend and Realtor, Sue, to check it out. Lindy accompanied us as well. I could only cry when we walked in the door. It was made for us, and my Father held it until I needed it. The builder had a lot of compassion, and told us I could actually start moving things into the garage immediately. Escrow would not close until Thanksgiving weekend, five weeks away.

Qualifying for a mortgage would be a little tricky considering my normal business income was still only $800 per month, plus child support and alimony. In fact, my unbelieving next-door neighbor asked his wife, "Now who on earth would ever give Patty a loan to buy her own house with the income she makes? It will never happen."

His wife, knowing the Lord the way I do, responded, "Has God ever let her down yet?"

Once again, He proved Himself faithful. I got the loan because of all the equity I was able to pour into the house from the profits I received on the sale of our much larger home. In addition, there was enough left over to have a nice patio poured and landscaping completed. I even had enough to buy some furniture. All this and a house payment well within my budget. Thank you, Lord!

Complete The Race

2 Timothy 2:11-13 *Here is a trustworthy saying: If we die with him, we will also live with him; if we endure we will also reign with him. If we disown him, he will also disown us; if we are faithless, he will remain faithful, for he cannot disown himself.*

We must complete the race.

The Lord is always faithful. We, on the other hand, waver in our faith depending upon the circumstances of life. Our obedience is the key that starts the vehicle of our journey with the Lord. We have to die to our old nature so that He can live through us. We have to be willing to endure through the trials and difficulties of life, knowing that He is there even if it does not feel like it sometimes. We must hang on for dear life so that, in the end, we can reign with Him. We can walk away from Him, but he will try to bring us back.

Lord, give me strength to endure until the very end. Thank You for the gift of faith that got me through those things that looked impossible. Increase my faith throughout life, so that I can live with You forever.

Jesus, The Judge

John 5:22,26,27,30 *Moreover, the Father judges no one, but has entrusted all judgment to the Son, that all may honor the Son just as they honor the Father... For as the Father has life in himself, so he has granted the Son to have life in himself. And he has given him authority to judge because he is the Son of Man... By myself I can do nothing; I judge only as I hear, and my judgment is just, for I seek not to please myself but him who sent me.*

Jesus is the Judge.

The Father has given His Son the right to judge the earth and everything in it. He knows the hearts of men. A pastor I know recently told me that he believes God no longer judges man or countries because He now operates in mercy. That is not correct. It is important to believe all of God's Word.

Lord, I pray that You will find me favorable in Your kingdom. Show me the areas that need improvement. Thank You that You are a Judge of fairness and mercy.

 ## Choose Intimacy

Luke 10:41 *"Martha, Martha, you are worried and upset about many things, but only one thing is needed. Mary has chosen what is better and it will not be taken away from her."*

Things and activities get in the way of intimacy.

Life gets so busy. I feel needed when I am asked to be a part of ministry, when someone requires counseling, or

198

when I am asked to help by being a leader. But, is it the Spirit or is it the flesh that says yes to these things. "Mary has chosen what is better." She sits at Jesus' feet to draw near to Him and know Him on a deeper level. I need to learn that, and to be content there, growing in the Spirit, being with my Lord.

What a lesson, Lord. Help me to say "no" unless You're asking me to say "yes." I don't want to keep Your salt in the salt shaker, but I need to check with You as my Lord, to see what You're directing me to do before giving a reply. Without Your answer to prayer, my own quick response can be so misguided.

A Supernatural Distraction

In the middle of packing to move during that devastating time of life, I received an unexpected phone call. I recognized the Irish lilt immediately.

"It's me, Joan! I have a favor to ask of you. Billy Graham is coming to Ireland but he's not coming up near Belfast. Could you contact him for me and let him know how much we need him to come here?"

I had to bite my lip to keep from laughing.

She went on, "You live in the United States and he lives in the United States. Isn't there something you could do?"

I tried to explain but, hearing her disappointment, ended with, "I'll see what's possible." *Oh my.*

A day or so later, I received another phone call from a different Joan, who also happened to be Irish. We had been in a Bible study together with some other women from our church. She wanted to let me know that there was a new study starting in a couple of days at her home. I told her briefly about my trip, promising that I would attend her study and tell more about it then. It was not until I arrived at Joan's home that I learned she had left our church and was now attending a different church in Danville. We had a great teaching and enjoyed catching up. I was prompted at the end of the meeting to tell her and the others about the Joan I had met in Ireland and the unusual request. I laughed and expected them to laugh as well. To my surprise, Joan told me that Billy Graham's nephew was on staff at her new church and that I should make an appointment to see him. *Oh my.*

Knowing that there are no "coincidences" in the kingdom, I decided to follow up, and was given an appointment with this young pastor the following day. I explained the situation to him, the great need in Northern Ireland, and the unusual phone call from my friend. He kind of shrugged his shoulders and left me hanging. *Oh well.*

I received a phone call that very evening from a friend who knew I had been away. Aware of all that was going on in my life, Diana just wanted to check in. I told her about my trip, the phone call from Ireland, the Bible study with our mutual friend, finally the meeting with Billy Graham's nephew, and then awaited her response.

"Well, you do know Marilee, don't you? She spoke at a meeting a couple of weeks ago (while I was in Ireland). Her father founded World Vision. Marilee knows Billy Graham well enough to call him Uncle Billy." *Oh my.*

She said that they were good friends and had been trying to get together to have lunch for some time. But, because Marilee's schedule was very hectic, they had not connected. Diana asked me if I wanted her to call and make another attempt. "Believe me, it will have to be the Lord to pull this one off," she laughed.

The phone rang again about a half hour later. "How does tomorrow sound?" *Oh my.*

The following day, I busied myself with lunch preparations knowing full well that I needed to get on with packing. Marilee Dunker was such a beautiful, warm, encouraging person. She was the one who actually persuaded me to begin writing down my life experiences. I explained the reason for their visit, and she gave me several leads. These were people to contact within the Billy Graham organization who would be interested and could truly do something to promote a visit to Northern Ireland. It was a great meeting and I so enjoyed this lovely distraction from my "real" life. When Marilee was preparing to leave, she gave me a signed copy of her book, "A Braver Song to Sing." I have always kept it to remember that special point in time, and how the Lord intervened in my life.

I went to work at one of my client's offices the next day, and was telling Bob all about the series of events that had transpired in less than a week. When I finished, one of his staff came around the corner with a twinkle in her eye to tell me that her parents had been part of the Oakland Billy Graham Crusade. They headed up the ministry to the deaf, not just in Oakland, but at other crusades as well. She also provided a couple of contacts. *Oh my.*

We were preparing for a women's meeting at our church that weekend, so my pastor's wife encouraged me to get the other women involved by giving them a short synopsis of this chain of events. We started a letter writing campaign that went to all the upper level management of the Billy Graham organization. I am happy to tell you that they did bring a simultaneous televised version of the Dublin crusade to Belfast as well. What an honor to be a part of this God-orchestrated experience, and what a great way to continue to realize the goodness of our Lord during a really tough time in my own personal life.

The Mouth Reveals The Heart

Proverbs 10:11 *The mouth of the righteous is a fountain of life, but violence overwhelms the mouth of the wicked.*

What comes out of the mouth reveals the heart.

That coarse jesting has to go. The negativity spoken about others is unbecoming to the righteous. Hatred and evil also do not belong to the upright in spirit. When violence is spoken, you have to wonder about the condition of the heart of the speaker. I know I have spoken many things that revealed my true character, and I was immediately ashamed. My heart is wicked at times; I need the Lord to change it. I would not even be aware of my own depravity if I didn't hear those words slip out between my lips.

Lord, I know I'll never be flawless, but I'd like to strive for that goal. Thank You for showing me the darkness of my heart so that I can confess and run in the opposite direction. Let the Holy Spirit continue to reveal my sin so that I can return quickly to You and Your righteousness.

Boast In The Lord

Jeremiah 9:23,24 *This is what the Lord says: "Let not the wise man boast of his wisdom or the strong man boast of his strength or the rich man boast of his riches, but let him who boasts boast about this: that he knows and under-stands me, that I am the Lord, who exercises kindness, justice and righteousness on earth, for in these I delight," declares the Lord.*

That about says it all, doesn't it?

Silly man! Why do you boast about your own accomplishments, your worldly wisdom, your muscles, your money? These things are bragging fodder, garbage, compared to our Creator, our Savior. The only thing we can boast about is in knowing our God. Even then, He came to get us; it was not our doing. If our focus is on our own accomplishments, they are very short-lived in the light of eternity.

Lord, You are the righteous One who exercises kindness and goodness to those who serve You and You alone. You overwhelm me with Your love.

Idolatry Comes In Many Forms

Jeremiah 10:3–5 *"For the customs of the peoples are worthless; they cut a tree out of the forest, and a craftsman shapes it with his chisel. They adorn it with silver and gold; they fasten it with hammer and nails so it will not totter. Like a scarecrow in a melon patch, their idols cannot speak; they must be carried because they cannot walk. Do not fear them; they can do no harm nor can they do any good."*

Idols come in many forms.

Back in the early 1980's, when I had known the Lord a year or so, we were finally able to build our "dream home." We had saved our ideas for many years, hoping that someday we would be able to accomplish this task. We worked so hard to put it together and the house became our focus. The Lord began taking a backseat position as this idol built with our own hands of wood, hay, and stubble rose up out of the dirt. It was beautiful and very creative, I have to admit, but it was certainly given more attention than was deserved. We must have just the "right" tiles, just the "right" flooring, just the "right" design. How can it be so wrong, when it seemed so "right"? Suddenly there was a financial downturn and we almost lost our dream. We worked extra hours to maintain and keep this home… for a season. Eventually, its importance cost us our peace, our joy, our family, and our marriage. We could have sold it to pay off the business debts, but there was too much pride to let it go. How foolish we were back then.

Lord, help me to let go of things much sooner than I did when that hard lesson of life hit me. You were there in the midst of the turmoil and I hung onto You during all the trials that came to pass. Thank You that You have never left me, though it seemed like I was so alone much of the time. You refocused my priorities and life went on. All the while, it looked like the end of the world. You have since rewarded me with a comfortable, simple home on the river, a great husband, and a wonderful life. Over thirty years have passed and I am grateful that You never let me go.

<u>Starting Our New Life</u>

I remember going to a furniture store where Chris and I were going to purchase our new living room furniture. His eye fell immediately upon a plush recliner where he could just envision himself sprawled in front of the television with his remote tightly in hand. I found a lovely floral couch that happened to go with his recliner. Chris groaned when he saw the flowers but we came to an agreement---he could have the recliner if I could have the couch. Besides, they blended perfectly with the mauve carpeting. What a switch from the black leather, overstuffed furniture I had been living with since 1972. I loved this new, more feminine look, though Chris was dismayed.

Next, we picked a small stereo and television to complete our entertainment unit. When it was time to write up the contract, I began filling out the paperwork. Everything was going okay until the question of marital status came up. Tears filled my eyes to the point that I could not see anymore and had to walk away to compose myself. I heard the salesman ask Chris, "Are you taking good care of your mom?" He just nodded. At that moment I felt like our roles were reversed.

Chris and I got moved into our own place on Thanksgiving weekend. I am still so thankful to our friends that helped us in that transition. I was emotionally paralyzed and could barely pack our belongings much less move them. If it were not for our neighbors, I would still be sitting there in a heap. Leaving our marriage and our home was something I never envisioned as a part of my life. On top of that, my grandmother died Thanksgiving night up in Oregon. My husband and I both worked hard to clean our house as we prepared to close the doors forever. When it was ready for its new owners, we hugged and cried together before we said good-bye. Believe it or not, I felt compassion for this man.

The Lord was preparing a new chapter in my life and, though it was a difficult one, He and I had a lot of great times together. First, I loved the new dwelling He had provided for us. He became my Husband and Maker, my Provider, my Healer. He was all I needed to get through. He helped me to raise my son and gave me wisdom in my business. I began to grow after all the struggles I had been through. Chris was a strong willed teenager and we had our ups and downs but, as I look back, he was excellent company and a great help during our transitional time. Life was beginning to be good. I threw myself into making our home one we could be proud of, entertain in, and be comfortable together in. My business was blessed with new clients, new types of work, and the people who could help me to understand what to do to improve it. There were many changes that pointed to a bright future ahead.

Abram Believed The Lord

Genesis 15:5,6 *[God] took him outside and said, "Look up at the heavens and count the stars---if indeed you can count them." Then he said to him, "So shall your offspring be." Abram believed the Lord, and he credited it to him as righteousness.*

Abram believed and God saw him as blameless.

We all know the story. He believed for the moment, but down the road he created Ishmael as he took the matter into his own hands. Ishmael's bloodline has been against God's chosen ones all these generations later. Waiting is the hardest thing for us. We hear God's voice; He gives us a glimpse into the future and then we wait… and wait… and wait some more. Will we continue to believe, or do we take things into our own control, making things happen as we think they should? If we do not trust God, we can bring disaster upon ourselves and, possibly, the generations following us. After all, Ishmael's bloodline became the progenitors of the Muslim world.

Lord, I've heard You. I'm sure of it. I'm trusting that in Your time, Your words will come to pass. I don't want to create any more Ishmaels in my life!

He Blesses Those Who Love Him

Isaiah 61:7 *Instead of their shame my people will receive a double portion, and instead of disgrace they will rejoice in their inheritance; and so they will inherit a double portion in their land, and everlasting joy will be theirs.*

Something to ponder...

My heart belongs to God. Because He loves me I can trust Him. What does He mean by "double portion"? A double portion of His Spirit, joy, or peace? What exactly am I inheriting? Is it for now or in heaven? I have known the shame of divorce, though it was not of my choosing. I am content now with all the Lord has poured out upon me. I cannot imagine more. Somehow this Scripture got my attention this morning, and I am not sure what to make of it. It seems greedy to want more...

The very morning that I wrote this, as I was proofreading my pastor's letter to our church, he talked about expecting more, having faith to believe that God wants to pour out more than we could imagine. He is looking for those who are ready to believe He is willing to give us enough to give away to others. The Lord had spoken the same theme to him that He spoke to me. Amazing. What a godly coincidence! The Holy Spirit did speak, not just to me, but to others about this subject.

We believe, Lord; now help our unbelief. You know our hearts. You know the plans you have for us. Is this new dream that we are praying about just that, a "dream," or is it You? I had forgotten all about this "godly coincidence" until it came time to type it up this morning, many months later. You are so awesome to remind me of Your hand moving throughout Your creation in the lives of Your people.

Pray BIG Prayers

Hebrews 12:2 *Let us fix our eyes on Jesus, the author and perfecter of our faith, who for the joy set before him endured the cross, scorning its shame, and sat down at the right hand of the throne of God.*

Keep your eyes on Jesus, your ears attentive to His voice, then pray BIG!

Thoughts have been mulling around in my head for a month. Dave and I have begun praying for a benefactor who would want to help people go to Israel. Once people get to Israel, see the land, place their feet on the same stones where Jesus walked, and get excellent teaching about those sites, they will never be the same. I am beginning to see that these may be Spirit-inspired thoughts and prayers, not just Patty ponderings.

Lord Jesus, our eyes are fixed on You. If this is You, it will come to pass. If not, it will fall by the wayside. We don't want what You don't want for us. But time is short; we must move out in faith on what we believe we are hearing from You.

A Sobering Moment

On January 12, 1989, I had come home from work to find the finalized divorce papers in the mail. All I needed to do was sign them and our marriage of 21 years would be over. My friend who lived across the street saw all the seething anger I had been trying to contain. She invited me to go play racquetball with her. This was exactly what I needed. We slammed that ball around the court for an hour until we were totally exhausted. It helped to get all the pent up energy out of my body. Then we sat in the hot tub to relax again. When I got home, I had barely walked in the door when the phone rang.

"This is the Emergency Room at John Muir Hospital. Your son has been in a very serious car accident. He'll be arriving here by ambulance shortly. He is alive."

Can you imagine? *Oh, my God! Please help me to get there! Oh, Father, please save my son! Please, Lord, don't take him from me.* I nearly flew across the streets of Walnut Creek to the hospital, arriving in a strangely calm condition that only the Lord could explain. Upon reaching the Emergency Room, I found it full of teenagers in a state of near hysteria. The E.R. nurse came up to tell me that the ambulances should be there any second. He asked me to try to quiet the kids down, that they were causing too much upheaval in their hospital. *Me? But I'm the Mom!* There was a peaceful assurance as I took the steps needed to gain control of the chaos within that crowded room. I can only tell you it was Jesus who brought the quiet needed for that moment.

About that time, the ambulances arrived. I ran outside and could see Chris on a gurney about to be rolled into the hospital.

"Chris, Chris! It's me, Mom," I yelled. "Can you hear me?"

Though there were police guarding the ambulance and I could not get nearer for the moment, my heart leaped when Chris lifted his head and I heard my son's reply.

"Yea, Mom, I can hear you. I'm okay."

There were three kids that left a party where there had been a lot of drinking, and one of Chris' friends was really proud of the way his small sports car could take the turns. This area of Walnut Creek is quite hilly, with a narrow road which winds its way down the foothills. To the right is a steep bank that drops off to a creek far below. Tommy missed the curve, and the car plowed between some oak trees, flipped end over end, landing upside down in the creek. Tommy was pretty much unhurt; Chris had bruised his leg and ribs pretty badly, but a girl in the backseat was injured very severely. She broke her back and spent quite some time in the hospital. As far as I know, she eventually made a complete recovery. The accident scene was a grizzly reminder of what can happen to young, seemingly invincible, teenagers.

When I finally got to be with Chris after he was settled into a bed in the E.R., I was crying in thankfulness that he appeared to be in pretty good shape. "You know, Chris, you could have been killed. The Lord protected you."

His response was, "I know, Mom, I know."

I realized that I needed to inform his father and brother about the accident, and that he was okay. I found a pay phone in the hall and called Erik. He was home alone at that point. His dad would be arriving at any moment. Chris was moved into a bed upstairs to spend the night. I stayed with him quite awhile waiting for his father to get there. As much time passed and Chris was resting comfortably, I decided to head home. Upon reaching my car, I looked up to find Chris' dad with a questioning look on his face. We talked for a few minutes as I gave him the details that I knew. I told him I had signed his divorce papers that evening and said good-bye.

Chris stayed in the hospital for the night and, after he was released, we went to take a look at the car. My knees crumpled as I was made quickly aware of the severity of the accident. *Oh, my Lord and my God! Thank You for sparing my son!* It is amazing that any of them even made it through the accident, much less with so little injuries. This was a very sobering moment in the life of my young man.

 ### "Bring Israel To The People"

January 12, 2010

The first words I heard in my spirit before I even opened my eyes were, "Bring Israel to the people." Dave has always said, "I want to bring people to Israel," so this was a new twist. Then, as I was getting out of bed, the words "black day" came to mind. I tried to push away the darkness and, as I was preparing to make our coffee, I realized the date. It was 21 years ago today that two very significant events occurred in my life, my divorce and Chris' car accident. What do I do with this information?

Lord, I think You're telling me to put it behind me and to not think on those things anymore. You have new and <u>wonderful</u> plans for us, <u>more</u> (there's that word again) than we could ever hope or imagine. I have faith to believe, but now help my unbelief. Please continue to work these things through me until I am completely focused on You. "Psalm 52" rang in my mind.

I turned to my Bible, not knowing what God's gift contained, and wondered if it truly was His voice I heard or if it was merely my imagination. God is in control, both in the lives of believers as well as unbelievers. When I got to verses 8 and 9, I <u>knew</u> this word applied to my life. Thank You, Lord.

Psalm 52:8,9 *But I am like an olive tree flourishing in the house of God; I trust in God's unfailing love forever and ever. I will praise you forever for what you have done; in your name I will hope, for your name is good. I will praise you in the presence of your saints.*

I could not have said it better myself.

In the weeks that followed since this formidable anniversary, I was asked to speak at our Mother's Day Tea. I gave a testimony about my life, and how God has worked through all the struggles and joys since childhood. I believe it blessed many of the women there and it gave them hope for their own life misfortunes. The Lord has certainly put my feet upon a new path, and He will for them as well, if they trust Him through it all.

Just How Close Is Close Enough?

Luke 6:13-17 *When morning came, he called his disciples to him and chose 12 of them, whom he also designated apostles: Simon (whom he named Peter), his brother Andrew, James, John, Philip, Bartholomew, Matthew, Thomas, James son of Alphaeous, Simon who was called the Zealot, Judas son of James, and Judas Iscariot, who became a traitor. He went down with them and stood on a level place. A large crowd of his disciples was there and a great number of people from all over Judea, from Jerusalem, and from the coast of Tyre and Sidon.*

Even though Jesus is "no respecter of persons," it appears that there are several layers of people who were interested in Him.

First, there were those who were His trusted friends, the twelve (really eleven) apostles. Even in that group, there were those who were closer. You do not hear much about Bartholomew, and Thomas almost always has a negative connotation. He doubted. Even though Peter also failed, Jesus knew his heart, and worked to encourage him more. Then there were the disciples who were interested and loved hearing His stories. They were there to learn and follow at a distance. They wanted to know who He was. After that, there followed the multitudes who were only present for the "signs and wonders." They were there merely for what He could do for them, the miraculous healings, raising from the dead, demons released from people's souls. What category do I fall into? What about you? I want to <u>know</u> Him, to hear His heart, to respond to

214

His voice. I fail at times; we all do. But my heart is knit with His. I trust Him, even when my prayers are not answered the way I would like.

Lord, I know that it is the journey and not the final destination that You have in mind for us. How are we going to respond to each bump in the road? What will we think and say when someone hurts us? It is all those life lessons that You bring our way that make us the people we are today. Hopefully, we won't be the same tomorrow or the next day, and will grow more into the people You created us to be. It's a lifelong process. Thank You that we can count on You in the hard times and the good times. We want to be so close that we're walking in the dust kicked up by Your feet.

 ## The Lord's Beautiful Creation

Psalm 19:1 *The heavens declare the glory of God; the skies proclaim the work of his hands.*

The Lord's beautiful creation is evident for all to see.

As I look up and see the beauty of God's creation, I marvel at His works. A gorgeous sunset or sunlight glinting off the snowy mountains around Redding can sometimes bring tears of thankfulness. How sad for those who do not know their Creator. They cannot begin to appreciate what He has done for them.

Oh, Lord, keep me alert to all that You've done in Your creation. Help me to see the raindrop falling from a leaf in the garden. I want to admire the new green shoots coming out in the spring, or the hawk that sits waiting for his next

215

meal to appear. We can get so caught up in the trials of life and the busyness, we forget to praise You for Your goodness. How sad for those who worship Your creation rather than the Creator.

$\dagger$ ### God's Intervention

[Abimelech took Abraham's wife, Sarah, because they said they were brother and sister. But God spoke to Abimelech in a dream, telling him she was married.]

Genesis 20:6 *Then God said to him in a dream, "Yes, I know you did this with a clear conscience, and so I have kept you from sinning against me. That is why I did not let you touch her."*

Abraham and Sarah were less than honorable in lying to Abimelech but it was because, "There is surely no fear of God in this place, and they will kill me because of my wife." [Genesis 20:11]

Abraham's actions were because he was afraid he would be killed. Here we have two believers lying to an unbeliever. Abimelech took Sarah, but did not sleep with her. Who knows what God did to prevent the sin that would inevitably have taken place? Though he was not one of His own, God protected Abimelech until he knew the truth and could reverse what he had done. Abimelech repented because of God's intervention.

Lord, how many times have You protected me from myself? I've made bad choices, but You have not let me reap what I should have sown. I bet there are a lot more than I know about. Thank You, Father.

A Time Of Weeping

Jeremiah 31:15–17 *This is what the Lord says: "A voice is heard in Ramah, mourning and great weeping, Rachel weeping for her children and refusing to be comforted, because her children are no more." This is what the Lord says: "Restrain your voice from weeping and your eyes from tears, for your work will be rewarded," declares the Lord. "They will return from the land of the enemy. So there is hope for your future," declares the Lord. "Your children will return to their own land."*

My heart was utterly broken, but the Word gave me hope.

Within weeks after my divorce was final, I had rushed home to pick up Chris on our way to the dentist. There was a message on the phone so I listened to it before dashing out the door again. It happened to be Valentine's Day and the message was from my now ex-husband. Hoping for the best, I called him back immediately, only to find that he was making plans to remarry within a month, and was taking Erik to live with him in another city. I began to cry and could not stop. *I'll let myself cry in the car until I get to the dentist,* I thought. *I'll let Chris go in first so I can pull myself together*, I thought. While in the waiting room, I tried to read my Bible, but nothing seemed to penetrate the grieving in my spirit. *I'll be okay when I get in the chair,* I thought. However, I never did pull it together. This was the final straw. The dentist worked on my teeth and his assistant dabbed tears for my entire appointment.

A year and a half later, I was looking at things I had written in my Bible and happened to run across Jeremiah 31 again.

217

I noted the date "2/14/89" written at the top of the page, and pondered, W*asn't that the date that I sat in the dentist's office bawling my eyes out?* This piqued my curiosity so I began reading the underlined Scripture. Oh, my goodness! That was me! I refused to be comforted, but the Lord was trying to give me hope.

This was such an encouragement as I reflected on how my relationship with Erik had changed since then. I would pick him up once a week after working for one of my clients in the area. Our connection was so strained for the first hour or so. Finally the hard exterior shell would be penetrated. We could begin to laugh and visit, and be ourselves once again, only to have to say good-bye for another week. I missed my son; he was always so joyful and fun to be around, but it seemed like that part of him was no longer there. After rereading the Scripture, I felt like I needed to have faith that the Lord was going to return Erik to me. I prayed and began proclaiming that I knew he was going to come home. My friends would ask me when this would take place. I had to admit, I did not know when, just that he would be home again… someday.

Only a few weeks later I received the call of a lifetime. It was Erik. "Mom," he started, "can I come home?"

I could not believe my ears. "Of course!"

"But," he began, trying to form the words, "I have one major request." He halted momentarily while my mind raced. "Can I go to a Christian high school?"

Be still, my heart! I promised that we would try to get him into his best friend's high school. I did not have a clue how we would be able to pay for it, but we would try. It was only a few days before school started, so I made an appointment with the principal to see what could be done. They had a scholarship program for kids in situations like ours. Erik began his sophomore year with his best friend at a wonderful, small Christian school not too far from where we lived.

After Erik returned to our home, he told me many stories about the nearly two years that he was gone, and how he bucked the system the entire way. I was grateful that this time of rebellion was well behind him, and that we had such a good relationship again. When he first moved away, I saw myself laying him on the altar, asking my Heavenly Father to care for him, protect him, and to have His way in Erik's life. It felt like an Abraham/Isaac moment. His earthly father did not follow through on many of the promises he had made. He was not on the same page spiritually either, even persecuting Erik for wanting to tithe on his earnings. Consequently, the time that Erik spent away from home grounded him more in his faith in God.

The three years Erik spent at the Christian school with smaller class sizes were very good for him. Erik met his high school sweetheart there, and they were married a few years later. They have blessed us with three great boys, one of which was born on my birthday. I call Jordan Patrick my best birthday present ever!

Faith In Christ Brings Good Results

Hebrews 10:38,39 *"But my righteous one will live by faith. And if he shrinks back, I will not be pleased with him." But we are not of those who shrink back and are destroyed, but of those who believe and are saved.*

Faith in Christ will bring us through everything we face.

I see people on television who talk of their faith, but faith in what? Is their faith in our Creator, in His Son who died on the cross for us? Or is their faith in a nebulous, wispy feeling, grounded in imagination? I remember when I was new in Christ and dabbled in the "word of faith" movement. How presumptuous is that? Your own words become what you put your faith in! This faith is hollow with no strength. Then, when God does not move in the way you command, you fall away.

Lord Jesus, our faith is in You, and that is what gives us strength and courage for our lives. We know You have our best interests at heart. Consequently, when our prayers aren't answered in the way we would like, we trust that You know better what we need. Our goal is to know You on a deeper level, keeping our eyes and hearts in Your Word, listening for Your instruction, following Your leading. You give us strength to do as You're asking, especially when we know we can't do it.

 ## And Speaking Of Presumption...

Numbers 14:44 *Nevertheless, in their presumption they went up toward the high hill country, though neither Moses nor the ark of the Lord's covenant moved from the camp.*

220

Do I presume upon the Lord?

As I go about my life doing my daily chores, working, writing, planning the future, do I presume that the Lord is going with me? Or do I stop every morning and invite Him to "be the driver of my bus," so to speak? I have found that I can waste a lot of time if left to my own devices. I do not ever want to take for granted that He is going to give me favor, that I will win every battle. He must truly be Lord over my thoughts, actions, relationships, and my life.

Father, I know I'm disobedient at times. My procrastination is not pleasing to You. Help me to be quick to repent and to never just assume that You are leading. Take me where You want to go today.

 ## Intentional Invitation

Matthew 25:38 *When did we see you a stranger and invite you in, or needing clothes and clothe you?*

The word "invite" keeps coming to me this morning.

Perhaps it is because of my recent experience with some people I really care about. We felt as though we were intruding, but we could stay if we chose to. Am I doing that unintentionally to the Holy Spirit? Is that why I am feeling estranged from Him at the moment? Am I not being intentional in my relationship with God? Am I expecting Him to show up just because I'm opening His Book? Then I put the two things together this morning, knowing how uninvited I felt. I realized that I can hurt the Holy Spirit by my laziness in being purposeful about inviting Him to share my day.

Oh, my Lord, forgive me for my lack of enthusiasm about desiring to draw near to You, to have You teach me day by day. Oh, God, I am so sorry about not even expecting You to show up. Lord, thank You for this course correction in my walk. Lord, change my heart to be looking for You every day, especially in the perilous times in which we're living. Thank You for teaching me this morning about how important a heartfelt invitation is. Oh, Holy Spirit, I'm living in expectancy of hearing Your voice, of seeing Jesus, of reading and loving Your Word.

The Lord Knows Us

Luke 22:60,61 *Peter replied, "Man, I don't know what you're talking about!" Just as he was speaking, the rooster crowed. The Lord turned and looked straight at Peter. Then Peter remembered the word the Lord had spoken to him: "Before the rooster crows today, you will disown me three times."*

Though we may surprise ourselves, the Lord is never surprised by our sinful nature.

I have thought I was so strong about my spirituality only to find myself saying something I shouldn't, doing something I shouldn't, or thinking things I had no business thinking. We all live with that fallen nature lurking inside waiting for the opportune time to trip us up. We cannot say, "The devil made me do it," because much of the time, it is our flesh and that of our own sin nature that gets us into trouble.

222

Lord, please fill me more and more with Your Holy Spirit so that there will be no room for my old self to rise to the surface. I need You, Jesus! Bring Your conviction.

 ## <u>Season Of Singleness, Part 1</u>

Being single was not anything I relished experiencing at this late date. I thought that being a Christian would make things simpler for me. Little did I know that, just because a guy calls himself a Christian, it does not make him one. Let's put it this way, I kissed a few frogs and Prince Charming never showed up. I had been divorced about six months when a man at my church began showing some interest in me. He seemed nice, but I had not been on a date with anyone now for over 20 years. After shopping to get a new outfit for this novel experience, I stopped at my friend Barb's to fill her in. She was immediately concerned about this man.

[First names of men have been changed to protect the not so innocent.] I told her, "Saul is a nice guy. We are just going to dinner."

"But what if he's a wolf in sheep's clothing?" she asked.

"Oh, don't worry. I'm a big girl," I laughed.

A few hours later, all decked out in my new dress, I slid into the passenger seat. Glancing at some business cards on the dash, I realized that his name was Saul <u>Wolford</u>! Barb was right. That should have been my first clue.

223

Saul liked to have fun; I liked to have fun. It was a good fit, right? We rushed into a romance and it felt so wonderful to be appreciated. I did not realize just how vulnerable I was. I had been married to a workaholic for 21 years, and now here was a guy that enjoyed doing things together, going new places, doing the unexpected. We dated for about six months and set a wedding date of December 30. I had not even been divorced a year. Looking back now, it seems so clear, and I know the Lord was warning me all along. I simply would not listen. I did not ask my friends' opinions, nor did I pray that the Lord would show me. I felt like I was doing the right thing. I was deceived. Lack of pain in a relationship does not make it love.

About a week before the wedding, I started getting very uncomfortable. On Christmas day we were at Bill and Barb's. Their two college-aged daughters were visiting from out of town for the holiday. They were beautiful girls I admit. Saul could not keep his eyes off of them. I watched this man flirting outrageously with them all afternoon. *Why haven't I seen this before? I'm making a big mistake here.* Oh…Did I mention that I was 11 years older than Saul? Did I think to tell you that he had never been married before, and that I could never give him children that he might want in the future? Or that my boys really could not stand the guy? Other than that, it was a perfect relationship. The icing on the proverbial wedding cake was when he asked me the next day what I was going to do when he backslid… not even if but when.

December 27 I went to bed in such turmoil, I thought I was losing my mind. After several hours, I got up, put on my wedding dress, the headpiece, and the shoes, looked in the mirror and began throwing up. I called him in the middle of the night, asking him to come over to reassure me that we were doing the right thing. When we talked early in the morning, I told him of my distress and fear and, finally, he told me that I was just not ready to get married.

"We will call everyone and cancel it, at least for now. Then, when you are ready, we can get married later."

I cannot tell you the relief I felt. We immediately began calling the caterer, the florist, the pastor who was marrying us, and all the wedding guests who were coming from Oregon, Nevada, the Midwest, Southern California, and everywhere in between. It was amazing (and God's hand) that we reached absolutely everyone within three hours. Not only that, not one of the merchants charged us a cancellation fee.

Chris, amazed that I was doing such a thing, told me I should go away for the weekend. He seemed so concerned to see his mother in this much turmoil. Come to find out, he had a big, blow out party planned for New Year's Eve while I was supposed to be on my honeymoon. Guess I spoiled that too.

It is never too late to call it off. Three days before the wedding is a little close, but I have never been sorry, nor have I ever felt so foolish. Within a couple of months, I was no longer seeing Saul, and it was a tremendous relief. I knew that my life would have been absolutely miserable had I gone through with the marriage. I hope he is happier

Having Coffee With Jesus

with someone else as well. I look back on those days with regret. I learned a lot about myself that I am not proud of, the main thing being how far I drifted in my relationship with Jesus. I am forever grateful for His faithfulness to me in overriding my own foolish, sinful nature.

I later found out that my friends were praying for me, that I would lose my peace of mind about getting married. Well, the Lord certainly answered that prayer! Thank you, my friends!

Season Of Singleness, Part 2

Deciding I could no longer trust myself, I did not see anyone for a couple of years. Then, one day in church, my friends introduced me to this gorgeous hunk of a guy named Rick. In my spirit I heard *"womanizer"* as he was saying hello. *No, that was just my imagination,* I thought. So, going on my merry way, I went out with him for a few months. He was only eight years younger, and had two small boys. To top it off, he was a former race car driver. We would go to the track and everyone seemed to know who he was. That was fun. I mostly saw him at church or going to his boys' baseball games. He had been a cocaine addict before he came to Christ, but was clean while I was seeing him. He had not known Jesus for very long, and I enjoyed showing him around the Bible. He appeared interested, so I felt that he had plenty of potential. I knew this would never work into a long-term relationship, but we enjoyed each other's company.

It was interesting that it seemed the main reason Rick was in my life was to find me a good car. Remember the previous guy who just wanted to have fun? Well, prior to our near marriage, he had a great idea.

"How about if we use the money you have been saving for a new car to buy ourselves a nice hot tub as a wedding gift?"

Well, it sounded reasonable to me, especially since he continued with, "You know, once we are married we will have two incomes and can get you a car then."

Since I never got married, I ended up with a hot tub that I rarely used, and my old Mustang that was almost on its last leg. Now, here was a guy that was determined to find me a car that I would be happy with. We looked and looked. One evening he called me with the perfect car, a 1987 Thunderbird, which I loved when they first came out; I never dreamed I would ever get to actually have one. I was thrilled.

Only weeks after accomplishing his mission, he ended the relationship. I was heartbroken, but mostly because of the timing. It was the fourth anniversary of my husband walking out on me.

Well, Rick did turn out to be a womanizer (and I mean hundreds of women). Though he was always very respectful of me, apparently he had quite a history. The last time I saw him, the sparkle was gone out of his eyes and he had a woman on his arm. It was apparent that they were both on drugs.

Season Of Singleness, Part 3

After Erik had returned home to live with us, he decided to sell his dirt bike. We went to the local advertising newspaper photo shoot on Saturday morning. In line behind us was a guy hobbling on crutches. I asked him if the crutches were the reason he was selling his motorcycle. He just grinned and nodded. We chatted with him awhile, had the motorcycle picture taken, and went back home.

The day the advertiser came out, we received a phone call. "This is kind of weird I know, but I wonder if you remember me? I was the guy right behind you in line getting pictures taken for the paper. There was just something different about you. Would you consider meeting me for a cup of coffee?"

Amazed at his boldness, I responded, "What's different about me is that I am a Christian and I don't go out with men who aren't."

He hemmed around for a moment and finally sputtered, "But... aren't you interested in saving a soul?"

I laughed and finally told him that if he would come to my church on Sunday, we could meet for coffee afterward.

This man had so much pain in his past; I told him that I did not see how he survived all that he had gone through without Jesus in his life. In one year he had experienced the loss of both parents, his daughter was killed by a hit and run driver, and his business burned to the ground. He was excruciatingly quiet, and I was amazed that he had mustered up enough courage to call me in the first place. He was content to be my friend and I saw him at church every few weeks; he knew right up front that I had no interest in anything but friendship. Finally, he asked me to a party at a ski club he belonged to, and wanted to pick me up in his car. When he showed up in a beautiful Corvette, I was quite surprised because he seemed so subdued. As I slid into the passenger seat, it brought to mind that very first date I had as a single woman. *What am I doing here?*

We headed north on the freeway, and things were going smoothly until he took an off ramp into an uninhabited area. As we drove away from the city lights, I felt my heart begin to thump faster and faster in the darkness. Slipping my right hand onto the door handle, I knew I was in real trouble. *Lord, oh God! Help me! Give me wisdom! What should I do?* There was absolutely nothing out there but blackness.

Finally Gene noticed my panic. "I can see you're afraid, but don't be. Our club is right over there in the distance. See those lights? That's where we're headed."

I was not at all reassured. When we arrived at the parking lot, I could see all the activity and my heart finally quit racing. I learned a lesson, however, that I will never forget. Who can you trust? I never should have gone anywhere alone with someone I did not know well except for casual conversation. It is not a safe world out there anymore. [And this was way back in the early 90's.]

He was a nice guy, though, and shared a lot of his wounded past with me. In the meantime, Erik and I shared Jesus with him. Finally he revealed that his parents were strong Christians. Ah ha! That explained it. I knew why we met.

"You know, Gene, your parents must have prayed for you a long time. I know they prayed that a nice, Christian woman would come into your life so that you could come to know the Lord."

He was amazed that this could be true. Being a mom myself, I convinced him that every Christian parent wants nothing more than for their kids to know Jesus as well.

He continued coming to church, but we spent less and less time together. Gene had lots of fun, expensive toys and found that they could not fill that void in his heart. He eventually moved away. I am not sure if he ever received Jesus as Lord of his life, but it was not because I didn't try. After all, way back at that first phone call, he opened the door to our relationship with, "Aren't you interested in saving a soul?"

Take Up Your Cross

Mark 8:34,35 *Then he called the crowd to him along with his disciples and said: "If anyone would come after me, he must deny himself and take up his cross and follow me. For whoever wants to save his life will lose it, but whoever loses his life for me and for the gospel will save it."*

In order to follow Jesus, we must be willing to give up all that is important to us.

My life is so different now than when I first gave my heart to the Lord. If left to my own decisions, wants, and dreams, I do not know what my stories would be like at this time. All I know is that it could not possibly be more satisfying than it has been for quite awhile. By giving up my rights, I allowed Jesus to have full control (well, almost), and He has taken me down paths I never dreamed possible. He has so transformed me and my desires over the years that I am barely recognizable to anyone who knew me then. I think that is a good thing, though they may have different opinions.

When I try to tell people who I used to be, they cannot comprehend it. I know that old life is all under the blood of Jesus; it died on the cross. In return, Jesus gave me a new life, new goals, new desires. It is all about Jesus. I could never have made all these changes on my own. Nor would I have wanted to. I was happy being the center of my universe, or at least I thought I was. What is wrong with wanting a big house, nice cars, a successful husband, great clothes? Nothing, if you are living for SELF. The difference is that the Lord changed my focus. I no longer concentrate on those things. My heart is bent toward eternal values, not the things that will perish. The Lord Jesus has changed me there as well. He has turned my life around.

Thank You, Jesus. Though You slay me, yet will I serve You. Hard words, but I know that if it comes to that, You will also strengthen me to endure it.

Haiti And A Spirit Of Repentance

[Written after the devastation of the earthquake, January 2010]

Job 42:6 *Therefore I despise myself and repent in dust and ashes.*

The people in Haiti have collectively done that in recent days. It is not on the news but you can find it if you look.

The Holy Spirit has opened heaven over Haiti (which means "hell"). Six years before, the president rededicated Haiti to Satan. But now, after the shaking, the president called for three days of prayer and fasting. The missionary and radio engineer who sent out his report said that all the churches were full to overflowing everywhere they went. No work was being done and there were no signs of false religions being practiced, as is the norm. Everything stopped except for prayer, worship, and praise to our Lord. A spirit of repentance has fallen on the country. Hopefully, this heart change in the people will be a permanent thing. What will it take in our land for repentance and revival to break out? Only God knows.

Father, Your will is being done, on earth as it is in heaven. I'm sure the shaking will continue from the top down until You have our full attention in the U.S. as well. I cry out for repentance, that You would have Your way across this land, that the roots of America would be reestablished. Please, Lord, wake us up!

Sowing And Reaping

Proverbs 11:18 *The wicked man earns deceptive wages, but he who sows righteousness reaps a sure reward.*

Proverbs 22:8a *He who sows wickedness reaps trouble...*

2 Corinthians 9:6 *Remember this: Whoever sows sparingly will also reap sparingly, and whoever sows generously will also reap generously.*

Galatians 6:7,8 *Do not be deceived: God cannot be mocked. A man reaps what he sows. The one who sows to please his sinful nature, from that nature will reap destruction; the one who sows to please the Spirit, from the Spirit will reap eternal life.*

*God **cannot** be mocked!*

Yes, to be sure, Satan is running a wicked world, and it is getting worse all the time. Bad things happen everywhere, even to good people. But the Word states very clearly that we reap what we sow. If someone is doing things contrary to God's Word, they will reap the destruction that comes from that seed. Just as in nature, one seed yields a whole plant that produces much more fruit, we bring more destruction to our lives than we ever planned on.

In Haiti, they had been dedicated to serving Satan with every evil, despicable, foul practice under the sun. There are many missionaries there to try to bring the people to God but, in the past, it was almost a fruitless undertaking. With the shaking, "God, in His mercy brought this nation to

233

its knees, that He may raise them up to be a trophy of His glory." God allowed it to happen for salvations to occur.

As in the life of an unbeliever, who knows what they are sowing? But be assured that they are reaping what they have sown as well. And God, in His mercy, will use that fruit to bring them to Himself... if they are willing. I personally sowed a little good seed before I came to the Lord, but I also sowed much junk. It was the junk that brought me to my knees in shame and repentance. It was not the good stuff and blessings, though there had been many of those as well. The wheat and tares of life comprised who I was then, and they comprise my life now. The difference is that they are all under the blood of Jesus Christ.

Nevertheless, if I am dabbling in those despicable things the Word tells me about, even though I am saved, I will reap the consequences. I probably won't lose my salvation if I am still in love with Jesus, but there is a price to pay. My walk won't be as fruitful and my relationship with the Lord won't be as rewarding.

We leave a door open for the enemy of our souls to come in to rob, kill, and destroy... our peace, finances, health, relationships, country, whatever we hold dear. The Lord is our covering, our umbrella of protection, but we can step out from that covering by our behavior.

Oh God, we've drifted so far away from You in these latter decades. Most people don't even have a nodding acquaintance with Your Word anymore. Children are no longer being brought up in the church and, consequently, later generations of people will fall away even farther from the truth. Father, bring them back. We so need You and Your wisdom for this country. What will it take, Lord? Even the Israelites fell away for seasons and then returned in repentance. What will it be for us?

 ## Holy Spirit Prayer

Acts 2:18 *Even on my servants, both men and women, I will pour out my Spirit in those days, and they will prophesy.*

This happened for me on March 13, 2010.

I was going about my normal business when strange thoughts jumped into my head. *Fire near Chris and Karen's house... Frightening because it looks like it could be their home... Getting closer, it is not their house.* Disjointed thoughts made me wonder where they came from. I brushed them off and went about my day.

Dave was returning from the Bay Area that evening, tracking a huge, black plume of smoke all the way from Alameda. As he approached Walnut Creek, the thoughts that I had earlier in the day did come to him about how close it was to Chris and Karen's home. Piedmont Lumber burned to the ground, the place where I did a lot of business when my ex-husband and I were building houses.

A lesson learned: These were not just some random thoughts that roamed through my head. This actually was a prayer request from the Holy Spirit. He knew it was going to happen and needed intercessors. I did not understand then, but I do now. I am going to be more alert when "strange thoughts" enter my mind. If nothing else, I will pray in the Spirit when I do not know how to pray.

Thank You, Lord, for teaching me this so that I can take a more active role in kingdom life. I wonder how many other random thoughts I've just let go by when You had a purpose for speaking to me?

 The Lord's Provision

Joshua 5:11,12 *The day after Passover, that very day, they ate some of the produce of the land: unleavened bread and roasted grain. The manna stopped the day after they ate this food from the land...*

God provided for every day of their journey until they no longer needed it.

Why do we worry? Why do we fret and stew? The Lord is our Heavenly Father. He knows what we need before a word is even on our lips. What a beautiful example of God's love and care for us. He knows our needs and, if we are walking with Him, He provides in miraculous ways. He is our Covering, our Caregiver, our Provider. We do not want to squander His provision for us, nor do we want to horde. He will let us know when to save and when to give.

Lord, we listen for Your voice. We call out for Your direction, and for You to lead us through each day. Thank You for Your Holy Spirit!

Christ Is Our Strength

1 Corinthians 10:12,13 *So, if you think you are standing firm, be careful that you don't fall! ...And God is faithful; he will not let you be tempted beyond what you can bear...*

We think we are so strong, but it is only Christ that strengthens us.

There are obvious areas of weakness in our character that we know we have to guard, but it is the areas we think we have conquered that can get us into trouble. It is a little like Sampson; he did not realize his power was gone, but the strength of the Lord had already left him. The Lord is our conquering King. If we are not continuing to walk in Him, we will fall.

Oh, Lord, You are my strength and my rock. Show me the areas of my life that are eroding away without my knowledge. I need You to fill those gaps. Fill me with Your Spirit, Oh God. Give me Your strength and courage.

No Division In Christ Jesus

2 Thessalonians 2:1-2,13-17 *Now, brethren, concerning the coming of our Lord Jesus Christ and our gathering together to Him, we ask you, not to be soon shaken in mind or troubled, either by spirit or by word or by letter, as if from us, as though the day of Christ had come... But we are bound to give thanks to God always for you, brethren beloved by the Lord, because God from the beginning chose you for salvation through sanctification by the Spirit and belief in the truth, to which He called you by our gospel, for the obtaining of the glory of our Lord Jesus*

Christ. Therefore, brethren, stand fast and hold the traditions which you were taught, whether by word or our epistle. Now may our Lord Jesus Christ Himself, and our God and Father, who has loved us and given us everlasting consolation and good hope by grace, comfort your hearts and establish you in every good word and work.

The Thessalonian church was comprised of both Jews and Gentiles.

We have been part of the Messianic movement for many years, and have grown to love the Jewish people and their ways. When Jesus came to the earth to live, teach, heal and restore, and finally, to die and be resurrected, it was for <u>all</u> of mankind. He is Jewish, and He first came to the Jewish people. They, in turn, were to share Him with the Gentile world. Gentiles did eventually start coming into the synagogues to learn about this Man called Yeshua (Jesus in our culture), and they began believing in Him as well. They met on the seventh day of the week (Saturday), they shared meals together, they learned to dance the very worshipful dances. They learned about the traditional feasts that all pointed to the Messiah, and how Yeshua had fulfilled the springtime feasts by His coming, dying, and resurrection.

Perhaps this is why Dave and I so love the Messianic culture. We have learned how the Old Testament, New Testament, society, history, and the love of Jesus all tie together. The Father did not intend for man to be divided in their worship of Him. He did not intend it to be an "us against them" type of relationship. He sent His Son for <u>all</u> to love and worship. Unfortunately, as man so often does, new traditions became adopted, new days are now celebrated, and most of humanity looks at the Jewish people without understanding them.

We feel so blessed to be included in the numbers of Gentiles who get it, and have been struggling for the last several years to try to explain to our fellow believers that we are not trying to become Jewish; we just love the full picture. The Messianic congregations (churches) worship the same Jesus we do. They do not throw out the traditions that God first established, including the commemorations like Passover, Unleavened Bread, and Pentecost. These feasts were put in place for a reason, to show mankind what and Who to look for as time goes on. Jesus fulfilled the spring feasts in very interesting ways, and He will fulfill the fall feasts as well.

Man came in with his own ideas about which day of the week to worship, the day to celebrate the birth of Christ, the day He died, and the day He rose again. These celebration dates are rooted in paganism if you look into the historical accounts. Why not celebrate the days that God set down from the very beginning? These, after all, are His chosen feasts. Jesus celebrated them and fulfilled them. The Word never says to discontinue them.

Why can't we just be one in Messiah, loving each other, encouraging each other, and meeting together until He takes us home? Why must we debate our views and be so dogmatic? I guess that is the Jewish tradition; maybe in that way we got it right! There are many people in our churches and in the synagogues that have not accepted Jesus fully into their lives. As we love them, share with them, and encourage them, perhaps they will come to know Jesus (Yeshua) as Lord of their lives as well.

God never intended two religions; man, with Satan's leading, came in and divided people over the years. God wants unity in His Spirit, Jew and Gentile, one in Messiah. Now let's pray for our brothers.

Oh, Father, I have such a hard time trying to explain my heart on this one. Do I have Your heart of understanding? I know You love us all, and want us to trust You, serving You with our whole being. It's like, as a parent myself, the pain I felt when my sons argued and fought. We cry out for unbelieving people across this whole earth and pray, especially for our loved ones, that they will come to know and serve You. Oh, God, give us hearts of love and understanding for those that seem so unlovable. Help them to love us in return. It's Your love poured out for each of us that covers a multitude of sins.

 Small Beginnings

Judges 11:1 *Jephthah the Gileadite was a mighty warrior. His father was Gilead; his mother was a prostitute.*

Oh ye of small beginnings...

The Lord uses whom He chooses to accomplish His will. A mighty warrior birthed of a prostitute; who would have ever thought it as he was growing up? Rejected by his own family, only to be reinstated as their leader years later, he was given great success. The Lord blessed him with victory. He heard the Lord as he was going into battle, and the Lord gave him victory along with tragedy. Victory and tragedy both come into our hands throughout our lifetimes. Will we continue to walk with God no matter the outcome, as Jephthah did?

Oh, Lord, You give us opportunity and victory. We praise You through the obstacles of life. No matter how small Dave's and my beginnings were, a widow's son with not much formal education, and a little girl looked upon as trailer trash, You have blessed us with favor and we praise You!

A Love Story

During my season of singleness, I was asked to help head up the single's ministry at my church, Zion Fellowship in Danville. At first I thought they were nuts because I had no clue how to be single, much less how to help others along that road. This was a new phase of an already existing group of people who had been meeting together for years. I had just started attending, mostly to meet other single gals to hang out with. After all, my friends were married, as I had been, and I felt like the proverbial fifth wheel most of the time. As it turned out, I really enjoyed planning events, doing book studies, talking to younger women about the rules and regulations of male relationships, and teaching them how to love the Lord. God gave me a Monday night women's group that ran for several years. We saw many answers to prayer during that time, and our friendships deepened.

Pastor Larry was new to Zion Fellowship and one of his ministries was to the single's group. We became friends and I bounced lots of things off of him as far as leadership was concerned. He had a deep love for Israel, and many fascinating stories about a trip he took with a friend to see the land, just the two of them. They were attacked by Muslims, almost killed, and he received 42 stitches in his face from rocks thrown through their car windows. In spite of that, he still wanted to go back to Israel and began organizing a formal tour, which my mother and I immediately signed up for.

Once I got saved, I had this inexplicable love for Israel and its people. I just could not get enough, and Pastor Larry taught the Bible from a Jewish perspective, educating us all about the Passover, even teaching us how to do a Jewish dance. I loved it and could hardly wait for our voyage. As time went on, the tour was cancelled due to activities in Israel that would make it dangerous for tourists. A second trip was also cancelled, and I wondered if I would ever get to this beautiful, fascinating country.

One evening, I got a call from a lady I had never met who asked if I was a leader in the single's group. She had a quick wit, and explained that she was looking for other women to do things with.

Then she went on to describe her situation: "I just broke up with someone and, I know everyone has baggage from the past, but this guy has a 12-piece matched set!"

I laughed and knew immediately that she and I would really hit it off together. Sharon turned out to be a good friend that I could spend hours on the phone with, and who had much in common with me. We would organize dinner parties. She would cook most of the meal (she was a great cook), while I did appetizers and helped with the cleaning. We did a lot of things together, with and without the group. This was just what I needed, an unmarried friend who loved the Lord and knew how to be active, enjoying life as well.

One day she told me she had met someone. He sounded interesting. When she gave me his name, I was shocked because another woman in the single's group was also interested in this man. Of course, with Sharon's vivacious personality, cooking skills, and love of life, she won his heart. Soon she began telling me about the guy named Dave that her friend, Ruben, rented a room from.

"You know, I think you two would have a lot in common; he loves the Lord, plays keyboards on the worship team at another Foursquare Church in the East Bay and, best of all, he loves Israel."

One day we were at the Fourth of July Parade in Pleasanton and, every time an antique fire rig would go by, she would tell me a little more about Dave. "He's a retired firefighter…bet he'd love this parade."

Finally, at the end of the day, she told me her birthday was coming up on the eighth and Ruben wanted to fix a nice meal for her to celebrate. I guess he was a great cook as well.

"Do you want to come as my guest? Dave will be there. You could at least meet him."

Not anxious to get into the dating game again, but wanting to please my friend, I told her I would come.

First, though, I had an important phone call to make. "Pastor Larry, do you know a guy by the name of Dave LeMoine, who attended your church in San Leandro?"

His response was immediate. "Of course; he's the one who saved my life in Israel. He's a great guy."

I told him I had a blind date with him that week. He laughed, telling me that Dave was very shy around women, and not to expect much from this meeting. Thinking back on my previous "Prince Charming" experiences, I thought *at least he doesn't seem to be a frog.* For that, I was very thankful.

Unfortunately, I got a terrible head cold and felt so crumby on the day of Sharon's dinner party. Determined to go, I got ready and sniffed and snuffled my way over to Hayward, the other side of the tracks as far as I was concerned. What a snob I was! It was a nice, little house though, very neat and tidy. Sharon answered the door and was excited to introduce me to her friend, Ruben, but even more excited that I meet Dave. She was right... He did seem awfully nice.

While we were eating our delicious meal, I happened to glance up at a photo on the wall above the table. There was this beautiful, red 1964 Corvette. "Nice '64! Must be a 427, huh?" I asked.

His response surprised me because I thought I knew it all about old cars. "Nope, it was a 327."

"Then why does it have six tail lights?" was my next question.

"Because I added the extra set myself," came his cautious response.

I had his heart in my hand at that very moment. [For all you girly girls out there, I was referring to the engine size---427 cubic inches. Sometimes Corvettes with a 427 had an extra set of tail lights to show the world that they were extra special.]

The evening progressed nicely as we talked about all Dave's old cars, his years in the fire department, our common experiences, and a myriad of other topics. Finally Ruben asked if we wanted to go bowling. *Bowling?* Dave was not real excited about the prospect either, but we all prepared to leave for Ruben's favorite bowling alley. When he walked out with, not one, but <u>two</u>, bowling balls of his own, I lost it. *Sharon, are you taking notes on this guy?*

We did have a great time as it turned out, but not in the way Ruben would have expected. Surrounded by hard partiers, heavy smokers, and drinkers, Dave and I were caught up in our own animated conversation about the end times, the Rapture of the church, and the part Israel is going to play in the scenario. We couldn't care less if we bowled or not. Poor Ruben! I felt sorry for him, as Dave and I were on our own track. He got so frustrated trying to get our attention each time it was our turn to throw the ball down the alley. I liked Dave right away. He was very nice, and we did indeed have a lot in common. I decided he would make a nice friend.

Pastor Larry was curious about how the evening went the next time I saw him at church. I gave him a full report.

He responded with, "Well, don't expect him to call you. He's very shy."

I was happy to report that Dave had, in fact, already called me, and that we were going to meet in Pleasanton after church. Larry was quite surprised at that. What I did <u>not</u> tell him about was the phone call I had received from Dave the night before.

"Would you um... You probably are very busy... I bet you, uh, have a lot of plans for tomorrow... You wouldn't have time to..."

Finally, I interrupted with, "Do you want to meet in Pleasanton after church tomorrow? That's about halfway for both of us."

I am sure he was delighted that I made it so easy for him. I was actually happy that he was not some cocky, self-assured kind of guy. He was real.

We met for lunch and enjoyed our meal together. After that, I dragged him to a nearby furniture store that had a couch I was very interested in. This was my initial purpose for going to Pleasanton that day. It, too, was floral, but much better quality than the one I got with Chris at the outset of my season of singleness. When I asked Dave what he thought about it, he replied that it was very fem, but he had been surrounded by females in his first marriage and was used to that sort of thing. He said he liked it (he lied).

246

After I signed documents to purchase the couch, we took a long drive over to Alameda where he lived the first 52 years of his life. It was fun to see something that I had never experienced before. I could tell that he felt right at home there, though he now lived in Hayward because of his financial situation and divorce two years earlier. We looked at all the fire stations where he and his ancestors had worked over the previous generations. It turns out he was a fourth generation firefighter with quite a history.

During the afternoon, he had asked a casual conversation starting question, "So, what do you think you'll be doing with the rest of your life?"

Brother! What kind of question is that? I told him I was thinking of moving to Redding.

His response was the usual one, "But it's SO hot there. Why would you want to do that?"

I told him I was tired of the traffic, was thinking about somewhere not so crowded, and that both of my boys were grown. Erik was in the Navy, and Chris was planning on going to school in Sacramento. After a full day of never-ending conversation, we arrived back at the restaurant where we had started our date, but this time to have dinner. I liked this guy!

The following Sunday, Pastor Larry wanted an assessment of our time together. When I told him we bought furniture, he almost fell over. I still get a kick out of that one, all these years later.

Jesus, The Shepherd Of Our Souls

Isaiah 40:11 *He tends His flock like a shepherd; he gathers his lambs in his arms and carries them close to his heart; he gently leads those that have young.*

I think of those single moms.

My sister, Beth, loves the Lord and is doing what He has called her to do. He gives her wisdom about her business, and brings clients when she needs them. At times she feels overwhelmed, wondering what is going on. It reminds me of when I was a single mom with such a heavy load to carry. It is in those times, like the lambs in the field that become lost, when the Shepherd of our souls will pick us up and hold us near to Himself, close enough to feel His heart of compassion. He longs to comfort and protect. He will lead her and her daughter as they cling to Him.

Lord, I pray that this word of comfort will be an encouragement, not only to my sister, but to other single moms out there. Hold them close to Your heart.

Veiled Hearts

2 Corinthians 4:3,4 *And even if our gospel is veiled, it is veiled to those who are perishing. The god of this age has blinded the minds of unbelievers, so that they cannot see the light of the gospel of the glory of Christ, who is the image of God.*

Oh, God, rip off the veils of their hearts.

248

We have been teaching on the Passover Seder every year since we have been married. These have usually been small groups in our home, but we have been invited to present it to the church this year. We are expecting about 130 people; it is exciting! God is opening doors to us that no man can shut.

Lord, You are so good to us, to allow us to do Your Passover dinner in a large setting. What an awesome responsibility You have given us. We are so grateful to You. I know there will be many unbelievers in the room, and I pray that You will reveal Yourself to them tonight. Show them Your love.

✝ **Seek Godly Wisdom**

2 Chronicles 10:8,9 *But Rehoboam rejected the advice the elders gave him and consulted the young men who had grown up with him and were serving him. He asked them, "What is your advice? How should we answer these people who say to me, 'Lighten the yoke your father put on us'?"*

Be careful to whom you listen.

Rehoboam acted unwisely during his reign. He made up his own holy days, he worshiped calves and other unholy things. He was unruly and disobedient to the Lord. He rejected sound advice, making up his own rules.

Sounds like who I was in my early adult years. Thankfully, I was not ruling a country at the time. But I was putting my life in a shambles, and not making wise choices for myself or my young children.

Father, thank You for sending Your Son to rescue me from myself, for turning my life around, and for helping me to make wise choices.

Be Careful With Whom You Align

2 Chronicles 20:35 *Later, Jehoshaphat king of Judah made an alliance with Ahaziah king of Israel, who was guilty of wickedness.*

After all the greatness of Jehoshaphat's earlier days, he made a very unwise decision here.

We can never stop listening for the Lord's direction. If Jehoshaphat had taken time to seek God, he may not have made such a bad choice by aligning with Ahaziah. But, because of this decision, the ships were wrecked and his investment was spoiled. He went out on a bad note.

Lord, help us to listen for Your voice and Your instruction. You know the hearts of people who harbor wickedness. Steer us away from those wrecked (relation)ships. Give us the gift of discernment that will help us to make wise choices.

A Love Story Continues

Dave and I saw each other casually for two months or so, visiting about once a week, but talking on the phone almost daily. Chris happened to be home one afternoon, so I finally had an opportunity to introduce my new friend. While intently watching a football game, he nonchalantly unwrapped himself from the recliner to shake Dave's hand. After Dave left, I asked Chris what he thought.

He told me, "Well, he's a whole lot better than any of the other guys you've introduced me to… nice handshake."

What I did not realize until much later was that, when he shook Dave's hand, he purposefully gripped harder than necessary, which was returned with an even harder grip from Dave. Those two guys had a very meaningful conversation of which I was totally oblivious. Men! Who knew?

Dave was awfully nice, yet very timid around me; in fact, he had not once held my hand. I liked that… take it slow and appreciate the friendship. Pastor Larry was planning a single's retreat up on the Trinity River, west of Redding, for Labor Day weekend. I asked permission for his old buddy to come on the retreat with us and he was happy to oblige. On our way, we pulled Dave's utility trailer behind his car, stuffed to the gills with all the cooking utensils, food, tents, etc., that the group would need for the outing. We enjoyed talking, and I could tell that he was trying to be a little bolder about our relationship. We stopped at an ancient greasy spoon in a tiny mining town called Old Shasta for dinner on our way. Jay Bird's Café was amazing. It looked like people had been carving their initials in this place for generations. The tables were covered with various forms of graffiti. When Dave whipped out his pocket knife, I felt myself getting red in the face. *This is for kids*, I thought to myself. He was not to be discouraged by my embarrassment. He carved, "DL + PJ" (my first and middle initials) followed by "9–2–94" (the date). I promptly burst into tears.

He was surprised and exclaimed, "But… I thought you'd like it!"

I explained that it was seven years <u>to the day</u> that my husband had first walked out on me. We both sat there in stunned silence. Seven is God's number for completion. Could this mean that my season of singleness was over? We knew it was too early to tell, but it was an intriguing thought.

We had a great time at the retreat. Dave and Pastor Larry enjoyed getting reacquainted as well. My friends had met Dave before, and immediately started taking bets on how long we would go together before getting married. Most agreed that we would be married within a year, though Dave and I knew nothing about their wagering.

When my tent-mate found out that we hadn't even held hands, she began devising ways of showing Dave how it was done. While tubing down the river the next day, for instance, she grabbed my hand and yelled to Dave, "See, this is how we stay together in the water!"

That evening after dinner, we took a walk in the darkness where he held my hand for the very first time. It was sweet.

The weekend marked a turning point in our relationship, from friendship to courtship. We had many wonderful moments together, and I found that he was very thoughtful. For instance, in his car on the way home, he had a tape ready to play "Lady," sung by Kenny Rogers*. This quickly became "our song," and was requested at almost every event we found ourselves over the years.

He was having a retirement party later in the month, and I enjoyed teaching him how to dance so we could have fun there as well. The evening was amazing. I met his mother, stepdad, brother, and two of his closest friends, along with about 150 of his firefighter buddies, all in the same night. I had met his two daughters right after we started seeing each other, and they were there too. I could tell that they were proud of their dad. We had a ball and danced our feet off all evening. I never wanted the night to end.

*"Lady" was written and produced by Lionel Richie, and released on September 29, 1980 by Liberty Records. [Little did we realize this when we set our wedding for September 29, 1995.]

A Courtship

We had many special times during our dating, and I was thankful we lived so far apart, or we would have seen too much of each other to be proper. We had decided that our relationship would be above board on all accounts, setting many limitations for ourselves.

One evening, Dave came to pick me up from a client's office in Pleasanton. We went to see a movie and had a very sweet experience afterward. My car was still parked behind the office building, so he pulled his car into the otherwise empty parking lot. But, being Dave, he had the tape of "Lady" at his fingertips. He pulled me out of the car, held me close, and we danced in that parking lot to our song. When a street sweeper came barreling right through our romantic moment, we kept on dancing until the song was over. Laughing at ourselves, and the fact that the music was drowned out by the noisy machinery, the sweeper did his job right around us. What a fun memory!

One night, as I was getting off work in San Francisco, he picked me up with a surprise evening planned. He had heard about a place on the Bay right behind the yacht club. It was called the "Wave Organ." An artist devised all different lengths of pipes to go into the water and, when the waves hit the ends of the tubes, each made a different sound. There were many building capitols from demolitions piled up into creative cubbyholes as well.

The winds were howling and it was cold, but Dave had thought of everything. I was wearing high heels and a dress because I was unaware of his plan. He brought out his firefighter turnout coat and pants, along with a blanket that he threw over the roof of the car to cover all the windows. I went into the car and changed into this much warmer outfit. Then he brought a luscious picnic dinner that he had prepared beforehand, and we snuggled into a shallow cave to keep out of the wind. It was a very sweet evening. I remember watching the daylight ebbing away and the city lights coming on, one by one, in the cocoon of safety provided for us. He later wrote a poem about the evening. It was wonderful. Not to be outdone, I wrote him a poem about our relationship which MUST be read with a country twang and as much corn as possible:

254

A HOG HEAVEN POEM

I still remember that September day,
The day we began to court;
It makes me so happy, I frolic in glee,
And almost have to snort!

We took a walk; we just had to get out;
The next thing I knew,
We was snout to snout!

You made me feel so fine,
You was the best of swine, so divine.

We played on the swings,
Feeling like a couple of dorks;
We swung higher and higher,
Two flying porks!

We stretched out on your trailer,
Gazing up at the sky so big;
I couldn't have been one happier pig!

Ain't love grand?

Well, I didn't say that I had talent, just that he did!

Confidence In Christ

Psalm 143:5 *I remember the days of long ago; I meditate on all Your works and consider what Your hands have done.*

I remember all the wonderful things the Lord has done in my life.

When I read the Word and look at the things He did for His people when they were living uprightly before Him, it gives me confidence in what He can accomplish in my life. Then I look at all the things He has already done in my life, and I am grateful that He has rescued me, a lowly slave to the sinful nature. He has set my feet upon a rock, just as He promised, and has given me the desire to live a life pleasing to Him.

Lord, I am eternally grateful! You have changed my life, my desires, my very nature, now and forever more. I love You and so enjoy our life together.

Looking Toward The Future

Philippians 3:13b,14 *Forgetting what is behind and straining toward what is ahead, I press on toward the goal to win the prize for which God has called me heavenward in Christ Jesus.*

Keep looking to what God has prepared for you, both in this world and in the world to come.

It is good to look back to see what God has done in your life, recognizing His goodness, building your faith for what lies ahead. But it is even more important to look

256

forward to what He has for us, to watch and wait for those assignments that He has been preparing. The little "coincidences" of life that have us looking up in wonder at His goodness never cease to amaze me.

Lord, keep us alert to Your gifts in this life. Of course, our eternal reward and a relationship with You is the biggest gift. We also await the gift of a home in heaven. Thank You, Lord, for all that You have in store for us. And, thank You for those that we will get to bring with us through those opportunities.

Blessings For Obedience

Psalm 128:1,2 *Blessed are all who fear the Lord, who walk in his ways. You will eat the fruit of your labor; blessings and prosperity will be yours.*

Blessings come from the Lord.

When you walk with the Lord and follow His ways, He says He will bless you. I have seen that first hand. He has blessed us so much since Dave and I came together. He has prospered us, not just financially, but relationally, and in every way. It is a pleasure to serve the Lord. He is not a hard taskmaster. "His yoke is easy and His burden is light." Curses come when you bring them upon yourself, by turning away from Him, and not listening to, or reading, or caring about what God cares about.

Lord, keep us on track with You. Be quick to show me my sin so that I can change and lead a life more pleasing to You. Your opinion of me is really all that matters.

257

<u>An Engagement</u>

Dave and I had been seeing each other almost a year, and he asked me to marry him in a very romantic spot... the parking lot of a restaurant. It seemed he had this great plan, but just could not contain himself. He blurted out his proposal right in front of our car. And I said he was such a romantic guy? But, of course, I accepted, and we made plans to marry in a few months.

Since Pastor Larry had been in a relationship with Dave and his first wife, and had also been involved in our relationship from the onset, we decided to ask him to provide our premarital counseling. We really looked forward to our meetings with he and his wife, Becky. They were very enthusiastic about our relationship, in part because they had witnessed firsthand the difficulties in Dave's first marriage.

As our wedding date was about a month away, one of my clients gave me a lovely shower. It was a beautiful event; all the ladies were so happy for me and our approaching marriage. The evening went well and, when the song, "Lady" came on the radio, I got to share the memories that it brought up. I was so happy, and enjoyed opening all the generous gifts my friends had brought to start our life together. I called Dave when I returned home, bubbling about all the blessings we had received. I never dreamed that my world would be dumped upside down early the next morning.

<u>Our Lives Must Be Blameless</u>

<u>2 Corinthians 8:21</u> *For we are taking pains to do what is right, not only in the eyes of the Lord but also in the eyes of men.*

Our lives must be blameless to all.

Our testimony is being watched by everyone, even those that we are not aware of. We must be above board and without reproach in all that we do. If there is any question, we must answer and hold fast to the truth, whether it is in financial matters, moral matters, or any circumstance in which we find ourselves. We are not perfect, far from it, but if we make a mistake, we must correct it, and talk to the person we offended. We cannot leave them in the offense; it must be dealt with.

During our courtship, I often stayed at Dave's mother and stepdad's for the night. It gave us opportunities to get to really know one another, and we enjoyed those events. One evening, when Dave brought me over to his mom's, she had a twinkle in her eye as she reported that Chris had called, just to make sure I was really staying there over-night. She vouched for my credibility. I was so grateful that I did not have anything to hide. Life is so much simpler when you live by "The Book."

Lord, Chris was a little sheepish when I asked him about his phone call to Dave's mother, but he claimed he had a legitimate reason for trying to reach me. I pray that he learned about how important honesty is in every relationship we have throughout our lives. Thank You for keeping us on track with You. [As I just reread this story, I have to wonder if there was a party at my house that night. I am so gullible!]

Fear Of Life

Psalm 91:7 *A thousand may fall at your side, ten thousand at your right hand, but it will not come near you.*

We must not look to the left or the right in fear.

We are looking at our neighborhood, and watching beloved friends lose their homes in these tumultuous financial days.

We must keep our gaze firmly fixed upon the Savior of our souls. He knows what He is doing in every life around us, as well as what He is doing in us. I picture a hunting dog… she is poised, waiting for <u>her</u> master's voice. As others in the hunt are giving directions to their dogs, she listens only to her owner's instructions. God has the needed wisdom we require for a life of enrichment, fulfillment, and peace in the storms.

Father, though others may fall at our side, we rest in the palm of Your hand of protection during these times. We must try to encourage those that are suffering. Fear cannot overtake us.

 ## An Unexpected Visit

It was early Saturday morning, and I was looking once again at all the beautiful things we had been given for my wedding shower the night before. Suddenly there was a tap at the door. Looking out the window to see Dave's car, I was excited that he was there to enjoy the moment with me.

But when I opened the door, I found him obviously in a state of grief.

"What on earth…?" I asked as he came inside.

He blurted out that he could not go through with our marriage plans, that he truly loved me, but the Lord had been convicting him all night that he had to try to reconcile once again with his first wife. I refused to believe what I was hearing. I just had this beautiful shower, our wedding was only a month away, we were deliriously happy, everything was wonderful. Wasn't it? I could not console him in any way. He was convinced that the Lord would not allow him to go through with our wedding at this time.

It happened that Lindy called from Redding to find out how the shower went the night before. When I began crying and telling her what was going on, she calmly asked to talk to Dave. He explained to her everything he had told me.

When he finally gave the phone back to me, Lindy's words rang in my ears, "It sounds like the Lord to me."

This confirmation was not what I wanted to hear. Dave and I cried together, got on our faces before the Lord and prayed together, and finally said good-bye. It was gut wrenching.

After Dave left, I called Lindy back. She suggested that I come up to Redding for a visit. In the meantime, one of my friends from the single's group called to see how things were going and immediately came over. She called three other close friends who also shortly arrived. They were all dismayed with Dave, and shocked over what had just

261

happened. I did decide to go up to Redding. My friends told me they wanted to clean my house for me while I packed. After I left, they put everything away that would remind me of Dave, re-boxed all the shower gifts, and blessed me by straightening my home. I was so grateful for them.

I arrived at Lindy's very late in the evening and I am sure she was shocked at my appearance. To put it truthfully, I was a wreck. After settling into my room for the night, I decided to write Dave a letter expressing my love for him, but also releasing him from all obligations he had made to me. I realized that, if we had proceeded, our marriage would have never been a good one. Filled with guilt and depression, there would have been a dark cloud over our lives from the very beginning. When I was finished, as I crawled into bed, the Lord spoke to my heart. *"He will be back and it will be your choice."*

The next day, Lindy told me that the couple I had counseled with for years in Marina, Pastor and Mary Perryman, happened to be up on the lake vacationing. She asked if I would like to see them. Of course, that was just what I needed. I met them and told them the whole story. Now Pastor and Mary really liked Dave, especially compared to some of the guys I dragged by them in my singleness. After I finished, they began to pray for me.

Afterward, Pastor stopped, not realizing he was confirming what I had received the night before, "You do know that he'll be back, don't you? Is he worth waiting for?"

"Yes, Pastor."

"The number four keeps coming to mind and I'm not sure what that means. Can you wait four years for him? Would you take him back?" he asked.

"Yes, Pastor, I can wait four years," I cried.

"Then just hide it in your heart; don't talk about it now to anyone," they replied.

The Lord Disciplines Those He Loves

Psalm 94:12,13 *Blessed is the man you discipline, O Lord; the man you teach from your law; you grant him relief from days of trouble, till a pit is dug for the wicked.*

When we are serving the Lord and following His ways, we will be disciplined if, and when, it is needed.

Though we stumble, we will not fall, for the Lord upholds us with His hand (Psalm 37:24). He brings us times of relief from the stresses of life when we walk with Him. Eventually, the wicked will fall into their own pit, possibly even the pit they dug for us (Psalm 35:7,8).

Your discipline is welcomed, Lord, compared to the punishment the ungodly try to lay on us. They don't like to see us succeed. Failure and ruin are what they have in mind for us. But we serve You, our awesome God, who will gently guide us in the direction You're leading. You won't let us fall into the pit when we're walking with You, and You will take care of our enemies.

His Mercies Endure Forever

Psalm 25:7 *Remember not the sins of my youth and my rebellious ways; according to your love remember me, for you are good, O Lord.*

The Lord is good; His mercies endure forever.

He is merciful and He loves me in spite of my rebellion. I know that, no matter what my children may have done to me in the past, the moment they would come to me and ask for forgiveness, my arms would open to them. If I have that kind of love, imagine the depth of love He has for us. It is truly amazing, unfathomable love. He wants to spend time with us, so that we can know Him on a deeply personal level. He is <u>good</u>, His love is perfect and unconditional.

Father, guide me in Your everlasting way. You know the path and the direction of my journey. Though my earthly family may fall away because of You, You've given me others who share in Your love who have become mishpochah (Hebrew for family).

 ## Waiting Upon The Lord

I returned home from Redding after a few days and dug into my work for my clients. I felt so foolish having to return all the shower gifts for the second time. (Remember the wedding I bailed on a few years before? Marriage just didn't come easily for me, apparently.) Everyone was so kind and puzzled over this latest twist. Work became everything I focused on in order to keep myself going forward. After about three weeks, Barb, who happened to be a nurse, came over one evening for a visit and suggested that my faithful dog, Bonzai, did not look well. I told her Bonzai was grieving with me; that was all.

"No," she insisted. "You need to get her checked out."

The next day, Bonzai was noticeably more lethargic so I followed through on her suggestion. The doctor took X-rays and found something wrong with her kidney. They asked to keep her overnight and started hydrating her immediately. I began praying, *Please, Lord, don't take my dog. She's all I have left. Oh, Father, I'll pay up to $1000 if you'll save my Bonzai.* Alerting my friends to begin praying for Bonzai, I went back the next day where I was told that she needed surgery. Giving permission, I stayed as long as I could and they scheduled her operation for the next morning.

I went to work that day, but was very worried about my girl. They called to let me know that she had drunk radiator coolant which had crystallized on her kidney. They were not sure she would make it. When I came down later in the day, the vet seemed much more hopeful.

I told him that my friends and I had been praying for her and his response was, "Well, that's what must have done it because dogs don't usually come out of something like this."

Bonzai was very weak, but they said I could take her outside on a leash for a few minutes where we walked around the parking lot. The next day she was doing so well, she was free to go home. The veterinary office was amazed at how quickly she was recuperating. With that, they presented me with the bill, $1020, and the $20 was for the special food I needed to feed her during her recuperation period. At that point, I wished I had prayed, *Oh, Lord, I'll pay up to $300 if you'll save my dog.* But I was very grateful.

After I got Bonzai situated in the car, I began to drive home with prayers of thankfulness on my lips. *Oh, thank You, Lord, thank You for Your faithfulness to me. Thank You for saving my Bonzai. Oh, God, I am grateful and happy to have her back. You have been so good to me. But, Father, I miss Dave. I pray that You would return him to me soon as well.* The date was June 8, 1995. I had a feeling that Dave was very close to me all day. We had always celebrated the eighth day of every month because we met on July 8, 1994. Earlier in the day, while at work in San Francisco, I looked out the window, longingly wondering if he was somewhere near. I was still in touch with Dave's folks, who knew that Bonzai was in bad shape, so called them when I arrived home. They were delighted, as I was, that my dog would live.

About a half hour later there was a knock at my door. I opened it to find Dave standing there with my wedding ring in his hand. He had had a day full of miracles himself, which all pointed to his returning to me; his first wife confirmed once again that she would not <u>ever</u> want him in her life. A friend he had not heard from in a long time sent him a letter saying that she, for some reason, always thought of him when she heard a certain tape by the Brooklyn Tabernacle Choir. She had been meaning to write him for months. Though she knew nothing of our situation, she felt the Lord was telling her to contact Dave and tell him that it was time to move forward in his life. He had done all he could to save his first marriage.

Yes, I agreed that this was all quite amazing. No, I would not run off with him right then and there to get married. It was now just four WEEKS since he had called off our wedding.

I brought Dave to church with me on Sunday morning and one of my friends, who had been there the morning he broke up with me, hauled off and punched him in the stomach. In anger, she called him "Boomer." The name has stuck to this day. She felt as if he had boomeranged back into my life. Fortunately, she has forgiven him, and we hear from her every Christmas. Dave and I married about 3-1/2 months later, standing on a cliff overlooking Pismo Beach at sunset, with Pastor Larry and Becky officiating. Jim and Lindy flew in from Redding to stand up for us. It was a very private ceremony, just what we wanted. Though our original plans weren't exactly God's plans, we did slow down to conform to His desires for us. I am happy to report that our life has been GOOD, and that little one-month hiatus proved to be a blessing though it was very painful at the time. Wait upon the Lord! His timing is <u>always</u> perfect.

♪ **Fear Of Man**

1 Samuel 15:24,25 *Then Saul said to Samuel, "I have sinned. I violated the Lord's command and your instructions. I was afraid of the people and so I gave in to them. Now I beg you, forgive my sin and come back with me, so that I may worship the Lord."*

Fear of man can cause us to hold back on what the Lord has called us to do.

This was a hard lesson for Saul. Even though he repented, he lost the gift God had given him. The Holy Spirit left him, and an evil spirit came to fill that void. Thinking he was self-sufficient, it was not until God left him that he realized how empty he really was. There is a big difference between pride in our own self-sufficiency versus humility in what God is accomplishing through us.

Oh, Lord, thank You for the wonderful opportunities You have given us. Thank You for Your faithfulness in showing us that we could not have accomplished Your tasks on our own. Give us the boldness to complete the jobs at hand, regardless of what man might be saying against us.

 Fear Creates Bad Fruit

1 Samuel 18:29 *Saul became still more afraid of him, and he remained his enemy the rest of his days.*

Fear can cause hatred and jealousy.

Perfect love casts out fear. The only <u>perfect</u> love comes from God. When we allow God to fill our lives, fear cannot remain. If Saul was serving God with his whole heart, he would not have been so completely controlled by fear, jealousy, and anger.

Lord, I know that jealousy can rise up in me if I allow it. It's the fear that someone will be more favored over me. I recognize it, and I give it to You. Pride would want to keep me puffed up when the humility you ask for is what is far more important. Give us humble hearts and contrite spirits as we serve You.

The Pearls Of Life

As we were talking about the distresses that life throws our way, I saw grains of sand in my mind's eye. Like an oyster, these grains are irritations being used by our Father to create pearls in our lives to draw us ever closer to Him. Sickness, finances, relationships, work---whatever brings discomfort and even fear---are all being used to draw us into His Word, to sit at His feet, and to know Him on a deeper level.

We do not try to run and hide from these realities of life, but face them head on with our Father. By looking into His face and listening to His voice, pearls are being formed within us. These pearls, that are formed through great trials, will be used to help us know Him and His will for our lives. They will build the trust, peace, and joy that He desires as we walk through life with our Heavenly Father.

One day, the day of His own choosing, He will create a masterpiece out of the pearls He has allowed into our lives. It may be while we are still walking this earth that He will bring them all together to form a beautiful necklace of greater understanding to share with others. Or it may be that these pearls will be used to create the crowns that we will eventually lay at the feet of Jesus, the Author and Finisher of our faith.

Father, it helps to know that the painful circumstances in which we find ourselves have an eternal significance.

Then There's Dad

John 5:39,40 *You diligently study the Scriptures because you think that by them you possess eternal life. These are the Scriptures that testify about me, yet you refuse to come to me to have life.*

Then there's Dad, who never, ever studied the Scriptures.

We had been praying for Dad all this time and finally had the opportunity Sunday, April 11, 2010 to talk to him about heaven, and life after we leave this earth. He prayed with us to accept Jesus as his Lord and Savior while in the hospital. He really does not have a deep understanding of what he did, but he nodded his head to say yes to Jesus, mostly for the free gift of eternal life. This, in itself, is such a huge change in his attitude. Talk of Jesus used to make him angry before this illness.

Lord, please draw Dad near to Yourself. Help him to sense Your presence. God, show us that he is indeed a changed man, that the fear of death is gone by Your Holy Spirit that now lives in him. Father, I am not so sure. Give me the confirmation I need so that I don't have to doubt anymore. I pray that You will reveal Your angels or, even better yet, Yourself, to him before his death from this cancer that is ravaging his body.

Filled With Joy

Acts 16:34 *The jailer brought them into his house and set a meal before them; he was filled with joy because he had come to believe in God---he and his whole family.*

In my text notes on *filled with joy*, it says, "the consistent consequence of conversion, regardless of circumstances." This is what I hope to see in my father this visit, an unexplainable joy regardless of his illness and the consequences of cancer.

Oh, Father, I pray that You will show us Dad's heart. I pray it is beating for You now, and that You are the center of his life. I pray that You have wiped away his fear of death. Father, please confirm Dad's salvation to us so that we can relax, knowing that You're in control. [Written 5/16/10 before our trip south.]

[5/20/10] Praise the Lord! Dad is walking in peace. He <u>has</u> received Jesus and the difference is evident. He is telling certain family members about his prayer with us, and the difference it has made in his life. My dad, the evangelist! Jesus is the answer. We must never quit praying for our loved ones.

[7/11/10] Dad went to be with the Lord today.

⚔ Be A Leader In The Kingdom

Jeremiah 15:19 *Therefore, this is what the Lord says: If you repent, I will restore you that you may serve me; if you utter worthy, not worthless words, you will be my spokesman. Let this people turn to you, but you must not turn to them.*

Be a leader, not a follower, so that the Lord can use you.

When we have turned away from our former lifestyle, we must not go back into that darkness to try and drag our friends out. Let them see and observe our new life, and come to us to find the answers to their questions. They might try to lure us back to their level if we persisted in returning to the former life.

Dad, until later in life, was an alcoholic, yet he still enjoyed going to the bar to hang out with his buddies. For a year he drank soft drinks with them while they guzzled beer. On the one-year anniversary of his sobriety, they held him down to pour beer down his throat. This, of course, dragged him back into the pit. What a picture of the unrepentant heart and how the enemy of our souls can hold us in bondage!

Father, it's the job of the Holy Spirit to convict of sin, and to change their hearts. Let people see You and come to ask us what makes us so different. I know I'm not to return to my old lifestyle to try and change them. Lord, remind me to pray continually for those You want to bring to eternal life.

 ## Evil Has No Place In You

Psalm 97:10 *Let those who love the Lord hate evil, for he guards the lives of his faithful ones and delivers them from the hand of the wicked.*

Love the Lord with all your heart so that evil has no place in you.

When we love the Lord and put our focus on Him, we have no desire for evil in our own lives. We get disgusted when we see others who are serving the devil, and we want no part with them. But, the love of Jesus compels us to pray for them, that He will bring them out of the kingdom of darkness into His eternal light. We know how it hurts our Father to see His creation being dragged into the pit. We must have a hearing ear to know the ones He would have us reach out to touch, as Jesus touched the "unclean" during his lifetime.

Father, thank You for Your love, and the love You have poured through us to others. Thank You that You guard our lives and keep us faithful to You.

Worship Jesus

Luke 11:27,28 *As Jesus was saying these things, a woman in the crowd called out, "Blessed is the mother who gave you birth and nursed you." He replied, "Blessed rather are those who hear the word of God and obey it."*

Woe to the Catholic Church.

If Jesus wanted us to worship His mother, this surely would have been the place to instruct us to do that. If He would have wanted us to pray to her, He would have said so. Unfortunately, an entire worldwide church has been built on a false premise. Jesus wants us to know the Word and to know the Father through Him. He represented the Father "with skin on" for 33 years. God knew we could relate better if we could see Jesus in action. Then He actually died on the cross for us, which proved His love for humanity. His death was followed by His resurrection, which represents, for us, our eternal life as well.

Thank You, Father, for sending Your Son here to live on earth with us for a season. It's so wonderful to read what

He spoke as a man, so that we could know You, and Your heart for mankind.

<u>The Holy Spirit, Our Property Manager</u>

By the time it was done, we knew beyond a shadow of a doubt that God was relocating us to Redding. Never would we question whether this was His plan. Dave and I had been married five months when his home sold. Consequently, we moved to my house in Walnut Creek until it, too, sold. Three moves in the first eight months of marriage was a bit much, I agree, but it was essential as we began our new life together.

When we put my house up for sale, we knew we could not accept less than $220,000 for it because we had found a house in the Redding area on the river.

Dave's one stipulation for moving to Redding was, "If we can find a house on the river, we can live there for three years to see if we really like the area. If not, we'll move back."

My home in Walnut Creek was cozy. I loved it as a single mom, but it was a bit small for both of us with all our belongings. One evening, a nice man, who was renting about a block from us, rang the doorbell. He was very interested in my house, but could not pay more than $200,000 for it. We had a great visit and learned that he also was a Christian.

The house we found in Redding was located on a wonderful acre with lots of trees, and the Sacramento River flowing at the edge of the property. Though the backyard was fabulous, the home itself was a real fixer upper. The owner decorated with dirty diapers and cardboard boxes. Laundry piled in every room completed the picture. It was dark and filthy. If you listened closely, you could almost hear a puppy bark when you pushed the doorbell. It was a real dog. Through the crud, we could still see the potential that this house held.

We put in a contingent offer that we would sell both of our homes to purchase this one. That lasted a short time, and we finally decided to forget it. A few months later, quite unexpectedly, we got a call from a businessman who lived in Chico explaining that the owner of the house we wanted owed him a lot of money. He finally agreed to sign over the property to pay off this debt. Mr. Chico had several rentals in the Redding area, but really did not want a house on the river. Would we be interested in trading my house in Walnut Creek for this one? We agreed, so he came to Walnut Creek to take a look at my place.

When he arrived, we were surprised to find that he was a quadriplegic and could not even go upstairs to take a look. That did not slow him down a bit. His driver, a trusted friend, checked out the upstairs and gave her okay. He looked at the backyard, and seemed to be happy to make the exchange. My home would make a good rental for this investor. Of course, we were delighted as well, because we had already given up on the riverfront property. Coming from the Bay Area, who would ever think we could own a house on a river, and that it was in our price range. In the process, we agreed to drop the price $20,000 on both of our houses to lessen the taxes.

On the very morning that we were preparing to come to Redding to sign papers for this real estate trade, we got a call from the Christian man who had been interested in my house several months before. "The Lord is prompting me to call to check on your house. What's going on with it?"

Wow! What timing. I explained what we were doing, and that this man from Chico was going to use it as a rental.

"Great! Call him and tell him that I'd love to rent it from him. I'll take really good care of it for him, and he won't even need a property manager," was his response.

Instead, we gave him the phone number to make the call himself. By the time we got to Redding to sign the papers that afternoon, these two had negotiated to do a third trade. You see, since we had both dropped our prices $20,000, Mr. Chico agreed to sell my house to Mr. Walnut Creek at the $200,000 he had originally wanted to pay us for the property.

Whoever heard of a three way real estate trade between three different cities? Only the Lord could have arranged this one! And we were all happy.

 ## Encourage With The Love Of Christ

1 Thessalonians 2:11,12 *For you know that we dealt with each of you as a father deals with his own children, encouraging, comforting and urging you to live lives worthy of God, who calls you into his kingdom and glory.*

God gives us people to teach and exhort; we need to do it <u>His</u> way.

276

When we meet with people, we need to be respectful of who they are. We need to meet their needs in gentleness and love, just as the Lord does with us. We need to exhort them in Christ, encouraging them to do better, not in a spirit of negativity and criticism. We need to let the love of Christ flow through us to them in a manner that will lift them up and show them a better way. Hopefully, the result will be that they desire to live a life pleasing to the Lord.

Father, You have placed so many younger women in my path. I want to make sure I am doing my very best, giving them what You desire in their spiritual growth. I do not want to waste a moment of their time. Lead me, Lord! Let Your love flow through me to encourage them. Help me not to walk in a critical spirit.

 ## Waking Up In A New Place

1 Thessalonians 4:13 *Brothers, we do not want you to be ignorant about those who fall asleep, or to grieve like the rest of men, who have no hope. We believe that Jesus died and rose again and so we believe that God will bring with Jesus those who have fallen asleep in him.*

I had an experience much like we will face at our death and resurrection.

I went in for surgery, and the sedative they gave me knocked me out before they even anesthetized me. When I woke up in a different room, I did not even know that I already had the operation. We will all die here on this earth (unless we are in that group that is raptured out), but we will wake up in a new location, and a much more glorious place than a hospital recovery room.

Lord, for those that love and serve You, You have created a beautiful place for us to come home to. You have promised us a new home in heaven so that we can dwell with You forever. What an unspeakably joyful time awaits us!

<u>Oh, For A New Dwelling</u>

<u>**Romans 7:23,24**</u> *But I see another law at work in the members of my body, waging war against the law of my mind and making me a prisoner of the law of sin at work within my members. What a wretched man I am! Who will rescue me from this body of death?*

Of course, the answer is Jesus!

Our lives here are short compared to eternity, and we have to live in this wretched, saggy tent... And it sags and wrinkles more as time goes on. Our bodies started out serving ourselves as infants first: "Feed me! Change me! Clothe me!" Then, as we grew up, we began to take notice of others around us. Finally, God got my attention and I began to serve Him. But my flesh, that saggy, wrinkled tent, still battles to be at the center.

Jesus! Give me strength to say no to the frivolous, to the superfluous. Help me to say yes to You and Your desires. You are the answer to a fulfilling life. Make me Your prisoner and servant, as You rescue me from this body of death.

Out Of Control

Proverbs 6:16-19 *The Lord hates: haughty eyes, a lying tongue, hands that shed innocent blood, a heart that devises wicked schemes, feet that are quick to rush into evil, a false witness who pours out lies and a man who stirs up dissension among brothers.*

Most, scratch that, <u>ALL</u> these are members of a body out of control.

Sin enters the body, first as a thought, followed by actions. If we refuse to be led by the Spirit of God, wickedness soon has control over our thoughts, our tongue, our eyes, our desires, our hearts. I have known people like this, even in the church setting, and have chosen to steer clear of them for my own protection. The spirit that motivates them hates the Spirit of God.

Father God, keep our hearts and minds set on You and Your plans for our lives. Help us to walk in Your Spirit. Give us the gift of discernment when it comes to those who don't have our best interests at heart. Remind us to pray for them because we know You love them. But, give us wisdom to protect ourselves.

A Wasted Opportunity

We loved the house that we built in 1982 although, almost immediately, it became a struggle just to keep it. After only a few months, I realized that I needed to get a part-time job to help with the finances. I had always been a secretary in the past and now, because of our own business, I also had some bookkeeping skills. Off I went, nervously applying for work. I quickly found a job with a Realtor in town. Having previously signed up for a Bible study class, I was praying that I could have Tuesday mornings free. As it turned out, that was fine with him also, so I started right away.

Thinking back to when I was putting my husband through college by working in the Mathematics Department at Cal Poly, I wondered how I could ever have gotten to where I was now. The Department Head had offered to let me audit a math class during my lunch hour, so I decided to take their simplest class, more for agriculture students than anything else: 5 cows plus 2 cows equal how many cows? I was taking the class, typing my own tests... and flunking out! I just did not have the aptitude or desire for it back then. Now here I was working as a bookkeeper. Imagine that.

As it turned out, my boss and his wife were Christian Scientists. I had some wonderful occasions to share with them during the time I was in their employment. As an example, after working for him for a couple of years, it became apparent that he was very ill. His coloring was pallid and he had lost all his strength. Being very concerned for his health, I kept encouraging him to at least go home to rest. Of course, with their religious training, to divulge illness was tantamount to admitting to great sin, and he simply would not go to a doctor. As it turned out, a doctor finally confirmed that he had a severe heart attack five days before, and it was a miracle that he was not already dead. I shared the gospel message with them at that time with great concern for their souls, but neither one was ready to accept God's love and forgiveness. It saddened me greatly. I left their employment shortly after that because he needed to downsize his office.

Three years later, after I had my own business, they contacted me about coming in every four weeks to help them with their month-end closing. I was shocked when I saw my former boss; his weight had dropped considerably, and he was obviously very ill. I helped them the first month and was impressed to speak to him again about Jesus, but failed to follow up on it. *I'll be more prepared next month when I come in,* I thought.

Regretfully, only two weeks later, I got word that he had died. The sorrow I felt, knowing I missed that opportunity, engulfed me. After his memorial service, I began to tell his wife about my concern. Reassuringly, she told how, shortly after I had previously left their employment, they had a falling out with their church and, in the process, had come to know Jesus. Thankfully, God had orchestrated their salvation. Then and there, I vowed that I would never let opportunities slip through my fingers again. What a blessing to know that they will both be in heaven one day.

More On Unforgiveness

Colossians 3:13 *Bear with each other and forgive whatever grievances you may have against one another. Forgive as the Lord forgave you.*

Forgiveness is hard, and that is the reason God talks about it so much in His Word.

The Lord commands us to forgive and love one another, especially within the body of Christ. If we do not forgive, the Father will not forgive us either. We <u>all</u> need forgiveness. I am dealing with a friend who is new in the Lord. She came from a hard life, and is still using those tactics she learned as an alcoholic to survive and control people in her surroundings. That tormenting spirit would try to isolate and drive people away from her. The Lord wants to teach her and mold her into His likeness. Is she teachable yet? Only He knows.

Father, I pray that the Holy Spirit would be so present in our meeting today, and that peace would prevail. Help me to help her find forgiveness.

[Praise the Lord! God did work it out so beautifully, though I had to say some very hard things. She wants more meetings like this. She <u>is</u> teachable!]

Be Fruit Inspectors

1 Corinthians 5:11 *But now I'm writing you that you must not associate with anyone who calls himself a brother but is sexually immoral or greedy, an idolater or a slanderer, a drunkard or a swindler. With such a man do not even eat.*

Paul is not talking about those outside the church; he means people who call themselves Christians.

None of us is perfect, but when a believing friend has been rebuked, warned, and admonished about a certain behavior and they continue in it, action must be taken. Their behavior degrades Christianity in the eyes of unbelievers around them. You need not intentionally associate with them. You do not have to subject yourself to their slander or other sin. However, be sure to pray for them. Above all, make certain your heart is right toward them. Of course, we will see them at church or other events, but that is different than purposely associating with them on a personal basis. We are not to judge, but we definitely need to be fruit inspectors!

Father, this is a serious business and we need the Spirit's direction, especially in this kind of relationship. Please give Your wisdom in each situation.

I Was Needy

Psalm 110:30,31 *With my mouth I will greatly extol the Lord; in the great throng I will praise him. For he stands at the right hand of the needy one, to save his life from those who condemn him.*

I was needy and He saved me.

I have had many opportunities to share the blessings the Lord has poured out upon my life. Whether it is in a group or in a one-on-one setting, I love to tell the stories of God's faithfulness. It gives such pleasure to recount the almost miraculous interventions I have experienced, and I believe it gives the listener hope that they, too, will see similar answers to prayer in their life situations. I love to encourage people by sharing the joy of the Lord with them.

Oh, God! You are the miracle worker, the orchestrator of our lives, to bring about events that bless us and bring glory to Your name!

 Lead By Example

Titus 2:3 *Likewise, teach the older women to be reverent in the way they live, not to be slanderers or addicted to much wine, but to teach what is good.*

We're never too old to learn.

The older women (where I now find myself) lead by example. As the Lord shows me how to live... not to gossip; not to slander; not to be addicted to anything, I try to present that example to the younger women I know. When given the opportunity to model this behavior for them, I try to do it. When given the opportunity to verbally teach them, I try to do it. This is a responsibility not to be taken lightly. These younger women in the faith will eventually be older as well. Then they will set the example for the next generation.

Father, remind me of these words throughout the day so that I can live what I write. Help me to be that godly example You're teaching me about. Without the Holy Spirit, this is an impossible task.

 Ye Of Little Faith

Psalm 74:21-24 *When my heart was grieved and my spirit embittered, I was senseless and ignorant; I was a brute beast before you. Yet I am always with you; you hold me by*

my right hand. You guide me with your counsel, and afterward you will take me into glory.

God upholds us even when our faith is small.

The Spirit of the Living God guides those that belong to Him; He gives counsel when we have no idea which way to turn or what to do. At times, when our spirits are all but destroyed, we feel alone and that God has abandoned us. This is not true. He is there to hold our hands and to guide us through the troubled waters. At those times, our faith is small but our God is LARGE! I have dated and underlined in my Bible those places where God has spoken to me. It is a diary of sorts. I can look through it, and marvel at all the times He's rescued me throughout life. I can check to see if He has answered those prayers yet; if not, am I still patiently waiting?

Oh, God, as I read my Bible and see all the places where You have spoken to my heart, it is such an encouragement. Your Word has been the lifter of my head, and water to my parched soul.

 <u>Give A Sacrifice</u>

<u>Hebrews 13:15</u> *Through Jesus, therefore, let us continually offer to God a sacrifice of praise---the fruit of lips that confess his name.*

Sacrifice of praise---in the good times, bad times, and in between times.

We are to continually (at all times) give God our thank offerings of praise. Sacrifice is to "give something precious for the sake of something else" [Webster's Dictionary]. We are giving our precious gift of praise to God to see that He gets the glory and honor due Him. It is a sacrifice sometimes, when life is tough, to lift praises to His name. But that is when we need to praise and trust Him the most. It is easy to praise when things are going great; it is not a real sacrifice in those moments. It comes naturally. It is a sacrifice when we do not know the answer, but we continue to praise because we do know our God.

Father, I do not praise You enough. I need to lift up Your name continually, and I don't. Remind me daily just how much You long to hear my praises.

 ### Jesus, The Coming Lord

Luke 3:16 *John answered them all, "I baptize you with water. But one more powerful than I will come, the thongs of whose sandals I am not worthy to untie. He will baptize you with the Holy Spirit and with fire."*

Jesus, the coming Lord, is the One we are intently watching for.

John knew the people were looking for their Messiah. He wanted to quash rumors in the bud so that they would not look to him. The ascension of Jesus would open the way for the Holy Spirit to come and permanently indwell His believers. Flames rested on the heads of those being filled with the Spirit (Acts, Chapter 2), just as the flames were on Mt. Sinai when the Lord descended to give the Law (Exodus 19:18). Pentecost was looking back at the giving of the Law, known as Shavuot; how appropriate that the fulfillment of the Law, with the outpouring of the Holy Spirit, was given on that anniversary, and with fire. The return of Christ speaks about His eyes being "like blazing fire" (Revelation 1:14 and Revelation 19:12). What a vision! The people in John's day were looking for Messiah, and we are looking for Him to come again.

Lord, the imagery You use in Your Word is alive, a living, breathing testimony of You.

A Word From The Lord

Several years ago, as the summer was winding down, the Lord put it on my heart to start a new Bible study in my neighborhood. None of my neighbors knew the Lord, so I was excited to see what He would do. There were five of us for that first meeting, where we studied about Jesus and the Holy Spirit. It was a good teaching, and toward the end of the evening, I heard in my spirit, *"We all need Jesus, because we never know what tomorrow may bring."* I dutifully mouthed those words, and continued on with the teaching. When the ladies were preparing to leave, I heard it again, so spoke it again, "We all need Jesus because we never know what tomorrow may bring."

The next morning, my sister called, waking me up early crying, "The World Trade Center is falling!" I never could have guessed, but God knew.

The following week, the little gal that I was most anxious to reach for Christ, arrived early. She was very upset, and wanted to find out how she and her children could be assured of going to heaven. I took the opportunity to pray for her and her family before the others arrived.

She moved away shortly after that, and I heard from her about three years later. She was happy to report that she and her entire family were now walking with the Lord, in a good church, leading a Bible study, and her marriage was now thriving. There was a true revival in her heart, and in the hearts of her family members.

✝ <u>Can These Bones Live?</u>

<u>Ezekiel 37:1-3</u> *The hand of the Lord came upon me and brought me out in the Spirit of the Lord, and set me down in the midst of the valley; and it was full of bones. Then He caused me to pass by them all around, and behold, there were very many in the open valley; and indeed they were very dry. And He said unto me, "Son of man, can these bones live?" I answered, "O Lord God, You know." [NKJ]*

History repeats itself.

While watching a video on the dry bones with poignant music in the background, there appeared a vivid sketch of skeletons all tangled together. Suddenly, my mind saw the pictures of the Holocaust victims' tangled and mutilated skeletal remains thrown into a shallow valley dug for them. These Jewish people, and those that once stood with them, were the first seeds being sewn into the promise of their own land, though nobody realized it at the time. Vibrant lives had been snatched and destroyed at the whim of a madman. These people had worshiped together, eaten together, married and had children, just as the people of this generation are doing now. These were God's children, the apple of His eye.

The country of Israel was born again out of the corporate guilt offering given by the British and the United Nations. The guilt was heaped upon the shoulders of those who had turned to look the other way; yet they could not escape the horror of what they had done. This Holocaust was a burnt offering that could not be ignored. The word, Holocaust, in Hebrew, means to burn up in smoke. For almost 2000 years, the Jewish people had been the brunt of many unforgiveable atrocities. To appease their collective consciences, the United Nations voted to give the Jews a land which had previously been given to them by God Himself thousands of years before.

Will we be guilty? Will we simply close our eyes so as not to see the torture and destruction that is taking place once again, only a half century later? Surely we must not let history be rewritten to eliminate the truth. If we don't overcome unrighteousness, who will? We must stand with Israel, a mere sliver of its former self. God, after all, gave them a much larger slice of land than they currently have. Yet, the Muslims are not satisfied until that tiny piece also belongs to them. These dry bones have revived, and they are the people of the land. They live in the land, and God will breathe His Spirit into them. They will have a full understanding of what He did, and continues to do, for them.

To quote a Holocaust survivor, "For these twenty centuries, we Jews were always the object of history. That is, an object where others made decisions for us. As of this date onward, we suddenly became again a subject of history where we make decisions for ourselves."

Father, I weep when I see what has been done to Your people. My heart cries out for them over all the centuries of mayhem. We know the end times are at hand because we see so many Jews coming to know Your Son. Prophecy is coming to pass. Help us all to continue to pray for the peace of Jerusalem and the salvation of Your people. We know that the peace of Jesus can't come until they know Him.

Listen And Be Obedient

Acts 8:26,29 *Now an angel of the Lord said to Philip, "Go south to the road---the desert road---that goes down from Jerusalem to Gaza"... The Spirit told Philip, "Go to that chariot and stay near it."*

Listen and then obey.

We must choose to listen. My friend, Yvonne, is deaf and cannot hear people speaking, though she hears the Lord perfectly. Her ministry gives much hope to those the Lord touches through her. We have many distractions (the radio, television, internet) that keep us from hearing and respond-ing to Him. What is it in your life that keeps you from spending time with Jesus? What distraction do you allow that you know the Lord has spoken to you about? We all have them, little habits that seem so harmless. But, if the Lord has put His finger on them, we need to get rid of those things for our own good. Believe me, I am speaking to myself as well.

Jesus, I know those things in my own life that keep me distracted, not able to focus on You like I'd like. I can't be rid of them without Your help. I need Your holy conviction so that I can be successful in this. Please help me, Holy Spirit.

Alive Or Dead?

1 Peter 1:24,25 *For, "All men are like grass, and all their glory is like the flowers of the field; the grass withers and the flowers fall, but the word of the Lord stands forever." And this is the word that was preached to you.*

Flowers fade but You are new every morning.

I saw my flowers in a vase that, only a week ago, were beautiful and standing tall. Those same flowers are now dying and drooping in their pretty container.

That is an encapsulated picture of our lives here on earth. As I am getting older, thinking about how quickly our lifetimes come to an end, I also see my little plants in my garden. In the heat of summer they must be watered daily to survive. They sprouted but the roots are shallow. They have never produced the flowers that I planted them for. The frail, small shoots have been a disappointment to this gardener. I pray that my life has not been a failure to my Creator. Are my roots deep in Him? Am I being fed often enough by the streams of Living Water? Am I producing the fruit that He gave me life for?

291

Though I tend those delicate plants in my garden, I could never begin to care for them as much as He cares for me. Those pitiful, withering clumps of green are not even concerned about what I think. They do not have an interest in pleasing me at all, in fact. They do not know that I exist. Many people on this earth go about their lives in the same way, totally unaware of their Creator. Some are successful by the world's standards and some are not. God's standards are not of this world, however. I am looking up, straining to get out of the shadows, for more of the Son-light. I desire to please my Maker, to accomplish what He made me for.

Oh, Father, I want to know You in all Your glory. I want to see Your face. I want to live for You. I don't want to be another wasted life that withers, and finally fades away.

More On Self-Control

1 Thessalonians 4:4 *...that each of you should learn to control his own body in a way that is holy and honorable.*

Self-control is a fruit of the Spirit.

Even those little things must be under the control of the Holy Spirit. Things that are seemingly harmless will take control of us if we refuse to control them first. The things we watch, what we eat, the times we sleep, the books we read; all these, and more, need to be under His control. My mouth utters less than pleasing words when I think nobody is listening; my mind wanders, distracting me from what I am reading; I am hungry and grab some junk food. The God of the universe lives in us. Do I believe it? Do I want to live a life pleasing to Him while honoring the temple He lives in? Or am I only writing these words to bring conviction to others? If this sounds legalistic, forgive me. But we have to think about these things; the Holy Spirit is here, within us.

Convict me, Lord. I am helpless without You! Give me a repentant spirit. Let my heart be bent on pleasing You at all times.

Worshiping The Lord

Psalm 84:1,2 *How lovely is your dwelling place, O Lord Almighty! My soul yearns, even faints, for the courts of the Lord; my heart and my flesh cry out for the living God.*

The Psalms are God's songbook.

Maybe I am old fashioned, but there is a lot of music these days that I just cannot seem to worship to. It may be nice music, I grant you that. But that does not make it worshipful. The Lord provided an entire songbook in His Psalms for us to worship Him. When we sing God's Word back to Him, He must be pleased. And a lot of that music resonates in our hearts as well. It's a win, win situation. Thankfully, there are all types of music for all types of people.

Lord, my heart loves to worship You, but it's hard getting there at times. Thank You that You have provided ways for all of us to draw near to You.

Be On Guard

Matthew 13:24-26 *Jesus told them another parable: "The kingdom of heaven is like a man who sowed good seed in*

293

his field. But while everyone was sleeping, his enemy came and sowed weeds [tares] among the wheat, and went away. When the wheat sprouted and formed heads, then the weeds also appeared."

I am seeing a little differently….

I have always seen the tares amid the wheat, just standing there, a little taller, a little more slender, and hardly noticeable. Now I'm seeing the damage they are there to accomplish in the church. The whispering of evil intent often repeated to the wheat around them brings bitterness and distrust of others. The wheat, if left unguarded, receives these thoughts as their own, and begins regurgitating them to one another. It is no less damaging than a raging fire among the field. A small spark ignites one after the other, so that there is discord resonating where once there was harmony. The enemy has carefully placed his people so that they can do the most damage, wolves in sheep's clothing if you will.

The wheat and the sheep react innocently. They are unsuspecting of the danger that has invaded their fields. Damage has been done, thinking has been subtly changed, and whisperings among the innocent have been repeated enough to now have credibility. There is disharmony and backbiting among the family.

It is not until the chief shepherd or the farmer stands up and says, "STOP!" that things are put in their proper perspective. In fact, if the tares have succeeded in their assignment, the shepherd and his carefully chosen helpers are the most suspect of all. People have lost their trust. Is it too late?

Have the whisperings made the damage irreparable? Will people leave the flock, taking their grumblings and accusations with them where, eventually, the next field will be burned and charred beyond recognition as well?

It is not too late! We must recognize those tares among us, with the wagging tongues that James, Chapter 3, so aptly describes. None of us is perfect, no, not one. Pray for our brothers and sisters that they might be restored. Learn to recognize the enemies among us and refuse to allow them to get a stronghold in your life or the lives of your friends. No, we are not to go blindly to the stream of red poison for a drink. Test what is being taught by the Word of God, pray for one another; repent of your own tongue's grumblings; listen to the Holy Spirit; go to the person you have offended; embrace them with the love of God who resides within you. If we all behave in this way, the tares will be exposed for what they are… the enemies of our souls.

Father, this is all found in Your Word. We know the Word, but do we follow what it says? We need to be doers of the Word, not just hearers. Sometimes it is very difficult, and it takes tenacity to accomplish what You require of us. But, in the end, the reward is so much greater. Give us strength, give us courage, give us Your truth, so that we can be equipped to tackle the enemy of our souls. Let us not be victims, but victors!

Be Equally Yoked

1 Corinthians 7:32–34a *I would like you to be free from concern. An unmarried man is concerned about the Lord's*

affairs---how he can please the Lord. But a married man is concerned about the affairs of this world---how he can please his wife---and his interests are divided.

It is vital to be equally yoked.

When a man and woman come together in marriage, it is important that their walk with the Lord is on the same page. When Dave and I met, it was because friends saw that we had the same spiritual interests. In addition to loving Jesus, that is what has held our marriage close, the same goals and desires. We both enjoy teaching in small groups; we both have a passion to demonstrate the Passover Seder to show Jesus through the entire Bible, and we love how it presents communion so clearly. We also have both been given the gift of hospitality, so we work well together while entertaining. We are both writers and musicians so encourage each other in that way. Of course, we have our differences, too, but the important things are agreed upon.

I know a couple who enjoys prayer and that is their ministry together; yet another couple loves to see marriages thrive, so they like to work with young couples. It would be better to be single than to be unable to work together, each straining to pull the other in the opposite direction.

Thank You, Lord, that we can talk, laugh, and weep together about the things that affect our lives and Your people. We're so grateful that our marriage has worked out beautifully and that we waited for Your plan.

Christ Is Our Strength

2 Corinthians 12:10 *That is why, for Christ's sake, I delight in weaknesses, in insults, in hardships, in persecutions, in difficulties. For when I am weak, then I am strong.*

Christ is our strength.

I have said this before, but it bears repeating. When we get to the end of ourselves, and see how pitiful we really are, we realize our true strength is in the Lord. When we find ourselves in the hardest times, we know that they help us to grow spiritually. It is then that we come under the Lord's covering for our protection, clinging to Him for our lives. We realize our own weakness and His strength, no matter what the hardship may be: financial, emotional, physical, or relational. It could be anything. We get driven into a closer relationship with our Lord. First we beg that we might come to know Him more. Then, when hard times come, we beg that He will take them away. Well, which is it? Do I want to know Him and His strength, or do I want smooth sailing? I usually cannot have both simultaneously.

Oh, God, I have certainly been there. It's those difficult times that make me who I am today. Thank You that You have turned my mourning into dancing!

When You Give

Matthew 6:3,4 *But when you give to the needy, do not let your left hand know what your right hand is doing, so that* *your giving may be in secret. Then your Father, who sees what is done in secret, will reward you.*

Not *if* you give to the needy, but <u>when</u>.

The Lord has gotten my attention about giving to those in need. There are so many clamoring for their "wants" to be met, my heart has become hardened to them I'm afraid. They are the ones who expect a hand out in spite of the fact that they have primarily brought poverty upon themselves by foolish choices. I need to have a hearing ear and a soft heart, so that, when the Holy Spirit whispers, "She needs a hug," or "He needs a sandwich," I can hear and obey.

Father, please highlight someone, or better yet, a family, that needs help. Give me a heart of giving and generosity to serve those You are showing us. You have been so generous to us and have met our needs; please give opportunities for us to share Your goodness.

The Early Years

When I was a kid, my dad worked for a concrete construction company that traveled from one dam site to another (and, yes, that <u>was</u> a play on words). Consequently, we lived in a trailer and had to have a heavy, nice car that would be able to pull it from trailer park to trailer park. These new Oldsmobile or Cadillac cars were my Dad's pride and joy. As our family grew, I remember how excited Dad and Mom were to buy a newer, larger trailer to accommodate the six of us. This trailer was 40 feet long and 8 feet wide (which translates to 320 square feet of living space). Mom and Dad slept on a hide-a-bed in the living room while we kids shared the bedroom, four kids to a double bed, two at each end. I was the oldest and got really good at feet fights. We have lots of good memories, although I attended 17 different schools while growing up because we moved so often. I guess it helped me in the long run; I'm not shy in any way as an adult.

We had lots of pets over the years, one of which was a parakeet who was so smart. He would harass our cat by sitting on her head and picking at her whiskers. She would just sit there, ears flattened, knowing that she had better not touch that bird. This parakeet had quite a vocabulary thanks to my mother, and knew lots of tricks. He would sit in his cage and call, "here kitty, kitty, kitty," which I am sure the cat would have been happy to oblige if only those pesky bars were not in the way. The bird would come out with other quips like, "Stand back! I'm an eagle!" Or, addressing the late night talk show host of the 50's, "Go to bed, Tom Duggin!"

His favorite trick was to push a miniature cup and saucer over the edge of the counter and watch as the brass holder, cup, and saucer all clattered to the floor. Mom would put it back in place, and he would nudge, nudge, nudge with his beak until it fell to the floor again while he looked on. He would be released occasionally to fly freely around our small quarters, eventually sitting on the edge of the sink to watch Mom do dishes. To entertain himself, he would peck at that other bird in the shiny, chrome faucet. Once in awhile, Mom would put the cage outside on sunny mornings until, one day, my little sister lifted the cage door and cried out, "Fly away, birdie!" He did, and we never saw him again. We were all heartbroken over our loss.

Life was good for us. We did not think we were poor because we had always lived in a trailer and never experienced anything else. I remember in fourth grade, while living in Columbia, California, that one of my friends lived in a real house and had a room of her very own. I was so impressed! Columbia was a great little community, and we would hike all over the hills having wonderful adventures.

We usually lived in little one-horse towns out in the middle of nowhere, places that had one gas station, a grocery store, and three bars to accommodate the construction workers. I remember places like Boron, California, where Borax is mined. Just think, I actually lived four miles outside of Boron in the Mojave Desert.

We were in a new trailer park, and Dad and his buddies poured concrete slabs for patios at each trailer site. Once the concrete had cured enough, the kids ran water over it and slid to our hearts content in the hot summer sun. We would make tree forts in the sharp, cactus-like Joshua trees (Mom must not have loved us very much), and dug underground forts, covering them with corrugated metal we found laying around. It was not only scorching in there but, one day, a mother scorpion and her babies took up residence, leaving us fleeing for our lives. We loved catching horned toads, constructing houses for them out of shoe boxes. I'm sure they were thrilled too. We would follow sidewinder tracks in the desert sand but, fortunately, never found the snakes that they belonged to.

I will never forget the day we moved to our first house without wheels, in Port Hueneme, California. It was during Christmas vacation in fifth grade. We were all sick with the flu, and barely able to put our new bunk beds together so that we could crawl into them to recuperate. Our Christmas was very low key, but we were all excited to have a real house with three bedrooms. My brother got a room all to himself, while we three girls shared a room. It felt like heaven. I remember getting our very first telephone with a partyline. Dad talked so loud into the phone, I'm sure whoever he was talking to could have heard him without that black mouthpiece! In addition, I learned how to be so quiet that the other people having their conversations couldn't hear me listening in.

We made a lot of good memories; I thought I was settled in for life. What a shock it was, only a year and a half later, to find that we were moving again. Dad had gotten a job in Lompoc, working at Vandenberg Air Force Base, pouring concrete for missile silos. Thankfully, we stayed there until I grew up, got married, and moved away.

Lompoc was a great place to live during my junior high and high school years. We had lots of adventures, and it was a comparatively safe place to grow up at that time. We could ride our bikes for miles and, as I got into high school, all the guys had hot cars because there simply was not anything else to do. Cruising H Street and Ocean Avenue was the name of the game then. We would see how many kids we could sneak into the Valley Drive-In Theater. It helped that one of my best friends worked at the ticket booth. We loved to dance, and even invented new dances when we went to the after-game hops. It was all good, clean fun.

I played clarinet in band in junior high. My teacher tried to encourage me to join the high school marching band a little early, but I was too scared, so declined his offer. That was the year our high school band got invited to march in John F. Kennedy's inaugural parade in Washington, D.C. What a heartbreak that was! Ah, the fruit of the decisions we make. If only I had not let fear hold me back, I'm sure I would have some wonderful stories to tell about that trip.

Do Not Fear

Psalm 91:5,6 *You will not fear the terror of night, nor the arrow that flies by day, nor the pestilence that stalks in the darkness, nor the plague that destroys at midday.*

Fear abounds in these last days, but we are not to fear.

Arrow, pestilence, and plague translate to finances, Ebola, Islam, or health care in our times. There are so many things to be fearful of... if we do not trust our Lord. But He is greater than all these terrors. He is our covering. We will stand tall under His direction; there will be no need to cower in anxiety. He will guide, instruct, protect, give wisdom, and He will strengthen us in the days ahead. There is no fear while walking in Jesus.

Oh, Lord, for 40 years You brought Your people through the desert. Though we may be taken into captivity by this world, we trust in You in these latter days. Dayenu (it is enough). You are enough, Lord. As we focus on You, and not all that's going on around us, we can have peace in the turmoil, joy in the midst of any circumstance.

<u>Casting Pearls</u>

<u>Hebrews 4:2</u> *For we also have had the gospel preached to us, just as they did, but the message they heard was of no value to them, because those who heard did not combine it with faith.*

The gospel is nothing to those who are perishing.

If there is no faith involved, the gospel means nothing to those who hear it. They cannot respond properly. The Holy Spirit needs to be drawing them, or we are casting pearls before swine.

I think of an acquaintance I have known for years. She has been so cold to God all her life. Now, in the middle of terrible circumstances, she seems to be listening a little more. The sad part is that she is listening to <u>anything</u> that seems "spiritual," but I have to ask her, which spirit is it? I have given her a Bible that I am sure she's barely opened, yet she states that Yoga class she's taking has helped her to breathe deeply, to stretch her mind, and her spirit. She says she has a relationship with the Lord, though it is different than mine; she does not need to be born again. She thinks that she is going to heaven just because she is a "nice person." And she <u>is</u> a nice person. I have given it my all with little results. I realize that the Lord has to do it, so I have to continually put her back into His hands. Even now, she really doesn't want the answer that I have to offer, and that is Jesus.

Father, I pray that the Holy Spirit is working on softening her spirit. Please show her how much she needs the gift of Your Son to make it through, not only this temporary problem, but her eternal problem as well.

A Powerful Promise

Jeremiah 24:6,7 *My eyes will watch over them for their good, and I will bring them back to this land. I will build them up and not tear them down; I will plant them and not uproot them. I will give them a heart to know me, that I am the Lord. They will be my people and I will be their God, for they will return to me with all their heart.*

This Scripture is a powerful promise!

We have prayed these verses over our family for so many years that I have memorized this passage. God is faithful and, when we use His Word as a pattern for prayer, I am sure He is pleased. We pray, believing that our family will come to know Him in a deeply personal way. We pray for everyone related to us by "blood, marriage, remarriage, and adoption." That covers multitudes of people for many generations.

Thank You, Lord, for giving me this very creative prayer. I am blessed and excited to see the results from heaven's standpoint. It's wonderful when I hear about a distant relative coming to know You; I never would have thought about praying for them individually and yet, in part, their salvation is an answer to this prayer.

Our Children Will Return

Isaiah 49:22 *This is what the Sovereign Lord says: "See, I will beckon to the Gentiles, I will lift up my banner to the peoples; they will bring your sons in their arms and carry your daughters on their shoulders."*

God calls our loved ones home.

I am hopeful that God is changing the hearts of families, that relationships would be restored. Nothing is too difficult for God. We know that our Father is working in the lives of families. He has given us many promises, like Jeremiah 24:6 and 7, that we continue to stand upon. I know of many broken relationships that are crying out for healing. We have seen some beautiful answers to those prayers in recent years, and I am sure there will be many more to come as the Lord gathers His end time harvest.

Father, we know You care about families; You designed them, after all. We know You are faithful, and Your Holy Spirit is at work in the lives of each of these family members to bring about restoration. We will keep watching and waiting.

Prompt Obedience

Genesis 15:10,11 *Abram brought all these to him, cut them in two and arranged the halves opposite each other; the birds, however, he did not cut in half. Then birds of prey came down on the carcasses, but Abram drove them away.*

Abram is worshiping God and being obedient, but the enemy tries to disrupt.

Isn't that the way it still is? We try so hard to be obedient to God. We hear something in our spirit, then stop and pay attention. Next, as we begin to follow His direction, a distraction comes flying right into the middle of it all. We must be like Abram. We must drive the enemy away. Those arrows of thoughts like, *not now; I don't have time right this minute; maybe tomorrow; I will have the opportunity later,* need to be squelched as we obey our Lord.

Father, forgive my disobedience. I want to be prompt to obey before the moment is lost in the confusion of life. Lord, help me to drive the enemy out in the power of the name of Your Son.

Retracing Our Roots

When Mom and I had planned on going to Israel, and were disappointed with cancellations twice in a row, we decided to travel to Norway instead, retracing the roots of our family. We had a wonderful time, and I had ample opportunity to practice the few Norwegian words that I knew, "it is raining outside." I have to admit that Mom was as sick of hearing those words as I was of the opportunities to use them; it rained almost steadily while we were there. But it is an absolutely beautiful country, with lush green mountainous terrain, and gorgeous waterfalls cascading over the rocks. The fjords were everything I could have imagined.

While traveling on a train through the beautiful landscape one day, Mom turned to me quite unexpectedly and asked, "You do know that we were Russian Jews who fled into Norway long ago in our history, don't you?"

I sat there, too stunned to even speak. *What? How could I have not realized this?* Mom explained that her family was ashamed of their Jewish past, and chose to keep it a secret, hidden even from me, a lover of the Jewish people. Having lived through World War II as a teenager, and with the knowledge of concentration camps, she was afraid to let the truth be known. It was when she had received Christ in her later years, that she understood it was indeed a privilege to acknowledge her heritage. I could not have been more thrilled. This explained why, from the time I accepted Christ into my life, I had a love for Israel and the Jewish people. I called Dave from Norway to let him know this new treasure in my history. He, of course, was delighted as well.

When I returned home, I called my youngest sister, Kay, and asked her if she was aware of this "minor" detail in our bloodline. To my surprise, she responded that she did.

"Now, how could you know and I didn't?" I questioned. Her response made me laugh.

"Remember how Grandma always used to say she had just enough Jewish blood to make her a good shopper?" And I thought she was only kidding...

Follow THE Light

Isaiah 50:10,11 *Who among you fears the Lord and obeys the word of his servant? Let him who walks in the dark, who has no light, trust in the name of the Lord and rely on his God. But now, all you who light fires and provide your-self with flaming torches, go walk in the light of your fires and the torches you have set ablaze. This is what you shall receive from my hand: You will lie down in torment.*

Whew! A strong warning!

There are times when we feel as though not much is happening, that maybe the word we had received was in error. We have visions and goals that we were sure came from the Lord, but we still find ourselves making tents in the desert. Even if our dreams don't come to fruition, we don't want anything that the Lord doesn't want for us. We continue to walk with the Lord because we know His timing is perfect, and we do not want to create Ishmaels in our lives. We have plenty of experience with unforeseen results from going ahead with our own plans. Then, right around the corner, comes a "suddenly!" Suddenly the pieces begin to come together. The train that has seemingly been derailed begins to move once again, slowly at first, but gradually building up steam until it has got momentum and purpose. What a beautiful reward for trusting in and waiting upon the Lord.

Those that are looking for a more exciting journey, by chasing after other spirits, will lie down in torment. They create false light, demonic flares that entertain for the moment, but quickly burn out. Like an addiction to any-thing, the satisfaction is short lived and they must search for something new, and maybe even a little farther away from God's plan for their lives. Before they know it, they are lost.

Father, we trust that You will show us, that You will guide and lead at the right times. You will let us know when to stay and when to go. You will warn us to be careful; we will listen and <u>obey</u>.

Jealousy Brings Bad Fruit

Numbers 12:1,2 *Miriam and Aaron began to talk against Moses because of his Cushite wife, for he had married a Cushite. "Has the Lord spoken only through Moses?" they asked. "Hasn't he also spoken through us?" And the Lord heard this.*

Envy and jealousy cause bad thinking and bad fruit.

309

These two had a great part to play in the Exodus of God's people. Yet they were not satisfied with their roles alone. They were jealous of their brother, Moses, a humble man. The Lord was not going to put up with this and dealt with it immediately. As a result, Miriam was stricken with leprosy.

Lord, help us to not look at others' gifts and talents and covet them. Help us to be satisfied with the role You have given us in life. We don't want to become ugly people filled with jealousy and envy. Help us to complete the tasks You've given us, and to be content in that. Draw us ever nearer to You.

Partial Obedience Is Not Obedience

Joshua 10:40b *He [Joshua] left no survivors. He totally destroyed all who breathed, just as the Lord, the God of Israel, had commanded.*

But it seems so inhumane, so cruel!

Joshua had to destroy all of them, as he had destroyed all of the people in the southern cities. If he had not, in time, they would have regrouped and come back to conquer Joshua and his nation. God knew that, so He commanded total destruction upon the enemies of His people. If Joshua had not obeyed God totally, he would have been in sin, and they would not have been victorious. Partial obedience is not obedience. Joshua was blessed because he did all that God commanded.

Lord, forgive my laziness, my lackadaisical attitude, and my disobedience to You. I know You have a plan and want my total attention. I am not as strong as I want to be. Strengthen me, Lord.

The Lord Is My Stronghold

Psalm 37:39,40 *The salvation of the righteous comes from the Lord; he is their stronghold in time of trouble. The Lord helps them and delivers them; he delivers them from the wicked and saves them, because they take refuge in him.*

The Lord is our deliverer.

The Lord has delivered me from so much since I first received this Word in May of 1984. I have seen Him set me free time and time again. The fowler's snare has tried to entrap me; my various enemies have laid nets for me; they have gloated over their victories. Then, in sometimes miraculous ways, the Lord has delivered me in situations that only He could orchestrate.

Thank You, Lord, for Your hand of covering and favor over my life. You have blessed me in so many ways. I will never forget Your goodness to me over the years.

Sowing The Seeds Of Faith

Matthew 13:37–39 *He answered, "The one who sowed the good seed is the Son of Man. The field is the world, and the good seed stands for the sons of the kingdom. The weeds are the seeds of the evil one, and the enemy who sows them is the devil. The harvest is the end of the age, and the harvesters are angels."*

The enemy of our souls has surely infiltrated the church at large.

We don't know for certain who truly belongs to God. People can look good on the outside, carrying their Bibles, attending church, doing the Christian "stuff." Only God knows the hearts of men. As we share the love of God around us, we may win even those that we thought were already saved. Those tares planted in our wheat fields could come to salvation.

Lord, help us to let people see You in our lives. Let Your Light draw them to Yourself. Let there be less of us and more of You so that You can sow seeds, even in the hearts of those that we mistakenly believe to be our brothers and sisters in Christ.

Keep Your Eyes On Jesus

Luke 9:62 *Jesus replied, "No one who puts his hand to the plow and looks back is fit for service in the kingdom of God."*

I've been looking back, haven't I, Lord?

And in my spirit the Lord replied something like this: *"I have so much in store for you but, if you keep looking back at the hurts and disappointments, your path gets off track from Mine. If you will only walk in My footprints, not looking to the left, the right, or worse, behind, you will keep your focus on My plans for you. The rewards are many and the joys are great. Looking back brings distraction and bears no fruit. Looking at Me keeps you going forward and gives much hope."*

Lord, I am so sorry for focusing on those hurts, both in the distant past and the current time. You have brought me out to bring me into Your plans and a future with You. I want to help others who are dealing with the same types of damage to point them to You, and the hope that only You can bring. If I am looking back like they are, we can only console each other and wallow together in the mud. You are the lifter of our heads as we keep focused on Jesus.

Armor Of God's Protection

Ephesians 6:10-12 *Finally, be strong in the Lord and in his mighty power. Put on the full armor of God so that you can take your stand against the devil's schemes. For our struggle is not against flesh and blood, but against the rulers, against the authorities, against the powers of this dark world and against the spiritual forces of evil in the heavenly realms.*

I saw a picture in my imagination this morning. We are hidden in Christ in the full armor of God. If we are in Him within that armor, those fiery darts just bounce off and cannot get a hook in us. However, I opened the face mask of my helmet to look back at the past. A hook came in to destroy my peace in Christ through the opening in my armor. I had allowed it.

Father, You are so creative in the ways you deal with your sheep, especially the ones who are disobedient. Thank You for Your holy conviction. I so need that. I don't take Your Word lightly. The only way I can be strong in Your kingdom is to be obedient to stand against the devil's schemes.

313

Be Alive In The Spirit

Romans 8:9,10 *You, however, are controlled not by the sinful nature but by the Spirit, if the Spirit of God lives in you. And if anyone does not have the Spirit of Christ, he does not belong to Christ. But if Christ is in you, your body is dead because of sin, yet your spirit is alive because of righteousness.*

These changing bodies will eventually give way to our eternal bodies.

All this worry about underarm flab, a few pounds here and there, wrinkles, and age spots is pointless. All this will pass away. Yes, we should take good care of these old tents we live in because they are the tabernacles of the Holy Spirit. But our flesh is decaying for a very good reason. It is not our permanent home; the Lord does not want us to desire to stay here. Heaven is our home, and our spiritual life is to be the focus. Our relationship with God will provide a permanent home that does not decay, lose hair, and get flabby. Praise the Lord!

Thank You, Father, for Your promise of eternal life. I so look forward to not having to live in this old tent anymore! Maranatha, Lord Jesus!

Mary Pondered

Luke 2:19 *But Mary treasured up all these things and pondered them in her heart.*

I am sure Mary spent a lot of time pondering. She had a lot to think about!

314

There are so many miracles in Luke 1 and 2, from John the Baptist's birth being foretold by an angel; Zechariah's silence due to unbelief; Elizabeth's pregnancy in old age; Gabriel visiting Mary with the foretelling of Jesus' birth; the Holy Spirit coming upon Mary; the baby leaping in Elizabeth's womb after hearing Mary's voice; Elizabeth being filled with the Holy Spirit and prophesying over Mary before Mary even told her anything, and so forth.

All of these events are miracles in themselves in preparation for Jesus' birth. We zero in on the manger, angels, shepherds, Bethlehem, and miss all the other supernatural actions that led up to the birth of our Lord. But the part that gets my attention the most is Mary. She simply pondered these things in her heart; she was quiet, unassuming, and gentle. She didn't stand up at a podium to tell everyone how great she was. She kept it silently to herself. She sang a song glorifying her Lord and praising Him for all He had done for her people and for her, His humble servant.

Lord, You've given me promises and I rest in them. If it was truly You, Your timing is perfect, and mine is not. If I am mistaken, it will become evident. My trust is in You, and I will obey as I ponder Your goodness to us. I am Your servant, so help me to also walk faithfully through the short time we have left here on this earth. Mary suffered greatly because people did not understand her circumstances. Yet You were with her through it all, just as You will be with us no matter what comes our way.

315

Jesus, The Truth Teller

John 3:3 *"I tell you the truth, no one can see the kingdom of God unless he is born again."*

John 3:5 *"I tell you the truth, no one can enter the king- dom of God unless he is born of water and the Spirit."*

John 3:11 *"I tell you the truth, we speak of what we know, and we testify to what we have seen, but still you people do not accept our testimony."*

Jesus is the way, the truth, and the life.

He <u>always</u> tells the truth. He cannot lie. But, even when He speaks the truth, people refuse to believe it. They refuse because they do not want to change. They prefer to remain in the darkness where their sins stay hidden. Heaven is so foreign to them that they refuse to believe it is real. How can they believe in something that is so ridiculous and be expected to give up their old life for a place that seems to be a fantasy to their unspiritual thinking?

Once we finally give up and receive the free gift of eternal life, we come out of condemnation and darkness into the Spiritual Light. When the veil has been lifted, we no longer want to stay in darkness. We long for the Light of Jesus Christ and choose to put away those things that disappoint Him because they bring separation from Him. We long to hear His voice, to see His face, to feel His presence. He is real, His words are real, and heaven is real. Ask for the gift of faith to believe. He will give it to you. Once you have fully received Him, you will never be the same. I promise!

There is so much to behold in the future that the darkness will not have the same appeal it once did. Jesus comes to help you with all the details in your life. He longs to be a part of every decision, every relationship, and your Teacher as you come to Him every morning to read His Word. But the best is yet to come! You will never die but, once you cross the threshold of what we on earth call death, you will be more alive than you have ever been!

Jesus, I remember thinking that walking with You was a fantasy experience. But that was before. Thank You for making my life so exciting. I love to see what You have planned each day. It is those unexpected meetings, where I see Your hand at work, that give such pleasure. You orchestrate even the most mundane of days to suit Your needs, to bring about confirmations, encouragements, and things we did not even know we needed. Better yet, You place us where someone else needs ministry. We are blessed to be part of the answer for them. You are awesome!

Man Pleasing Again

Luke 6:22,23,26 *Blessed are you when men hate you, when they exclude you and insult you and reject your name as evil, because of the Son of Man. Rejoice in that day and leap for joy, because great is your reward in heaven. For that is how their fathers treated the prophets ...Woe to you when all men speak well of you, for that is how their fathers treated the false prophets.*

We all want to be liked by others.

We want others to think and say good things about us. It looks to me, though, that this is not always a wonderful thing. Am I willing to compromise my walk with the Lord to make or keep friends? My walk is with Jesus first, and my life must be pleasing to Him.

Father, it is a tightrope when it comes to my unbelieving friends and family members. I know that I cannot say too much because they will walk away forever. But I still need to stand for You wherever possible. I know they sense You living in me without my even saying a word, but I am tired of leaving the best part of my life in a closet just to keep the peace with them. Show me what You want me to do. I definitely need to hear from You on this one.

It Is A Misunderstanding

Mark 12:29 *"The most important one," answered Jesus, "is this: 'Hear O Israel, the Lord our God, the Lord is one.'"*

"Hear," not "here"!

All this time I have been "hearing" and reading this Scripture the wrong way. I have been interpreting it as, "in this place," here. Then, during a Bible study, my error suddenly came to light. Jesus was saying, "Listen, all you people; pay attention, perk up your physical and spiritual ears!" How often do I misunderstand and not even realize it? This was a big one. Yes, I know this is a quote from Deuteronomy 6:4–9, the Shema to the Jewish people. As I looked at the notes, I learned that it is not only the Jewish confession of faith, but Shema actually is the Hebrew word for "hear"!

Father, I felt like such an idiot! Thank You so much for teaching me something I thought I already knew. Your patience is amazing.

Yet Another Play On Words

John 12:12,13 *The next day the great crowd that had come for the Feast heard that Jesus was on his way to Jerusalem. They took palm branches and went out to meet him, shouting, "Hosanna! Blessed is he who comes in the name of the Lord! Blessed is the King of Israel!"*

Palms versus palm trees.

When we were at a church to present a Passover Seder, the pastor was teaching about Palm Sunday that morning. He talked about the crowds waving palm branches (and lulavs) at Jesus. I suddenly realized that Jesus' own palms would be nailed to the cross a few days later. That, for me, was revelation.

I told Lindy about it, and we began discussing Isaiah 53. Verse 4 came up: *"Surely he took up our infirmities and carried our sorrows, yet we considered him stricken by God, smitten by him, and afflicted."* To smite means beaten with the hand. Figuratively, God's palm allowed the beating of His only Son through the depravity of man. Nothing happened to Jesus that had not come first through His Father's fingers. All this occurred so that we may have eternal life. *"For God so loved the world that He gave His only begotten Son, that whoever believes in Him shall not perish but have eternal life."* (John 3:16)

Oh, Father, the pain You must have felt as You watched Your Son being beaten. Those palm branches that were being waved as they declared Him King over Israel meant absolutely nothing a few days later when they nailed the palms of His hands to a tree to die for our sins. But You knew that already, didn't You? Your plan was conceived before the creation of the world. Thank You for Your unconditional love for us.

The Author Of Life

Mark 12:1–11 *Vs. 6 "He had one left to send, a son, whom he loved. He sent him last of all, saying, 'They will respect my son.'"*

God sent all the prophets in the Old Testament and they were not well received.

Finally He sent Jesus, His beloved Son, to bring them into salvation. They murdered Him, too. Little did they realize that they were playing into God's hand. Jesus had to die and rise again in order to bring the gift of salvation to all of mankind.

As we learned of The Harbinger by Jonathan Cahn*, we again saw God's hand at work in Isaiah 9:10. The people are playing into His plan. The script has been written by the Author of Life. Human beings, in their depravity, are actors on the stage. Will God get our attention for the end-time harvest? Will we play our part? Will we pray; will we speak up to tell what we know? Or will we sit idly by waiting for the end to come?

Father, you made it very plain to me that we are to give away copies of The Harbinger books, CD's, Dave's study on the subject, anything that confirms to others that we need to be interceding for our country during this most tumultuous time that we are blessed to live in. Show us how to continue to be creative in praying for our land.

*The Harbinger, by Jonathan Cahn, Copyright © 2011, published by Front Line.

Answered Prayer

Romans 9:25 *As he says in Hosea: "I will call them 'my people' who are not my people; and I will call her 'my loved one' who is not my loved one."*

God sees those that will become His.

Oh, if we could see the future like that. If we could only know that our loved ones will one day be walking with Him. We must pray as if we do, with no doubt or worry. Our trust is in our God, not in our loved ones' behavior or attitudes that we see. God knows their hearts. He knows what it will take to break the stones around their hearts to expose the soft tissue inside, so that the Holy Spirit can fill them with Himself.

Lord, we continue to pray and thank You for making our loved ones 'Your people,' though we see only the seemingly hopelessness of the situation. We praise You for Your faithfulness.

Answered Prayer, An Illustration

Saturday, May 3, was declared a 24 hour prayer time at our church. I had signed us up for the one-hour slot right before some friends, just like we did last year. We wanted to have some fun with them afterward. However, a few days before the designated hour of prayer, I discovered that our pastor's daughter had a soccer game that I had promised to attend. And, wouldn't you know, it began right in the middle of our prayer hour. Consequently, when I saw that the 10:30 – 11:30 time slot was now empty, I moved to that location, enabling us to attend her game in the afternoon.

The event was very well organized with certain stations and time frames allotted to each station for specific prayer concerns. Dave and I spent 20 minutes at Station 1, then moved to Station 2, to find that this was prayer for families. Not thinking much about it, we began praying for our granddaughter, Macee, and Dave's daughter, Bree, followed by many other family members. These are familiar prayers spoken daily for protection and the salvation of our loved ones.

That evening, the Lord put it on my heart to text Macee to see if she was recovering from the illness she had been under for several days. I usually do not text just to see how she is doing, but did so at that moment. She responded that she was almost in a serious accident that day. The students in one of her college classes were on a field trip to Pt. Reyes. She was supposed to ride in a prearranged car as a foursome but, at the last minute, changed to ride with her boyfriend instead.

As the group was caravanning to their destination, Macee noticed a strange sight, a cross bar swinging on the electrical wires without the support of a pole. Then she noticed the cloud of dust that accompanied this spectacle. The driver of the car in which she was supposed to be riding misjudged the speed of an approaching vehicle, pulled out in front of it, and was clipped in the rear. Spinning wildly off the road, the back of the car crashed into the electrical pole, breaking it to pieces. The back window shattered with the force of the impact, and the trunk of the car was totally demolished.

Macee told us that one of the girls in the backseat, where she would have been sitting, was bleeding profusely from the head, and needed medical attention. Macee, instead of being the victim of the accident, now found herself calming both girls. Unexpectedly, a bicyclist pulled up. Declaring himself a paramedic, he immediately went to work to stop the bleeding. Another motorist, who happened to be a paramedic also, arrived on the scene. The girl who received the most injuries was transported by ambulance to the hospital and stayed there for a full day receiving the care she needed.

What was the time of this incident? Just before 11:00, the time we were praying for our family members.

Thank You, Jesus, for keeping Your hand of covering and protection over our granddaughter. Thank You for the gifts You have given her, mercy and the ability to react responsibly in an emergency situation. Lord, show her Your

323

love through this event, and help her to recognize answered prayer in her behalf.

The Prophetic Voice

Isaiah 42:8,9 *"I am the Lord; that is my name! I will not give my glory to another or my praise to idols. See, the former things have taken place, and new things I declare; before they spring into being I announce them to you."*

The Lord can announce things to us in advance.

I need to move back into that place again, where I can hear the Lord. The Lord did not go anywhere; I did. I need to get back under the shelter of His wings where He can speak to me, and I can listen. It was so beautiful then, though the circumstances often were not. He gave me warnings, comfort, and preparation for what was ahead.

Oh, God, I miss our relationship of that time. Draw me close to You. I know what the difference is. I don't have as much upheaval in this part of my life. I certainly don't pray for more troubles. Lord, I want the closeness without the trauma.

Weaker Church Members

Acts 5:13 *No one else dared join them* [the apostles]*, even though they were highly regarded by the people.*

The general populace had heard about Ananias and Sapphira, and their immediate deaths. They were afraid!

The church continued to grow but the weak ones, the half-hearted ones, were afraid to meet with the apostles and other strong believers because they were fearful that their hearts would be exposed, and they might meet the same death. They knew they were not sold out for Jesus like the apostles. Maybe, in time, they made a real, wholehearted commitment but, at this point, they were not ready.

Jesus, show us where we are lagging back; show us our half-heartedness and lack of commitment. Purify our hearts and draw us near. We don't want to be hypocrites in any way.

Focus On The Heart

2 Corinthians 5:12 *We are not trying to commend our-selves to you again, but are giving you an opportunity to take pride in us, so that you can answer those who take pride in what is seen rather than what is in the heart.*

Focus on the unseen rather than the outward appearance.

We must give favor to the heart rather than flashy flam-boyance. Those that are meek and mild, but have hearts searching after God are often overlooked. Sometimes the most outspoken, busiest, fingers into everything types are given places of honor. We must examine the motivation behind the actions. Do these showy ones actually spend time with the Lord, and do what He is calling them to? Or are they after self-aggrandizement and power?

I loved being the church secretary; I felt needed. I loved praying with people and ministering to them. Almost always my motives were good, but there were a few times when I operated in the flesh. I might have been smiling on the outside, meanwhile thinking, *Go away! Can't you see I have bulletins to prepare? I'm under a deadline here!* That was the part seen by the Holy Spirit. I am sure He was not pleased.

Oh God, forgive those times when I was less than what You desired me to be. We cannot hide anything from You. You see everything, including our hearts, more perfectly than we do.

The Word Points To Jesus

1 Corinthians 13:12 *Now we see but a poor reflection as in a mirror; then we shall see face to face. Now I know in part; then I shall know fully, even as I am fully known.*

As I was reading the Word this morning, the thought came to me, ***"As wonderful as God's Word is, it only <u>points</u> to Jesus."***

What if, in biblical times, I was sitting there reading about the creation of the world and Jesus came up and tapped me on the shoulder. Would my response be, "Not now, Jesus. I'm busy"? Or would it be, "Speak, Lord, Your servant is listening"?

Today, after the Holy Spirit has been given to all believers, we have the same dilemma. I am reading the Word to learn about Jesus and the Holy Spirit. The Holy Spirit prompts me to get Dave a cup of coffee, but I say, "Not now, Lord; I am busy learning about You." It sounds ludicrous, doesn't it? It happens all the time as the Holy Spirit is awakening us, guiding us, and helping us through life, though we have often not been paying attention. Has He put a check in your spirit that you have not heeded? Has He prompted you to write a letter, call a relative, or see a neighbor? Have you been obedient, or have you told Him, "Not today, Lord"?

What is my focus? What I pay the most attention to becomes my god if I allow it. Let Jesus draw you into a closer walk with Him. He wants to fill your life with all the gifts He longs to give you. We have often talked about wanting to give more to our kids when they were younger, but did not because they were not ready and responsible to receive. Am I ready to receive? I desire to be expectant and fully ready.

Father, open our hearts to the promptings of Your Holy Spirit. Help us to trust and obey You no matter the outcome. We desire to see You face to face. We don't want to have to shield our eyes, the windows to our souls, from Your gaze. We don't want to hide from You. Purify our hearts and help us to know Your Son on a deeply personal basis.

Perseverance!

Revelation 2:2,3 *I know your deeds, your hard work and your perseverance. I know that you cannot tolerate wicked men, that you have tested those who claim to be apostles but are not, and have found them false. You have persevered and have endured hardships for my name, and have not grown weary.*

We must be strong and persistent!

I was so enjoying my morning with the Lord, totally engrossed in my reading. A movement caught my attention. I glanced up to find six Canadian geese right up next to the pool! The <u>nerve</u> of them! We have allowed these geese to overrun the lower yard this year for the first time, thinking that they would be content with that. But, no, they want more. I immediately thought of spiritual warfare. We are aggressive in our battles, running off the demons, only to find that, as soon as we quit fighting, they're b-a-a-ck. We must continue to persevere until they realize our God is bigger than theirs, and they move on for good.

Another analogy is Israel. They keep giving up more land to their enemies thinking that, eventually, they will be able to coexist. However, the reality is that the Muslims want it <u>all</u>---they want <u>everything</u>. Without the love of Jesus in their hearts, they will never be content to share. They can be accurately identified as, "those who do not play well with others." In fact, they don't even play well with their own Muslim brothers!

Lord, thank You for showing us the need to keep fighting the battle. We will always have a fight here on earth until You take us home. You will win the war, but each skirmish takes the strategy, strength, and wisdom that You provide.

The Act Of Obedience

Acts 8:31–33 *"How can I," he said, "unless someone explains it to me?" So he invited Philip to come up and sit with him. The eunuch was reading this passage of Scripture: "He was led like a sheep to the slaughter, and as a lamb before the shearer is silent, so he did not open his mouth. In his humiliation he was deprived of justice..."*

Let the Holy Spirit have His way.

I was watching the pool sweep today. It had a mind of its own for several minutes at a time. Periodically, the power box would kick in and drag it where it did not really want to go. But it submitted and laid still so that the box could have its way for the sweep's good. You see, the sweep occasionally gets hung up on the steps or its own tubing and is stuck in one position until the reverse box frees it up.

Analogy: The Power Box in our lives is the Holy Spirit. If we are going along okay, He lets us proceed. On the other hand, if we are headed in a direction that will make us "stuck" or ineffective, He stops us to redirect our path. Do I go limp at those times, or do I fight Him to have my own way? He allows me to win because He has given me free will. Do I will to follow Him wherever He leads, or do I refuse to submit, to my own detriment?

Father, if I only <u>knew</u> it was You every time, I'd be more cooperative. It's when I'm not certain that I battle the circumstances. You have been teaching us on perseverance with the huge riverfront spiders and the geese. We are thinking we must persevere in those areas, and in spiritual warfare as well. Please let us know equally when You want us to give up and give in on other issues. We need more discernment, Lord.

Hardness Of Heart

Proverbs 29:1 *A man who remains stiff-necked after many rebukes will suddenly be destroyed---without remedy.*

Don't be a stiff-necked follower.

329

After sharing my pool sweep story with a friend who has a pool business, she gave me more food for thought. In the winter, when the hoses are cold, they are no longer pliable, but become rigid and sometimes crimp up. Do you hear the correlation of that? We must stay warm to the Holy Spirit to be able to follow Him freely. If we become the "frozen chosen," not even listening for Him, we are too rigid to be open to the change that He might be asking of us.

Lord, please make us aware when we are being stiff-necked. Sometimes we do things that we think make perfect sense, but we do not want to be operating in our brains alone. We want to be listening in our spirits for Your wisdom in every situation.

Take A Gander At Those Geese

Psalm 8:6,7 *You have made him ruler over the works of your hands; you put everything under his feet: all flocks and herds, and the beasts of the field, the birds of the air, and the fish of the sea, all that swim the paths of the seas.*

Let the Holy Spirit lead and teach His way.

It started on May 12, 2013. We had been battling the geese on our property for months already. We wanted to protect our yard from these evil trespassers because we have so much company, and wanted to shield the children from goose droppings. We shared this with the home group on Friday night and Lindy's husband, Jim, gave us the above Scripture. The same evening, Dave made a comment about spiritual warfare. He just could not see it; the spiritual realm didn't seem real to him.

The following morning, I began praying for my husband, that the Lord would open his eyes. The Holy Spirit dropped a thought into my head. *"Treat the geese as a type of spiritual battle."*

Hmm, I pondered. We always pray a hedge of thorns and wall of fire around our property to protect us from every fiery dart that would try to disrupt our lives and the peace that the Lord has given us here. I remembered how God had opened the eyes of a servant (2 Kings 6:15–17, with Elisha) to see the invisible realm. I asked Him to make the wall of fire visible to the geese so that they would not even want to come here.

Beginning to do spiritual battle with loud authority, **"In the name of Jesus, the Lord rebuke you..."** etc., I sensed the Holy Spirit saying, *"No, no, no, not like that. Talk to Me about it, ask Me."*

So I rephrased my thinking and spoke aloud, "Father, You have dominion over the earth and Your Holy Spirit lives in me. I am asking You to remove these geese."

I got the impression, *"Don't watch them; trust Me with them."* Over the next week, I kept praying in the way He instructed, and began seeing results. The geese did not seem to want to hang on our property. They would pass right through without stopping to eat, poop, or nest. One morning, though, there was a family that apparently had not gotten the message, so they stopped for a few nibbles.

"Okay, you geese," I shouted, "I command you to leave here right now! Get out of here, you **fowl spirits!**"

331

Then I realized that these are birds... fowl! I had a good laugh right then and there, realizing that some spirits are like those geese; they are more stubborn, and you have to work a little harder to keep them away.

The glorious moment happened, though, a couple of weeks later. A whole "herd" of geese was running at breakneck speed toward our yard from downstream.

In a panic, I asked the Lord to stop them in their tracks, "Lord, please send them into the river!"

Amazingly, they stopped right around our property line. Again, I sensed, *"Don't watch; turn away and let Me handle it."*

I obediently went back to my reading. In a couple of moments, I glanced up to see that they were gone! *Where did they go?* I wondered. Thanking the Lord, I went back to my book when, a few moments later, some movement caught my eye upstream. There were the geese, coming out of the river two doors up from us. They had actually gone around our yard. Meanwhile, Dave was watching all these things happen so that he could literally "see" in the spiritual realm.

Dave and I have both learned many lessons through this amazing, almost unbelievable, process. Our Lord loves us, and the Holy Spirit is our teacher. Isn't it much better than chasing geese on the tractor, blowing horns, shooting birdshot, yelling, and clapping (all with zero results)? A neighbor made the comment, "Thanks for whatever you're doing to keep the geese away."

I answered, "Well, we're just praying." He replied, "Oh... That's good."

But I took note of the puzzlement clearly displayed on his face.

The Never-Ending Parody Of The Geese

Those geese! I just got back from chasing the stubborn ones off our property... again. They <u>look</u> so pretty, don't they? They appear so innocent, and yet sometimes they will not budge unless you get right up on them with a harsh word and a vigorous, aggressive manner. They have their own agenda, which seems good to them. But the side effect is the waste they leave behind with the healthy grass being pulled up as they graze along so serenely. They leave behind a barren wasteland, devoid of any good vegetation, and nothing for the other riverfront critters to eat. They are the devourers. One goose will come in all alone to taste and see if there is a place for him. If left to wander freely, he calls all his buddies from upstream to join him, until there are innumerable "foul spirits" to literally take over and get the control they so desire.

The landlords must hang tough, praying against these unwanted inhabitants, or they will keep coming, bringing ever more of their kind with them. Humans must stand their ground.

It is scriptural that in Luke 11:24–26 *"When an evil spirit comes out of a man* [yard]*, it goes through arid places seeking rest and does not find it. Then it says, 'I will return* *to the house I left.' When it arrives, it finds the house swept clean and put in order. Then it goes and takes seven other spirits more wicked than itself, and they go in and live there. And the final condition of that man [yard] is worse than the first."*

On another day, I entered in my journaling, "Prayed against one lone goose this morning, asking God to turn him around or to pass quickly through our yard. At that moment, a bunch of his buddies flew onto a lawn upstream, honking to announce their arrival. He promptly turned back to join them, leaving our property in peace."

As silly as all this sounds, is it also helping you to see into the spiritual realm better? I hope so. I am continually amazed to see God's hand at work in these simple illustrations. You may think I am a little crazy, but I am convinced that the Lord can use <u>anything</u> to teach His people if they have a heart after Him.

Thank You, Lord, for teaching us in a way that only You could.

Man Looks At The Outward Appearance

1 Samuel 16:7 *But the Lord said to Samuel, "Do not look at his appearance or at his physical stature because I have refused him. For the Lord does not see as man sees; for man looks at the outward appearance, but the Lord looks at the heart."*

Birds teach us more lessons.

334

I heard about a single turkey out on the golf course the other day. He kept trying to make friends with the other birds, without success. Finally a pure white peacock allowed him to "follow." Because the peacock was beautiful, the turkey was more than happy to submit to his leadership. What the turkey did not realize was that the peacock had been rejected by his own kind because of the blandness of his feathers. He just didn't fit in with that vibrantly colored group.

What an awkward pair they were! I can just imagine the peacock displaying his grand tail feathers followed by the turkey presenting his meager imitation. The turkey allowed the peacock to call all the shots and really gave up his own rights to seek after this stunning leader. How like man---we will follow someone because he looks good, speaks well, and appears to be telling the truth. Do we actually check him out? Do we look into his background before we allow him into our pulpit or our White House? Apparently not, and our country, and many churches, are suffering today because of it.

Lord, help us to give equal time to those that might not be as popular, or as pretty, or as articulate; after all, they belong equally to You as do the others. In fact, like David, they may not be as showy, but they may have a heart that searches after You in a much deeper way because they don't have the self-confidence that they would have had otherwise. If that turkey knew better, he would have realized that just being with You was enough to keep him happy and contented. I know that's where You have me right now.

Judas Fulfilled Prophecy

Acts 1:20 *"For,"* said Peter, *"it is written in the book of Psalms, may his place be deserted; let there be no one to dwell in it,"* and *"May another take his place of leadership."* [Quoted from Psalm 69:25 and 109:8.]

Acts 1:26 *Then they cast lots, and the lot fell to Matthias; so he was added to the eleven apostles.*

Psalms and the prophets spoke of Messianic prophecies which people were looking forward to seeing fulfilled.

God's plan for His Son was written about from the beginning to end in His Word. Judas fulfilled prophecy too, in a negative sense, and they saw it happen with their own eyes. The problem comes with the next part, where Jesus' followers only gave God two choices as a replacement for Judas. In my opinion, God didn't really choose Matthias; He chose a Jew named Saul who they would have <u>never</u> considered at the time. Our flesh leads us astray when we are trying to be <u>so</u> spiritual. God has His plans and it's up to us to find out what they are, then follow His leading.

We have our plans... and God laughs! Lord, hold us tightly to Yourself. Give us godly wisdom about when to speak and when to be quiet, when to move and when to stay, when to pray and when to sing. Lead us as only You can.

Set Apart For The Gospel

Romans 1:1,5 *Paul, a servant of Christ Jesus, called to be an apostle and set apart for the gospel of God...Through*

336

him [Jesus] and for his name's sake, we received grace and apostleship to call people from among all the Gentiles to the obedience that comes from faith.

Sometimes, God sets us apart to be with Him.

I was feeling the isolation and loneliness that had become a recurring event in my life. I finally decided to get to the bottom of it, asking the Lord, *"Father, why is my phone so silent? Please help me to understand why people have removed themselves from my life."*

I sensed that this was the Lord's doing. He had removed people so that I could finish His assignment. I had put it off long enough. I had been retired 13 months, and thought I would get my book done pretty quickly. Things got in the way. Pretty soon, a whole year had slipped by and my project had not gotten any closer to being finished. I knew that the Lord had called me to write my testimony and journal. It is not my business what He wants to do with it. It is my business, however, to complete the task.

Meanwhile, in the ensuing months that passed, I kept trying to keep the relationships with my old friends going. Some had also left the church but many were still there. It finally became evident that people I had considered dear friends no longer wished to include me in their circle for whatever reason.

It reminded me of my oldest son saying, "Mom, what did you expect? You were the one who moved away."

I had the feeling that I was not to look back, but to keep looking forward to the new things the Lord had in store for me. Yet, I would think about the rejection I was feeling. Pain would override the peace I should have been experiencing.

On the precise morning when I was pondering all this, Dave came home saying, "I have a word from the Lord for you."

That really got my attention. I have never heard him say such a thing. Looking purposefully at me, he continued, "pillar of salt."

Oh, my goodness! There was no doubt that it was the Lord speaking to my hardening heart. I <u>had</u> to get about my Father's business.

In the weeks that followed, my time with the Lord became very precious. I began hearing Him in new ways and was hungry for a deeper relationship. My fellowship with peers had been narrowed down considerably, but it allowed me to have more time for Jesus and what He had called me to do.

He assisted me in buckling down to figure out what was to be included in this book and what should be left out. There was much that needed to be cut because of my own negative attitudes. What would be helpful to others? What was just grumbling and pessimism that I needed to get off my chest? Thankfully, because of His intervention, for the most part, you readers do not need to sort through all that!

Lindy had previously told me that I was seeing these absentee persons as friends. They were seeing me more as mentor, and I would probably hear from some of them when they needed prayer. Just this week, I got a call from one of my contacts that I had not heard from in a few months. I immediately recognized my young protégé's voice, and we got together for coffee.

The Holy Spirit met us in a beautiful way. I had asked Him to take the lead and help me be quiet unless He gave wisdom. That is exactly what happened. What a blessing for both of us. She got some ideas about how to handle difficult circumstances, and I learned that it's not so bad to be isolated so that I can grow in the Lord, helping others to do the same in the process. He does have plans and purposes. I am learning to walk in them even though His ideas are much different than what I would have expected. Who would have thought that He would meet us in a crowded Starbucks, of all places?

Oh, my God, what a Treasure You are. You are the Pearl of Great Price. We can search for You everywhere, even in the wrong places, but You are right here inside us to meet every need. You are worth more than rubies and gold. Nothing I desire compares to You. Obedience to You makes me content, although it so often goes against my flesh.

Let's Just Have Some Fun

We have been dealing with serious issues, so let's take a breather. Following are some great stories that I enjoy telling, and I hope you will also enjoy reading.

Though I have told part of this first story before, it bears repeating: It was a slimmer-than-none chance that we would meet, but God had special plans for Lindy (Slimmer) Checchi and me. I had come to the Lord in January of 1981 while we lived in Redwood City. Only six months later, while preparing for our move to Walnut Creek, one of my friends handed me a little green card saying, "When you are ready to meet ladies, and are all settled over there, just send this card in. Someone will call you for a Bible study." When she handed me the card, that still, small voice told me *"special gift."*

We moved to Walnut Creek on Father's Day into a rental home we had selected. I spent the summer with the boys getting established in our new location. In September, when they went back to school, I spotted that card in my Bible. I immediately filled it in, mailing it with anticipation to see what the Lord was going to do. Lindy, who called me about the new Bible study that was starting, ended up being a dear friend, in fact more like a sister. She was a more mature Christian, and I have grown tremendously through our close relationship.

Lindy arrived to get me in her pickup truck and we went to our first Bible study which was comprised of a small group of women. We hit it off right away; it was interesting that her first impression was that I had it all together, was so-phisticated and poised, an intellectual. *What a joke! Me?* (She must have that memory mixed up with someone else.) Our friendship grew, and we have had many memorable times together. This is the story of some of our funny recol-lections that we love sharing with each other, and with others we can hold down long enough to listen.

My husband and I were building our "dream home" on a shoestring during those first months of our relationship. One of the early remembrances Lindy and I always laugh about is going into Piedmont Lumber as we ran errands for the foreman. We walked in to find ourselves the only women encircled by many burly construction guys. When it was finally our turn, the salesman looked at me and asked, "What can I do for you?"

My response was, "I need six studs." After that came out, I realized we were <u>surrounded</u> by them. We started giggling, not able to contain ourselves. I became a regular customer at Piedmont Lumber over the next several years, but that first experience always stuck with me, and probably with them as well!

One day we were going to the Christian Women's Club luncheon at a country club there in Walnut Creek. Somehow, we got the time confused and showed up half an hour late. Everyone was dressed very beautifully, already seated, enjoying their lunch, and listening to the guest speaker. We cruised through the front door, which opened right behind the spokeswoman. That, in itself, was very awkward. There were at least 100 women in attendance that day, and a lady clear across the room motioned for us to join her table as she had two extra spaces. We "inconspicuously" traipsed around the perimeter to reach her. Our seats were separated, which is probably a good thing; they would have thrown us out for sure. As I was delicately seating myself, my fork clattered noisily to the wooden floor to add to the already humiliating situation. We began

341

quietly eating our lunch, and, in a few moments, I got a piece of chicken bone stuck in my throat. In a very discrete way, I began trying to cough it up. Think of a cat with a fur ball…. NOW you've got it!

As I recall, it was a Valentine's Day luncheon and there were little paper cups of cinnamon heart candies at each place setting. Of course, I wolfed mine down immediately but, Lindy, being the generous, loving sort, saved hers for her son, Mark.

As we were making our great escape, Lindy happened to see someone she knew. Of course she threw her hands up in surprise, to which her cup of little candies poured out all over the aforementioned wooden floor, bouncing in every direction. Always being the cautious one, I got down on my hands and knees to pick up every last piece before someone slipped and fell on them. It felt like a real Lucy/Ethel moment, one of many in our relationship. After this, we absolutely could not get out of that place fast enough. I am sure those sophisticates were happy to see the last of us!

We attended a ladies retreat at Old Oak Ranch where we were assigned our accommodations. We found ourselves getting very comfy, spreading all our things out, basically taking over the whole space, never realizing that this was a room for four. Once we were all settled in, two other women came through the door, maintaining that they were our roommates. The "**noive**," I tell you! We immediately started condensing our belongings to make room for our new guests. These two were very industrious, serious women, not at all like us. We were both wearing funny long earrings, Lindy's comprised of bunches of bananas, while mine were strings of colorful bell peppers. In the early morning, while they were scurrying around trying to get to the prayer meeting on time, we laid there in our jammies, pensively chewing on black licorice. After observing all their commotion, we leisurely got ready for breakfast, ignoring the prayer meeting altogether.

In spite of our love for fun, that was the year that I got Spirit filled, and God gave me a vision while Lindy prayed for me. I remember praying for her as well, to be able to cry. She had been unable to shed a tear for quite some time, but finally was able to after that retreat. It was a very memorable and life-transforming day in both of our lives.

What about the infamous time at Saks Fifth Avenue in San Francisco? I had gotten a gift certificate for Christmas from one of my clients, to have the works done at Saks. Meanwhile there was a coworker who declined hers, giving it to me, which I then passed along to Lindy.

We got on BART and rode over to the City from Walnut Creek. As we walked into this highfalutin place, there was a woman in a full-length mink coat, and I mean down to her ankles. While gawking at that, we checked in at the counter. In preparation for our massages, we were directed to "go over there, take off your sweaters, and put on bathrobes." So, while we were visiting and oblivious to everything around us, we proceeded to take our sweaters off over our heads. I turned around, arms still poised in the air, to discover that we were in full view of the foyer of the store. We should have just packed up and gone home at that point. But, no... and it only got worse.

First we had the massages, and that actually went okay. Next we went to the facial station where we had a beautiful Middle Eastern looking woman working on us. Her coloring was very dark and her makeup was exotic... on her. When she did *our* makeup to match *her* makeup, we were shocked beyond belief, but we did not want to hurt her feelings. When we walked out the door, and were standing on the corner trying to figure out where to go for lunch, Lindy joked that, if we weren't Christians, we could have made enough money to pay for our day at the spa. In San Francisco, where anything goes, everyone was ogling us! We found a nice restaurant and stopped in the bathroom first thing. We were laughing so hard, the tears made it easier to get some of that mask off our faces.

We have had such wonderful experiences over the years, and some not so wonderful. But I will save those stories for another time. At any rate, I will always treasure this sister in Christ.

Nothing Is Impossible

Luke 1:19,26 *The angel answered, "I am Gabriel. I stand in the presence of God and I have been sent to speak to you..." In the sixth month, God sent the angel Gabriel to Nazareth, a town in Galilee...*

Luke 1:37 *For nothing is impossible with God.*

Nothing is impossible.

I think back to a time in about 1991 when I was crying out for my oldest son, pleading for God to have His way in his life. I had prayed, _Father, put someone in Chris' life to give him unconditional love, someone who will build him up and not tear him down, someone to help him be the person You created him to be._

Though my son was attending a junior college nearby, he was also living with some very disreputable characters in a real party house. I knew they were smoking pot and drinking all the time. I recognized there were life lessons here that he could only learn by experience, painful as it was for a mother to watch.

That same evening, I prayed with a more experienced saint in the church. Her words to me were, "Nothing is impossible for God... in your household."

It gave me the faith I needed for that moment. I arrived home later that night and, moments later, received a call from my son.

"Mom, the police were here today, and they ransacked our apartment. They've boarded it up, and I've got nowhere to go. Can I come home, at least for awhile?"

Oh, God! When I prayed that prayer this morning, I didn't mean me, I silently cried.

From that moment on, I had to be aware of every word I spoke... Will this build him up or tear him down? We lived together successfully for several months and our relationship was much improved by the next time he went out to live as an adult. Today he has his own thriving construction business, is a great husband, loving father of two girls, and is doing well.

Oh, Father, when things look so totally hopeless, You are there. You orchestrate circumstances and people. You are the God over the impossible. I believe in You!

Put A Guard On My Mouth

Matthew 10:27 *What I tell you in the dark, speak in the daylight; what is whispered in your ear, proclaim from the roofs.*

Psalm 141:3 *Set a guard over my mouth, O Lord; keep watch over the door of my lips.*

Be careful what you say. Are you speaking words of blessing or of evil?

I must pay attention to the Holy Spirit when I open my mouth. In my flesh I have a quick wit, but am I building up or tearing down? I can go to "coarse jesting" pretty quickly all on my own. I need to be proclaiming what the Lord whispers in my heart. Those are the words that need to come out more often than not. James is so right about that small member of my body. It can be used for good or for evil. I need to let the Lord put a guard on it, so that nothing displeasing to Him is allowed out.

Lord, You know me; You know my wicked tongue. Change me, O God. Give me lips of righteousness.

A 50 Year Anniversary

Isaiah 52:13–53:12 and **Psalm 22:6–18** These Scriptures refer to our Savior, Jesus, who died a horrible, agonizing death for you and me. They were written literally hundreds of years before Jesus was born. We can skim over these verses and not let the reality of them sink in, or we can study what happens to the human body as it goes through this horrible tragedy called crucifixion. Our pastor recently did a three-part series describing this event so that we could fully appreciate what Jesus went through for all of mankind.

Today, however, I was reading about the 50 year anniversary of the assassination of John F. Kennedy. Tears immediately filled my eyes as I recalled that oh, so painful day. I was 16, and very enamored with the "King of Camelot" and his beautiful queen, as they were lovingly referred to. This couple seemed (from this young girl's perspective) to have it all together. And, yet, as time has gone by, we find that the man was anything but perfect. Still, the emotion welled up again within me as the pictures flashed through my memory.

Though our president died, changing the course of our country, it did not change the outcome of my life. Jesus, on the other hand, is sinless perfection who stepped down from the safety of heaven to live life on Earth for 33 years to show us what His Father looks like. Where Kennedy failed, Jesus has stood the test of time, about 2000 years. He was betrayed, lied about, spat upon, tortured to death, and bore the title "King of the Jews," at His birth and again at His death.

I pondered what brought the emotion this morning as I recognized the anniversary and the memories. Unlike the death of Kennedy, I realized Jesus' death and resurrection served a very real purpose, to give life to all mankind for those who would believe in Him. My Savior hung on a tree and He now indwells me by the power of the Holy Spirit. He suffered so that we wouldn't have to, an eternity separated from Him.

Oh, my Lord, I can't even put into words the gratitude I'm feeling this morning. I hope that Your Spirit will touch the hearts of my friends as You did mine today. It causes me to love You even more when I realize what You went through, BY CHOICE. Lord, I freely choose You today and every day. Though I'm anything but perfect, You are, and ever will be, sinless perfection.

A Pastor's Heart

Luke 1:45 *"Blessed is she who has believed that what the Lord has said to her will be accomplished!"*

Luke 2:19 *But Mary treasured up all these things and pondered them in her heart.*

These Scriptures have a double meaning in my life.

I have written on them, in shorthand, "pastor's wife" dated 12/20/91. I felt very strongly that the Lord had spoken those words to my heart. At the time, I did not want anyone to know. It seemed proud, arrogant, grandiose, too wonderful to believe.

I later had another experience which I have talked about before: Dave said that he could not keep our engagement. After I had written my good-bye letter to him, releasing him from all previous obligations, the Lord very clearly spoke to my heart before I fell asleep at the end of that tragic day. *"He will return and it will be your choice."*

The following morning, Pastor Perryman asked me, "Can you wait four years? Would you take him back?" (These, by the way, are the words written in shorthand in my Bible and dated 5/8/95.)

Pastor further stated, "Don't talk about this to anyone now, but do as the Scripture says, *'Mary treasured up all these things and pondered them in her heart.'"* (Luke 2:19).

The years have passed and, though Dave has not gone to seminary, he has a real heart to help others. And he has a heart for God. Men call upon him all the time for guidance in their firefighting careers, for Bible study, for wisdom about how to find the answers to their questions, for a Messianic Jewish perspective on events and the Word, for prayer covering when their families are going through difficult times.

The Lord has taught him all throughout his life as Dave has walked with Him. His journey has been different than most and, yes, very difficult at times. He has not always been understood, but he has never wavered from the path. Though he calls himself a "man with feet of clay," and the gift of faith eluded him at times, that grain as small as a mustard seed was honored by Dave's Heavenly Father. He holds on tightly to His sons and daughters. He will hold on tightly to you, too, if you accept His Son, Jesus, and reject the sins of your previous years by coming whole heartedly into the Spirit-controlled life.

Yes, I am a "pastor's wife" of sorts because of Dave's heart for people. Believe me, it has not been nearly as grandiose as I had envisioned! BUT it has been a good life. The Lord did a wonderful thing for both of us when He put us together.

Thank You, Father, for fulfilling the words You spoke to my heart so long ago. Sometimes the answers don't come in the way our finite minds expect, but we know You are faithful!

I Miss My Mom

Proverbs 31:28 *Her children arise and call her blessed;...* [written 9/5/12]

I woke up to the knowledge that it is already ten years today since Mom's passing. I think about how hard it was on this date, knowing that we might not have her much longer. And, yet, I had no idea that the end would come so quickly. Things progressed rapidly, with Mom pulling her feeding tube loose during the night, allowing the liquid food to drip into her lungs. At least she did not have to suffer for days on end because of it, only hours. I am so grateful that my sister, Beth, and niece, Taylor, decided not to leave to go back to Central California. We were all together when the final chorus was sung at her bedside, and then experienced the hush that followed as she took her last breath, her pulse diminishing to nothing. I think of Mom so often and, even now, want to call her for a bit of family history or her secret recipe. I still miss her, and look forward to spending eternity with her.

Father, I am so grateful that both of my parents are with You in heaven, although I can imagine Mom asking, "Bob! What are you doing here?" when he arrived. They each came to You later in life, Mom at 68, and Dad in the last couple of months before his death, at 84. Thank You that I got to be present at both of their salvation experiences. What a blessing! I miss them, but the knowledge that we will be together again soon makes the sting of their loss a lot more endurable.

The Final Conquest

<u>**1 Thessalonians 4:16,17**</u> *For the Lord himself will come down from heaven, with a loud command, with the voice of the archangel and with the trumpet call of God, and the dead in Christ will rise first. After that, we who are still alive and are left will be caught up together with them in the clouds to meet the Lord in the air. And so we will be with the Lord forever.*

As I sit here, cozy under my blanket in the cool of the morning, it makes me think about the beginning of my journey with Jesus. He would awaken me early so that I could get up, prepare my coffee and watch the sunrise over our little corner of the world. Prayers, deeply felt from the core of my being, would well up to Him; I would listen in my spirit for His answers, and for direction for our day. While reading the Word or a cherished devotional, He would fill my life with hope, giving me treasures that only He knew about, things that would guide my life for years to come. Here I am, still on that same path, as my husband lies sleeping in the stillness of the morning. This is my "real" food, the sustenance that strengthens my life.

Oh, my God, Father in heaven, this world is falling apart around us and the future is filled with the unknowns of life. We have been praying for our loved ones all these years. Perhaps the situations they find themselves in are stepping stones into Your kingdom. Maybe You are using the dark times of their lives to open their eyes wider to search for Your light. After all, isn't that what You did for me at the lowest part of my existence? Lord, as I listen to the geese honking overhead while they practice for their fall run south, they (and I) recognize the signs of the times. For them, it is only their annual trek to warmer climates. But for humanity, it is a choice between heaven and hell for all of eternity. We are standing on the final precipice and the choice is for each individual alone. Will the trumpet blow this year, Lord? Or will we still be here a decade from now? Only You know. Prepare our hearts and gather in those final members of Your eternal kingdom. May our loved ones be in that glorious group.

In the precious Name of Jesus, my Savior and Lord, Amen! Maranatha!

<u>About the Author</u>: Patty LeMoine resides in Northern California with her husband, Dave. She writes for her own personal growth and entertainment, but friends and family have urged her to publish her work so that others could be blessed as well. Patty came to know the Lord in 1981, and has been on a steady track with Jesus all this time. She began journaling on a regular basis in about 2000. As well as writing, she loves music, and has played the clarinet on her church's worship team. There, too, she enjoys co-leading women's ministries.

Patty has two sons, along with their wives, and five grandchildren. In addition, her family includes Dave's two daughters and one grown granddaughter.

Patty and Dave delight in entertaining, with ample opportunities to do so in their home along the Sacramento River. Life is full to overflowing with their passion for people and ministry possibilities. God has worked all things together for good as Patty loves and serves Him.

353

70281837R00202

Made in the USA
San Bernardino, CA
27 February 2018